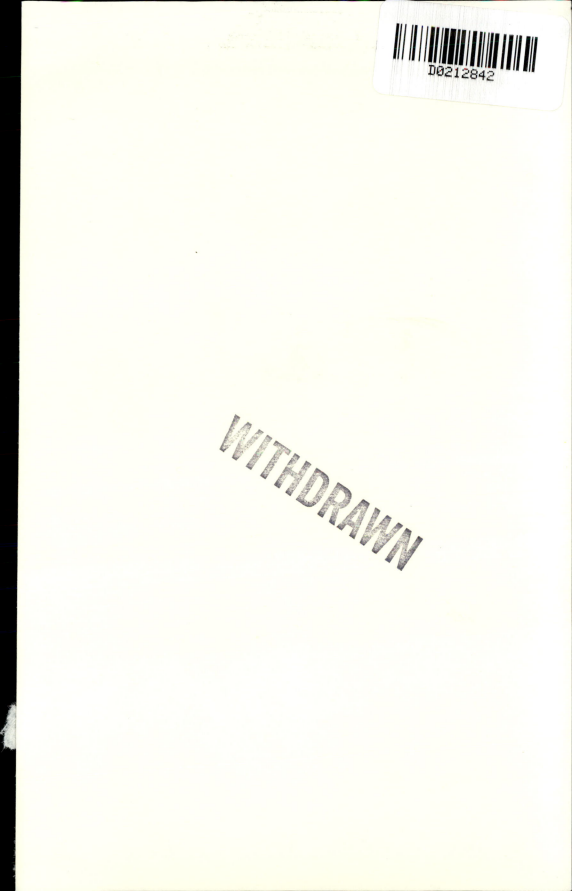

The Military Uses
of Literature

The Military Uses of Literature

Fiction and the Armed Forces in the Soviet Union

Mark T. Hooker

Westport, Connecticut
London

Library of Congress Cataloging-in-Publication Data

Hooker, Mark T.
    The military uses of literature : fiction and the Armed Forces in
the Soviet Union / Mark T. Hooker.
      p.   cm.
    Includes bibliographical references and index.
    ISBN 0–275–95563–X (alk. paper)
    1. Russian fiction—20th century—History and criticism.
2. Soldiers in literature.   3. Military art and science in
literature. 4. War in literature. I. Title.
PG3096.S64H66   1996
891.73′409352355—dc20   95–48318

British Library Cataloguing in Publication Data is available.

Library of Congress Catalog Card Number: 95–48318
ISBN: 0–275–95563–X

First published in 1996

Praeger Publishers, 88 Post Road West, Westport, CT 06881
An imprint of Greenwood Publishing Group, Inc.

Printed in the United States of America

The paper used in this book complies with the
Permanent Paper Standard issued by the National
Information Standards Organization (Z39.48–1984).

10 9 8 7 6 5 4 3 2 1

This book is dedicated to

Елена Петровна Поздеева
Elena Petrovna Pozdeeva

and

Лена Сергеевна Макушечева
Lena Sergeevna Makouchecheva

who first introduced me to the genre of military fiction at
The United States Army Russian Institute (USARI).

U.S. Army Russian Institute

Special thanks to my wife
Stella
without whose help, patience and support
this book would never have come into being.

Contents

Introduction

The Military Uses of Literature is a study of a little-known, made-to-order genre of Soviet literature that was written to fill the order for socialist-realist fiction about the Armed Forces placed by the Main Political Directorate of the Army and Navy (MPD). The book is divided into two parts: a historical study of the order placed by the MPD for military fiction, and a composite picture of how life in the postwar, peacetime Soviet military was depicted in the genre.

The first chapter examines the conferences and meetings that the MPD and its fellow travelers called to provide leadership to authors working in the genre. An individual conference or meeting, taken by itself, seems like only so much rhetoric. Taken as a whole, however, the history of the genre forms a background against which new issues stand out clearly, showing the changes in the mental landscape across which the MPD wielded the weapon of literature in the war for men's minds. It is the definition of the problems that military fiction was tasked to deal with, which is most surprising for the Western reader.

The MPD maintained tight control over the genre. Senior officers from the MPD were so frequently the keynote speakers at these meetings that an outsider could get the impression that they were members of the Writers' Union. This had a major impact on the genre, because many of its authors were either serving or retired political officers. While each individual author's work followed the Party line, it is the genre's changing (or, in some cases, unchanging) treatment of an issue viewed over time that provides the insights into life in the postwar Soviet military that this study offers. This type of comparison was one of the ways that the critical Russian reading public played the game of reading between the lines in the Soviet era.

The balance of the book is an examination of how individual issues were treated in the genre. It begins with the Soviets' changing relationship to the Germans in the aftermath of World War II, and ends with their relationship to the veterans of the Limited Contingent of Soviet Forces in Afghanistan as they returned home after a tour "across the river." In between, it takes a look at the impact of the retirement of the World War II generation of officers on the military; the effect of "Dear John" letters on combat readiness; the life of a military wife; living at remote posts; the significance of the military as a socializing institution; the use of lethal force by sentries; and attitudes toward: heroism, initiative and the suspension of disbelief to create realistic field training exercises. Each chapter looks at its topic from the viewpoint of a number of authors, so that the similarity or divergence of their treatment of the issue is highlighted. The conclusions drawn at the end of each chapter are not always those that the MPD intended the genre's reader to draw.

The Political History of Soviet Military Fiction

You cannot treat literature mystically, it is a weapon!
Furmanov[1]

There is a long tradition of military fiction in Russian and Soviet literature that is represented by such classic literary works as

- Tolstoy's *War and Peace* from the Patriotic War of 1812,
- Lermontov's *The Hero of Our Times* from the garrisons of the Caucasus in the 1830's,
- Serafimovich's *The Iron Flood* and Babel's *The Horse Cavalry* from the Revolution and Civil War 1917-1921,
- Polevoj's *Novella about a Real Man* and Fadeev's *The Young Guard* from the Great Patriotic War of 1941-1945.

Soviet military fiction is an excellent but neglected source for understanding the *weltanschauung* of the men defending the Soviet Union. The reason for this is the long and complex relationship between Soviet writers and the Main Political Directorate of the Army and Navy (MPD). From the beginning, the MPD took literature seriously as a weapon in the war for men's minds and made a continuing effort to organize and control it for almost seventy-five years. Looking at the MPD's efforts to control military fiction shows what goals the MPD hoped to achieve in shaping the mind-set of draft-age young men and compulsory service soldiers, the primary target audience of the genre.

The MPD began its relationship with Soviet writers in October 1919, when the predecessor of the Military Publishing House (Voenizdat) was formed as the Literary Publishing Department (Litizdat) of the Political Directorate of the Revolutionary Military

Soviet (RevVoenSoviet). Under the leadership of Dmitrij Furmanov, the author of *Chapaev*[2], Litizdat tried to draw together the literary forces faithful to the Revolution in support of the production of military fiction that would be favorable to the Red Army. Within a little over a year, Litizdat had published approximately 30 million copies of various titles for the Red Army.[3]

LOKAF, 1930

In June 1930, the MPD of the Workers and Peasants' Red Army (RKKA), joined together with members of the literary groups: the Russian Association of Proletarian Writers (RAPP), the Federation of Associations of Soviet Writers (FOSP), the All-Union Organization of Peasant Writers (VOKP), *Pereval*, *Kuznitsa* and *Rezets* to create the Literaturnoe Ob"edinenie Krasnoj Armii i Flota (LOKAF) [the Literary Association of the Army and the Navy].[4] The organizational meeting was held in the M. V. Frunze Central Officers' Club in Moscow.

The MPD's goal in forming LOKAF was to organize the fragmented literary groups of the thirties and direct their efforts to the production of works of literature with military motifs. The literature produced by LOKAF was intended to focus the attention of the workers on defense issues in the face of what was perceived by the MPD as a growing military threat from the capitalist world.

When the Writers' Union was formed, in April 1932, it absorbed LOKAF as the Commission on Military Fiction (CMF) and took over LOKAF's journal, changing its name to *Znamya* [The Banner]. This means that the CMF, LOKAF's successor organization, is the longest continuously active, genre-specific political organization of writers in the USSR.[5]

The Red Army viewed fiction as "one of the most powerful tools for the organization and education of the masses."[6] The broad program to eliminate illiteracy in the Soviet Union (LIKBEZ) had been waged, in part, to open up the minds of the masses so that they could be worked on with this tool. This program had been especially effective in the Red Army. It had produced an army that wanted to read, and fiction was what it read the most.[7] The nouveau-literate nature of the target audience can be seen in a statement by Dem'yan Bednyj, speaking at the first LOKAF Plenum. His primary characteristic of military fiction was that it should be as simple as possible. In order for an author to reach this audience effectively, he had to "know how to explain the most complex things in the simplest possible way," without lowering its artistic content.[8]

The demand for reading material for the Red Army was often expressed in the writings of literary critics of the period in terms of weapons or ammunition. Lenin had called the press "one of the most powerful weapons, which in a critical moment in the battle, can be more mighty and dangerous than bombs or machine guns."[9] During the Revolution, the directives of RKKA often contained the instruction "send literature urgently, on the same priority as ammunition."[10] In official literary criticism of the thirties, the sharp pens of Soviet writers were considered "as necessary to the Army as bayonets."[11]

From the military-political point of view, controlling what the newly literate Red soldier was reading was essential. The content had to support Red Army doctrine and ideology or the consequences could be serious. Controlling what was written made it easier to control what was read. Therefore, gaining control of the literary process was, logically, a very desirable goal for the military, and LOKAF was the organization through which they hoped to achieve it.

In their follow-up to the appeal to join LOKAF, FOSP strongly urged writers to support this initiative, pointing out that the life and work of the peacetime Red Army was a great source of literary material, "being one of the most important sectors in forging Socialist relationships, the cultural revolution and the re-making of man."[12]

LOKAF defined its basic tasks and literary-political line as:[13]

1. the mobilization of Soviet authors to write on military topics and thus improve the defense preparedness of the USSR;
2. the training of young writers still serving in the ranks of the Armed Forces, and organizing literary groups there;
3. the creation of literary works about the war and the Red Army with the correct Marxist-Leninist viewpoint;
4. the creation of a cadre of literary critics to combat non-Marxist-Leninist treatments of war in literature; and
5. the expansion of the number of works on military topics carried in the periodic literary press.

These five basic goals and the literary-political line set out for LOKAF in 1930 remained essentially valid through the dissolution of the MPD in 1991.

The first point in LOKAF's literary-political line was aimed at increasing the number of professional-quality authors writing on the contemporary, peacetime military. For those major authors, who were writing about the Red Army, it was the Red Army of the Revolution and Civil War, the period when most of them had cut their literary teeth, that occupied their attention. Works on the contemporary military were virtually nonexistent.

To correct this situation, LOKAF called for the formation of literary brigades of writers to visit military units in the field, on exercise and in garrison, just as writers' brigades were already being sent to factories, collective farms and construction projects so that they could write about them. Writers were also to be sent on temporary duty (TDY) to work in the military periodic press and to attend the military correspondents' course at the RKKA Military Academy. It was felt that, since most writers of the period were unfamiliar with life in the modern military, these TDYs would give them an elementary military-political foundation and help them understand the character and peculiarities of the modern battlefield, which, in turn, would make them equipped to write on the Red Army of the day.

This did not, however, suggest abandoning the topic of the Red Army of the period of the Intervention and the Civil War. Official literary criticism of the thirties countered theories that the topic had been exhausted and encouraged writers to continue working on it.[14]

The second point of LOKAF's literary-political line was also aimed at increasing the number of professional-quality authors writing on the contemporary, peacetime military. It sought to aid emerging writers still serving in the Armed Forces improve their literary skills so as to become the quality authors that LOKAF needed. LOKAF's approach to this aspect of the problem was for established writers, primarily from RAPP and VOKP, to offer guidance, leadership and literary consultations to local military writers and literary groups. It was these military men who became the first LOKAF authors to publish works of military fiction on the Red Army of the thirties.[15]

The third point in LOKAF's literary-political line detailed the desired approach to literature for writers to use in works on military topics. In his presentation at the first Plenum of LOKAF in April 1931, Leonid Degtyarev said that the literary method most appropriate for members of LOKAF was that followed by RAPP, "the leading organization of proletarian literature."[16]

RAPP was founded in 1925 to secure the leading position of the proletariat in the ideological struggle for supremacy in the creative arts. It supported realism, but from the proletarian point of view, which required pointing out

the class and international essence of the Armed Forces of the working class, the role of the Communist Party in leading the Armed Forces, directing military policies and the practices of the working class ... brutally unmasking the essence of chauvinistic and pacifist trends and tendencies, both in Soviet and in Western-European literature, instilling the workers of the USSR and the entire world with a burning hatred for capitalism and its lackeys and a readiness to destroy this class enemy.[17]

The fourth point in LOKAF's literary-political line called for the creation of a cadre of literary critics to combat non-Marxist-Leninist-

Stalinist treatments of war in literature. Criticism of military fiction remains a problem to this day. In the report on the CMF to the VIII Congress in 1986, the CMF was criticized for its failure to make a practice of thoroughly analyzing works of military-patriotic fiction and discussing them at committee sittings.[18]

Boris Leonov, the premier literary critic for military fiction, takes other critics to task for their reluctance to treat the genre seriously in his book of essays published in 1988. In his view, this problem is a result of the same cause that keeps big-name writers from working in the genre: their lack of experience with service in the military. Without it, they cannot have a well-developed system of ideas on "the essence of life in the military, on the variety of vital conflicts in the topic of everyday military life, which would be expressed as clear and objective criteria for judging how closely a literary work corresponds to reality."[19]

The fifth point in LOKAF's literary-political line resulted in the creation of a number of new periodicals serving as the organs of individual LOKAF branches. The official magazine of the Moscow branch of LOKAF was initially known as *LOKAF*, but in 1933, its name was changed to *The Banner* [Znamya] (referring to the Red Banner of the Communist movement), when it became the organ of the Writers' Union of the USSR. In Ukraine, LOKAF's official publication was *The Red Warrior* [Chervonij boets], which originally was the official organ of the Political Directorate of the Ukrainian military district. In Leningrad, LOKAF's publication was *Broadside* [Zalp], which became the journal of the Leningrad Union of Writers in 1933. In addition to these, LOKAF had materials placed in *The Star* [Zvezda], *Red Star* [Krasnaya zvezda], *Red Soldier and Red Sailor* [Krasnoarmeets i Krasnoflotets] and *On Literary Guard* [na Litpostu]. LOKAF's initial success in this area waned and the goal of increasing the amount of military fiction in the periodic press became a constant feature of the MPD's literary-political program.

The appeal for writers to participate in the formation of LOKAF,[20] and to write about the contemporary, peacetime Red Army, suggested the following topics as worthy of an author's exploration:

- the Red garrison, that gigantic factory where tireless supporters of the Socialist restructuring of the country were being manufactured from the masses of the uneducated peasant youth,
- the new Red commander,
- the new system of relations between superiors and subordinates,
- the heroic Air Force and brave Red Navy,
- the gallant, Red Banner, Far Eastern Army,

- the Red Army shock workers,
- the military Comsomol,
- the creative, guiding work of the military Bolsheviks,
- how hundreds of thousands of members of the Red Army in the countryside are demolishing mountains of backwardness, ignorance and unenlightenment, conducting a fierce battle with the Kulaks, a battle for collectivization and the Socialist restructuring of the countryside ... ,
- how Socialist industry is supporting the upgrading of the Army's equipment and increasing its defense capacity.

LOKAF PLENUM, 1931

LOKAF held its first plenum from 5 to 9 April 1931 in the Frunze Central Officers' Club in Moscow. In the short eight months of its existence, LOKAF had grown to 2,360 members, 126 literary circles and 690 professional writers. It had branches in Moscow, Leningrad, Ukraine, Belorussia, the Northern-Caucasus, Central Asia, the Far East and the Baltic and Privolga areas.

Despite these statistical successes, most of LOKAF's goals remained unfulfilled. In spite of the participation of writers from LOKAF in RKKA fall maneuvers, "the majority of the professional writers remain militarily illiterate,"[21] said Mate Zalka in his presentation. Leonid Degtyarev, for his part, noted the continuing lack of works on life in the modern-day Red Army and urged writers to take up the topic. LOKAF had, in fact, not managed to produce much of anything in the way of literary output, and one of the tasks facing LOKAF's Central Soviet was the creation of a concrete plan for increasing literary production.[22]

As preparations for the impending war soon became the order of the day for writers in the Soviet Union, the topic of the Civil War took on a new life. Writers tried to draw lessons from it for the imminent crisis that would become the Great Patriotic War.[23] In his speech at the I Congress of Writers in 1934, Aleksej Aleksandrovich Surkov called on the participants not to forget "that the time is not too far away that poems will have to move from the pages of literary journals to the pages of front-line news sheets and divisional newspapers. Let's keep our lyrical powder dry."[24]

The writers' purge of 1936-1938 followed soon after that and in it many of the founders of LOKAF and the Writers' Union that had absorbed it perished. Works on the peacetime military remained virtually nonexistent as the approaching war became the center of attention for writing activity. The war has held firm control of Soviet military fiction ever since.

II CONGRESS OF WRITERS, 1954

The II Congress of Writers in 1954 was the Party's attempt to reassert its control over literature after the death of Stalin. Aleksej Aleksandrovich Surkov, the First Secretary of the Directorate of the Writers' Union, stated this succinctly in his three-hour-long opening speech at the congress: "Literature is the sharp-edged weapon of socialist-political action. It is tightly connected to politics and is subordinate to the latter."[25] This is hardly a surprising assertion for one of the founding members of LOKAF, who survived the purges and the war.

At the congress, the military delegation, headed by Col. A. Vasil'ev, thanked the participants for their works on the Great Patriotic War, which had made a significant contribution to the inculcation of the Soviet people with the spirit of Communism, giving them the "courage, daring and firm belief in the righteousness of our cause, a limitless love of our Socialist Motherland and the Communist Party."[26]

At the same time, Vasil'ev complained that there was hardly anything at all being written on the postwar, peacetime military. In fact, in Vasil'ev's opinion, there had not been one significant work of military fiction about the postwar, peacetime military written in the almost ten years since the end of the war.

The situation in the fifties at the II Congress of Writers is essentially the same situation as when LOKAF was formed. In the thirties, most of the writers in LOKAF and, later, the Writers' Union were veterans of the Revolution and the Civil War, which was their topic of choice for writing instead of the peacetime military. In the 1950's, as Col. Vasil'ev himself pointed out, most of the congress participants were veterans of the Great Patriotic War, which had the same place in the hearts of the writers of the fifties as the Revolution and Civil War did in the hearts of the writers of the thirties.

Vasil'ev was sure, however, that the participants would take up the task set for them by the Central Committee of the CPSU in its message of greeting to the congress, charging them to

> inculcate young people, young workers and collective farmers, intellectuals, soldiers in the Soviet Army with the spirit of love of labor, cheerfulness, fearlessness, certainty in the victory of our cause, in the spirit of selfless dedication to our Socialist Motherland and constant combat readiness to soundly repulse the imperialist aggressors, if they try to disturb the peaceful labor of our people.[27]

Col. Vasil'ev goes on to criticize the literary journals for their lack of attention to military fiction. In particular, he attacks *The Banner*, which began publication as the organ for LOKAF, for giving up its tradition of publishing primarily military fiction. In his opinion, *The Banner* should return to this tradition, and other journals should accept works of military fiction as well.

Vasil'ev's complaints were very reminiscent of the original goals that LOKAF was established to achieve. It is not surprising, therefore, that the Commission on Military Fiction, LOKAF's successor organization, was disbanded and reformed shortly after the II Congress of Writers. [28] The CMF's main problem was that it had gotten out of touch with the military and that some of the manuscripts that it recommended for publication were inappropriate from a political point of view. In addition to that, the CMF had restricted its work to reviewing manuscripts that came in on their own, rather than actively encouraging writers to produce works of military fiction.

FIRST ALL-UNION CONFERENCE ON MILITARY FICTION, 1955

The reorganization of the Commission was followed by the First All-Union Conference on Military Fiction, which was held 27-31 May 1955 in the Frunze Central Officers' Club in Moscow. It was attended by over three hundred participants from writers' organizations all over the country, the MPD, publishing houses and literary magazine editorial staffs. Conspicuous by their absence, however, were many members of the leadership of the Writers' Union of the USSR.[29]

The majority of the conference participants' attention was focused on works of fiction about World War II. The popularity of the war as a topic with Soviet writers in the mid fifties is understandable. One in three of them had served in the Soviet military during the war.[30] The attendance figures for the conference show a similar breakdown with 238 of the 312 writers attending, having been in the war, 129 of them having served in line units.[31]

Just as the Revolution and Civil War had in the thirties, more than ten years after they had ended, the Great Patriotic War served as a prime source of literary material for writers of didactic, patriotic literary works in the mid-fifties. Mikhail N. Alekseev, an editor of the Military Publishing House, prophetically stated at the conference that "the utmost courage and steadfastness of the Soviet people, exhibited on the field of battle and in the rear, is an inexhaustible source of inspiration for our writers even in the postwar period."[32]

From the viewpoint of the eighties, the choice of the word "inexhaustible" as a descriptive adjective for the war as a source of literary inspiration was a good one, because new works about the war are still rolling off the presses of Soviet publishing houses. Molodaya gvardiya Publishing House, for example, has two recent publications, which contain new works on the war: issue number 33 of *Al'manakh Podvig* [Feat of Arms Anthology] (1989) has a number of works on the Great Patriotic War, and *A Soldier's Fate*[33] (1985), which is an anthology of novellas, short stories and poems about the war written by authors who were born after it ended.

At the First All-Union Conference on Military Fiction in 1955, General Lieutenant Shatilov, the deputy chief of the MPD, was not entirely happy with the description of the war in some of the more recent works of military fiction. Their depiction was not objective (a code word for the Party's view) enough. The treatment of the events in the initial period of the war was much too idealistic and did not touch on the errors and mistakes made by the Soviets then. These authors needed to take a Marxist approach. They needed to show the historic role of the Soviet people and their Armed Forces; to show the inspirational, guiding role of the Party led by the collective leadership of the Central Committee, but without ignoring the contributions of individual government and military leaders.

Shatilov's speech signaled the start of the thaw in military fiction that took Stalin out of the limelight of works about the war. This was a major change from "all the victories of the Soviet Armed Forces are bound with the name of Stalin," which is typical of coverage of the war during Stalin's lifetime.[34] The classic work of the thaw in military fiction is Lev Snegirev's *Thaw in Midwinter*, which parallels the plot in Dudintsev's novel *Not by Bread Alone* that attracted so much controversy in main-line Soviet literature.

The conference nevertheless devoted considerable attention to literary works on the contemporary, peacetime military of the fifties. Aleksandr Rozen from Leningrad criticized works on the modern military for locking officers and soldiers away from their civilian counterparts behind regulations and garrison gates. He wanted to see works in which servicemen face the same "ignorance, rigid views, careerism and the press of criticism" as civilian literary characters.[35]

In his remarks to the conference about the state of affairs of contemporary military fiction, lieutenant V. Yarchuk was critical of the number of works of literature that had been produced. He was able to name only three works of interest about the postwar, peacetime military: [36] • Vladimir Komissarov's *Guards Lieutenant*, • Vitalij Petl'ovannyj's *The Trumpets Play Retreat* and • Ivan Stadnyuk's *Maksim Perepelitsa*. Given the ten-year span of time since the end of the war, three works of interest on the contemporary military is hardly an impressive total.

Conference participants provided a number of reasons for the shortage of works on the contemporary, peacetime military:

- the baronial disdain for the genre in the Writers' Union of the USSR,
- the lack of contact between writers and the military,
- the weakening of contacts between the MPD and the Writers' Union of the USSR,
- the poor direction provided for the genre by the CMF,
- the lack of support for serving authors from the MPD,
- the lack of support for this genre by the Military Publishing House,
- the lack of serious literary criticism for the genre,
- the lack of a literary journal devoted primarily to military fiction,
- the "theory" that writing about the peacetime military is uninteresting and lacks romanticism.

In his keynote speech to the conference, General Lieutenant Shatilov repeated the task set by the Party in its message of greeting to the participants of the II Congress of Writers five months before, calling on the participants to

inculcate young people, young workers and collective farmers, intellectuals, soldiers in the Soviet Army with the spirit of love of labor, cheerfulness, fearlessness, certainty in the victory of our cause, in the spirit of selfless dedication to our Socialist Motherland and constant combat readiness to soundly repulse the imperialist aggressors, if they try to disturb the peaceful labor of our people.[37]

According to Shatilov, the development of this kind of inner strength was especially important on the modern battlefield, which had been changed by the Scientific and Technological Revolution. The appearance of nuclear weapons and other new military technologies made the postwar military much different than the one that had fought its way to victory in the Great Patriotic War. These changes needed to be reflected in modern works of military fiction.

These changes were at the heart of the problem of the loss of contact between the writers and the military. When the war ended, writers left the military and fell out of touch with it. Their concepts of life in the military were those left over from the war, but the substantial changes in the military in the intervening ten years meant that those concepts were out of date. Armaments had changed. Tactics and doctrine had changed. The people serving in the military had changed. Writers needed to reestablish their ties with the new, technologically advanced military of the nuclear battlefield rather than just try to use their wartime experiences to produce military fiction about the postwar military.

Despite the continuing criticism, throughout the history of the genre, of sending established writers on TDYs to tour military units and ships, this tactic remained a part of the MPD's and CMF's solution to the problem of getting more written about the contemporary military right up to the end. The arguments presented at the conference made it clear that the people most qualified to write on life in the contemporary, peacetime military were serving members of the Forces, whose duties allowed them but little time to produce literature.

In their presentations to the conference, Mikhail Alekseev and a number of other speakers attacked the "'theory' that writing about the peacetime military is dull and uninteresting."[38] The typical excuse for not writing about life in the military was that writers believed it to be bound by regulations and therefore there could not be any deviation from the prescribed norms or exceptional situations, which meant that there could not be any basis for an interesting story.

In countering this "theory", Aleksej A. Surkov, the First Secretary of the Directorate of the Writers' Union of the USSR, cites two specific topics that he believes would be interesting for authors to explore:

- the psychological changes in a young high school graduate, when he first encounters the rigors of military discipline, and
- the psychological changes in a brand new lieutenant, fresh out of a military academy, as he enters the unaccustomed world of a military garrison.[39]

The first of these topics had already been well treated in Stadnyuk's *Maksim Perepelitsa* (1952) and the second in Komissarov's *Guards Lieutenant* (1956). Later authors provided no-less-interesting but more contemporary insights into the changes young men undergo when they enter the military in works like Filatov's *Power Climb* (1975) and Kuleshov's *The White Wind* (1977).

General Lieutenant N. Radetskij offered yet another topic for writers to work on that required a better knowledge of the contemporary military: the struggle of the old and the new technologies, and how they affect the people in the military who use them.[40] The Scientific and Technological Revolution, as it was called, proved extremely popular with the writers of the seventies and eighties, providing such works as Biryukov's *Only Three Days* (1975), which is about the introduction of new weapon systems into the tube artillery, and Borich's *The Third Dimension* (1975), which is about the innovations in the submarine Navy.

Mikhail Alekseev seconded the suggestion of the Scientific and Technological Revolution as a topic of interest, but also added the topics of heroism and romance that are found in the peacetime service.[41] These later two topics have also been well treated by contemporary authors in such works as Godenko's *Eternal Fire* (1987), which relates the story of a reactor accident on a nuclear submarine, and Polyanskij's *The Right to Take Risks* (1978), which is the story of life in the airborne.

MEETING WITH WRITERS AND ARTISTS, 1964

On 7 February 1964 the Ministry of Defense and the MPD held a meeting with writers and artists to increase the role of literature and the arts in the patriotic inculcation of soldiers and young people at the Frunze Central Officers' Club in Moscow. Its keynote speaker was Minister of Defense Marshal Rodion Ya. Malinovskij, who opened his speech with an explanation of why it was "not just customary, but insistently necessary" for representatives from the military leadership to meet with writers and artists. It is because writers and artists hold the powerful weapon of the artistic image in their hands. As long as this weapon "is in good repair and aimed properly, it never misses its mark."[42] The purpose of this meeting was, despite all Malinovskij's protestations to the contrary, to aim the weapon at targets of the MPD's chosing.

As at the First All-Union Conference on Military Fiction in 1955, works of art and literature on the war were the primary topic of discussion. Marshal Malinovskij was pleased to note that many of the participants were veterans of the war and that some were even veterans of the Revolution.[43] That the war continued to be a popular topic with writers is demonstrated by the comment from the chief of the Main Political Directorate, Army General A. A. Epishev, that over the last two decades, more literary works had been written on the war than on almost any other topic.[44] A number of the speakers, however, pointed to the undesirable notes of pacifism in some of these works and the tendency on the part of some writers and artists to play down the heroism of the people during the war, and the leading role of the Party on the path to victory. This was the start of a very intense argument about the direction of military fiction on the war.

While the war loomed large in all the presentations, all speakers at the meeting touched on literary works on the life of the contemporary military. General Epishev was not satisfied with the number of works being written on this topic. His particular interest was in the International Duty of the Soviet Armed Forces and on their brotherhood in arms with the Armed Forces of the other Socialist countries. This was a new topic for military fiction. It had not been mentioned at the First Conference on Military Fiction in 1955, which took place only one year after the formation of the Warsaw Pact. The topic was, however, especially well treated in Stepanov's *At the Brandenburg Gate* (1973).

In their presentations, Arkadij Perventsev and Aleksandr Chakovskij noted the need to provide a better treatment of a topic that was a carryover from 1955: the romance of military service. Chakovskij's view was that the life and labors of soldiers are worthy of vivid works that will inculcate young people with a love of military service. The "romance" of the service, however, eventually became an overworked justification for the hardships that servicemen had to endure, as Pronyakin shows in his *Court of Honor* (1974).

From the standpoint of the nineties, Marshal Malinovskij's presentation in 1964 looks like a reading list of topics from successful works of contemporary military fiction, rather than a wish list. He addressed the rapid changes in technology taking place in the Armed Forces; changes represented by the creation of the Strategic Rocket Forces (Gorbachev's trilogy: *The Pull of the Stars*, *Give Me a Fulcrum* and *The Battle*, 1969 to 1977), making the National Air Defense Forces a separate branch of service (Pronyakin's *Court of Honor*, 1974) and the reorganization of the Army, Air Force and Navy (Kambulov's *Faithfulness*, 1965). In particular, Malinovskij mentions the conversion from tube to rocket artillery (Biryukov's *Only Three Days*, 1975); the introduction of new antiaircraft rockets in the PVO [Antiaircraft Defense] arsenal (Davydov's *The Assignment*, 1983); the introduction of supersonic aircraft to the Air Force arsenal (Sul'yanov's *The Zampolit*, 1982); the introduction of nuclear-powered submarines to the Navy (Perventsev's *The Island of Hope*, 1969); the introduction of new night-vision devices to enable all-weather, day and night operations (Belyaev's *The Runway*, 1979).

This new technology does not, observes Malinovskij, reduce the role of the soldier in war, but increases it. These new weapon systems are not automatic, but require men to work them. In the period since the end of the war, the number of engineering and technical specialists serving in the Armed Forces had tripled, and was still growing.[45]

The increasing numbers of technically literate soldiers was a particularly important change for the Soviet military. Numerous works of military fiction such as Borich's *The Third Dimension* (1975) and Babaev's *Conflict* (1986), touch on the conflict between the old brown-shoe army commissioned or noncommissioned officer and the new soldier-technician.

The introduction of modern and nuclear technology to the battlefield changed it substantially. This change has made it more necessary than ever for the serviceman to be psychologically hardened for combat. Malinovskij asks that writers create a work of literature that "can reach to the depths of the mind and heart, calling forth in them an elevated sense of citizenship and the resolution to dedicate oneself to the struggle for the happiness of the people."[46] Georgij Berezko's novel *Stronger than the Atom* was the first to treat this aspect of the change.

Marshal Malinovskij also directed the attention of the conference participants to military discipline and the "special importance of a soldier's unquestioning subordination to his commander." On the modern battlefield, it is "more important now than ever before to protect the commander's authority, strengthen it and to show the essence of unilateral command as an expression of the will of the *kollektiv*."[47] Soviet soldiers should see an order from their commander as an order from the Motherland and not fulfill it just because the law requires it, but because they are inwardly convinced of its correctness.

Marshal Malinovskij also raised the perennial issue of a lack of familiarity with life in the military on the part of authors and critics. He deemed that mere visits to units and ships were not enough to create good literary works on the military. His recommendation was a new approach. Local Writers' Union organizations should invite servicemen to participate in the evaluation of works in progress. He tasked the CMF to take an active stance on this issue.

CENTRAL COMMITTEE RESOLUTION, 1967

As if in preparation for the new law on the draft to be issued in October, the Communist Party of the Soviet Union (CPSU) Central Committee issued a resolution entitled "Measures to Improve Party-Political Work in the Soviet Army and Navy."[48] It shows the persistence of the issues discussed at the First All-Union Conference in 1955 and the 1964 Meeting. The criticisms and recommendations in the resolution could well have been taken from one of the conference or meeting presentations.

The resolution noted that military-patriotic topics had still not been done justice in literature. Some works of military fiction still contained elements of pacifism. The treatment of life in the military in others was only superficial. The resolution called on the Writers' Union to promote the production of high-quality works of military fiction in every way possible and to continue to aid writers to maintain contacts with the military.

The resolution stated that the changes brought about by the introduction of new weapons and technologies, as well as the changes in the organizational structure of the Forces, had increased the need for political inculcation of the troops. These same changes also meant that the methods and approaches of political inculcation had to be changed to take the increased educational level of the modern serviceman into account.

This is an interesting side effect of the success of the LIKBEZ campaign begun in the ranks of the Red Army. The target audience for military fiction had changed. Dem'yan Bednyj's rule of thumb—"explain the most complex things in the simplest possible way"—was no longer sufficient for the not-just-literate, but educated draft-age youngsters and servicemen of the sixties.

The resolution tasks the Ministry of Defense (MOD), the MPD and all political and Party organizations to raise the level and effectiveness of their ideological work in the Forces and to insure that not even one serviceman is left out of the program of political inculcation. In particular they should pay attention to:

- strengthening discipline at all levels,
- setting higher standards of achievement for subordinates at all levels,
- strictly adhering to regulations in every unit,
- insuring that Communists and Comsomol members set the example for others.

In addition to this, Party organizations were to heighten the ideological zeal of all Party members, insuring that they had

- zero tolerance for shortcomings,
- higher moral qualities and
- a sense of responsibility for fulfilling their Party and military duty.

The Central Committee recognized that there was some basis for these problems in the conditions under which the troops lived, and followed this list with an instruction to commanders and political workers to pay more attention to improving the living conditions of the troops as a prerequisite for improving discipline in the ranks. While this had been one of the subplots in Pronyakin's *Court of Honor*, and despite the Central Committee's concern, the problem was still unresolved in the eighties, as can be seen by the continuing stream of articles about it in *Red Star*.[49]

IV CONGRESS OF WRITERS, 1967

The IV Congress of the Writers' Union of the USSR was held 22-27 May 1967. In the eight years between the III (1959) and the IV Congress, the *Commission* on Military Fiction had been reconstituted as the *Soviet* [Council] on Military Fiction. The Soviet consisted of forty-seven writers headed by Konstantin M. Simonov, author of the war novel, *The Quick and the Dead*. The Soviet maintained contacts with all fourteen of the Republic Commissions on Military Fiction and the seventeen Regional Commissions. All totaled, there were over 600 writers working together with the Soviet, plus over 100 people from the publishing establishment, the other creative unions and the military political organs.[50]

The Soviet's report to the congress proudly details all the areas of its activities:

- discussing new books, plays and films on military-patriotic themes,
- daily discussion of the printing schedules of publishers of military fiction,
- regularly scheduled visits by groups of writers to units and ships,
- creative assistance to emerging writers serving in the Forces through more than 100 literary associations,
- organizing workshops for young writers,
- the publication of anthologies of works with military-patriotic themes,
- reviewing manuscripts (more than 650 were reviewed in the reporting period),
- helping veterans of the war and Revolution write their memoirs,
- detailing writers to work in the military press, where they cannot only improve their knowledge of the military, but also provide help to emerging writers,
- organizing meetings between the writers and members of the military leadership,
- holding conferences with readers who are still serving in the Forces,
- compiling bibliographies of military-patriotic works,
- holding conferences on military fiction and
- advising publishers.

While the Commission, now advanced in status to a Soviet, had greatly improved since it was dissolved and reorganized in 1955, the negative comments on the genre in the Central Committee Resolution, in the same year as this glowing report, show that there was still room for improvement in the genre.

In his speech to the congress, Simonov took a position that did not toe the current Party line in military fiction. He attacked political censorship and defended a true-realist rather than a socialist-realist approach to the topic of the war. He felt that literature cannot be rewritten just because the political wind is blowing from another quarter. Changes of that sort only weaken the impact of literature on its audience, which will be certain to notice the difference.

> I cannot imagine that next to all the works of Soviet art, read or seen on the screen by tens of millions of people, which have already told them one truth about the war, including the most bitter sides of that truth, new works could appear on that same epoch today in which the bitter sides of the historical truth were voluntarily or forcefully expurgated. That kind of art will not be respected nor will it be believed by the reader or the viewer.[51]

Simonov's stance was still a hotly debated topic of discussion some ten years later, when it was backed up by the Belorussian writer I. Chigrinov at a roundtable hosted by the organ of the Writers' Union of the USSR, *Literaturnoe obozrenie* [Literary Review]. Rather than supporting his view by the usual quotes from Lenin or Marx, Chigrinov goes outside the Soviet era to quote Lev Nikolaevich Tolstoy, the author of *War and Peace*.

> It would hurt my conscience to write about our victory in the battle with bonapartist France without describing our failures and our shame. Who hasn't experienced a concealed, but unpleasant feeling of embarrassment and disbelief, reading those patriotic compositions about 1812? If our victory was not by chance, and lies in the essence of the character of the Russian people and the Army, then that character should be much more sharply manifested in an epoch of failures and defeats.[52]

CONFERENCE OF WRITERS, 1969

A conference of writers working on military themes was held 10-11 March 1969 in the Frunze Central Officers' Club in Moscow. The topic of the conference was the effect that literature has on the inculcation of Soviet young people in the spirit of "limitless faithfulness to the people and the Motherland, in the spirit of constant readiness to stand up to defend our Socialist achievements."[53] The primary focus of the conference was military fiction on the war and how to return it to a more orthodox socialist-realist portrayal of that epoch.

This conference was sponsored, not by the Writers' Union of the USSR, but by the more conservative Writers' Union of the Russian Soviet Federated Socialist Republic (RSFSR), together with the Central Committee of the Comsomol, the Commission on the Press of the Council of Ministers of the RSFSR and the Academy of Pedagogical

Sciences. It was attended by representatives from the Central Committee of the CPSU, the Central Committee of the Comsomol, the MPD, the political directorates of the branches of service, DOSAAF[54] and members of the publishing establishment and the periodic press.

The keynote speech was delivered by the chairman of the Directorate of the Writers' Union of the RSFSR, Leonid Sobolev. Overall, Sobolev was pleased with the development of military-patriotic themes in literature, but there were three problem areas of concern to him:

- the image of the modern, well-educated, idealistic, military technician and engineer,
- the "truth-from-the-trenches" [*okopnaya pravda*] approach to writing about the Great Patriotic War and
- the lack of attention to the genre on the part of literary critics.

Sobolev felt that Soviet literature had succeeded in creating great images of the heroes of the Revolution and the war, but now it needed to turn its attention to the image of the modern military man. Sobolev specifically wanted to see more works on the military as a socializing process, showing how it helps to shape the minds of the young people who go through it.

The participants of the conference agreed with Sobolev and noted the special ideological value of works on the contemporary military in preparing young people to defend the Motherland. While Georgij Berezko, Gennadij Semenikhin, Nikolaj Kambulov and Nikolaj Gorbachev were held up as examples of good contemporary authors of military fiction, the conference, in general, felt that more could be done in the genre.[55]

"Truth-from-the-trenches" was a stark, realistic portrayal of war depicting all its horrors, fears and confusion. In Sobolev's view, the problem with this approach to the war was that it fails to show the inspiration of victory as coming from an internal force of personal will, but as being forced on the individual by a set of outside circumstances.

This approach runs counter to the Party position on which the whole of the program of military fiction is based: that patriotism and heroism can be taught. If the truth-from-the-trenches approach is correct, then it is only the circumstances in which an individual finds himself that count and not his mind-set or his previous inculcation. The MPD had no choice but to fight it.

Stalin was returned from his status as a nonperson in military literature on the war in 1969. This change from the policy set by General Lieutenant Shatilov in 1955 was signaled by a book review in issue No. 2 of *Kommunist*, which came out a month before the conference began. E. Boltin positively reviewed the memoirs of six of Stalin's marshals, who all spoke well of Stalin's role in the war. Drawing on the descriptions of each author's interaction with Stalin, Boltin debunks the "irresponsible assertions of his [Stalin's] military incompetence, of his plotting the war 'on a globe,' of his absolute intolerance for other people's ideas,"[56] which Boltin views as mere fabrications made up by enemies of the Soviet Union outside its borders.

Sobolev complained of the lack of attention to the genre on the part of the literary critics. Literary criticism was needed to bring the books to the notice of the reading public. Since it was not possible for someone to read everything that was being published, literary criticism helped readers to make choices about which books deserved their attention. E. Levakovskaya joined Sobolev in his complaint. She pointed out that, in the last few years, only five percent of the books with military themes had been reviewed in the press.[57]

There was a special session at the conference on creating closer ties with the military, which had been one of the original goals of LOKAF. Writers needed to know about the modern military if they were going to write about it, but past efforts to this end had been unsuccessful. General Major Tkachev of the PVO [Antiaircraft Defense], stated the obvious: "To write about the modern military, you have to know about it." [58] The pace of change in the military made knowing about it very difficult. The PVO of today was completely different from the PVO of ten to fifteen years ago.

Tkachev supported Mikhail Godenko's view that "to write about a sailor, you have to live with him in his berthing spaces, to respond to alerts with him, to see how tired he is after a six-month cruise, to listen to him as he reacts to events." You cannot invent fate. You cannot invent characters. You have to see them firsthand. The problem for Soviet military fiction was and remained finding people who were willing to do that.

Sobolev supported Dolmatovskij's idea for a new organization within the Writers' Union and also suggested conducting joint writers' workshops and detailing writers to work in the military press as a way to improve writing on the modern military.[59]

Working in the military press has certainly proven itself as an effective route to literary success in the genre. The authors of *Maksim Perepelitsa*, which is repeatedly cited by critics as a classic of the genre from the early fifties; of *The Corporal of the Guard Has Not Come Yet*, which was awarded the MOD prize for literature in 1968 for its description of the effects of the Scientific and Technological Revolution in the artillery; and of *The Mountain Pass*, which is one of the best novellas on the Soviet experience in Afghanistan; worked as editors for *Soviet Warrior*, the bimonthly organ of the MPD: Col. Ivan Stadnyuk, Lt. Col. Nikolaj Kambulov and Nikolaj Ivanov, a graduate of the Suvorov Military Academy and the L'vov Advanced Military-Political Academy.

On the question of reestablishing a journal strictly for military literature, Sobolev raised the possibility of making Molodaya gvardiya's *Al'manakh Podvig* [Feat of Arms Anthology] a monthly magazine that would be devoted to this topic.[60] *Al'manakh Podvig* had been established in 1968 as a journal strictly for military fiction, but on an approximately biannual basis. It never did increase its frequency to monthly. In 1991 it changed its name to *Derzhava*, a word for government, associated with the rule of the czar. This was a reflection of a Russian nationalist inclination which arose among the professional military in Afghanistan, which is a topic that is examined in Rybakov's *The Afghanies*.

In his closing speech to the conference, Sobolev reminded the participants of the success of "LOKAF, which had successfully prepared cadres of military writers," as an example to be followed. He argued that

> military might without people is nothing. The man who is the soldier is the determining factor in our military strength. Since man and literature are inseparable concepts, it is precisely our job to concern ourselves with the inculcation of our young people as genuine Soviet soldiers, who will be prepared for any difficulties, ready to defend the Socialist Motherland.[61]

V CONGRESS OF WRITERS, 1971

In preparation for the opening of the V Congress of the Writers' Union of the USSR, Boris Leonov published an article in the 29 June 1971 *Red Star* on military fiction. In works on the war and the Revolution, commanders and political officers inspiring their subordinates to accomplish feats of arms have been the main heroes. The key to successful works on the Revolution was to show how they establish the legitimacy of their authority. Authority is not simply given out along with the insignia of rank. It must be earned "by the personal example of a commander's conduct in battle, and by his professional knowledge, not only of how to wage a battle, but also how to win it." This is the example of heroes like Chapaev or Kozhukh from *The Iron Flood* or Vorob'ev from *Novella about a Real Man*.

In works on the contemporary, peacetime military, we see our soldiers "on the front line with imperialism," where events can still separate the quick from the dead. This can be seen in works like: Alekseev's *The Successors*, Berezko's *Stronger than the Atom*, Gorbachev's *The Pull of the Stars*, Seminikhin's *The Lunar Variant*, Perventsev's *The Island of Hope*, Kambulov's *The Corporal of the*

Perventsev's *The Island of Hope*, Kambulov's *The Corporal of the Guard Has Not Come Yet* and *The Rocket's Thunder*, Sviridov's *Victory Does Not Come Easy*, Rodichev's *Summer on the Amur River* and Vinogradov's *Surface—Air—Surface*. These works all show that there can be real heroes in peacetime, heroes who can inspire others by the example of their self-sacrifice. Despite the heroics displayed in these works, no one figure stands out as the image of the modern commander to match Kozhukh, Chapaev or Vorob'ev. Creating that figure is the task of the writers working on military fiction about the peacetime military.

The world of the contemporary peacetime military man is filled with powerful rockets, radars, nuclear reactors; all things that seemed like magic only yesterday. Amid all this technology, however, the important thing to bear in mind is that without men to run it, technology is dead. This brings us back to the commander and the political officer who still work with people. Today's commander cannot get by with only the force of his personal example for others to follow. He must be an expert technician and manager, who can lead the *kollektiv* that serves the complex weapon systems of today.

MEETING WITH THE LEADERSHIP OF THE CREATIVE UNIONS, 1977

A meeting between the MPD and the leadership of the creative unions was held in the Frunze Central Officers' Club in Moscow in April 1977. This meeting further examined the relationship between the commander and the *kollektiv*. When writing on the contemporary military, authors were not supposed to depict service in the ranks as leveling an individual and his spiritual needs, which to a great extent it was. The service was explicitly called the school of socialism by many military and civilian political figures, specifically because it helped to form members of the Soviet *kollektiv*. They were supposed to take a more corporate view of the Armed Forces as a system that cannot function without a highly developed organizational structure and discipline. Service in the ranks was to be depicted so that the troops would fulfill the requirements of their oath, the regulations and the orders of their commanders out of a sense of conscience. In the context of this discussion, the use of conscience as a motivator for adherence to orders in the face of some reluctance on the part of the troops is very reminiscent of Engels' definition of freedom: the recognition of necessity.

The military *kollektiv* is a complex set of social interactions. It is built from the unity of the wills of the commanders and their subordinates. The superiority of the Soviet Armed Forces is based on the communality of ideals and political convictions of the Soviet people and their defenders, the members of the Armed Forces. The construction of the military *kollektiv* is the duty of the officer corps, and literature and the arts are called upon to help them in accomplishing their mission.

ALL-RUSSIAN CONFERENCE OF WRITERS, 1977

An All-Russian Conference of writers working on the contemporary military was held in December at the Moscow Military District Officers' Club. It was sponsored by the MPD and the Writers' Union of the RSFSR.

Sergej Mikhalkov, the chairman of the Directorate of the Writers' Union of the RSFSR set the tone for the conference by quoting article thirty-one of the new Constitution: "The defense of the Socialist Fatherland is regarded as one of the most important functions of government and is the job of all the people of the land."[62]

Mikhalkov felt that the primary subject for literary exploration in the contemporary military was the interaction between man and technology in a period of scientific-technological progress. Primarily this exploration should focus on the personality of the story's character, on his ideological convictions, his social engagement, his moral qualities. In this regard, noted Mikhalkov, military fiction is no different from literature depicting life in other areas of society.

> An aspiration for Communism, dedication to the ideas of internationalism, patriotism, an aspiration to make your best effort for the good of the interests of society are equally characteristic of the man in an army greatcoat as they are of any other of our contemporaries, working at a factory, at a construction project, on a state farm, in a laboratory, in a scientific facility.[63]

Nikolaj Gorbachev, a widely read and respected author of contemporary military fiction, joined Mikhalkov in recounting the ideological underpinnings of the genre. Gorbachev reasoned that need for military fiction was dictated by the continuous military threat under which the USSR lived.

> Whosoever is forced to build a fortress and constantly strengthen it in order to remain strong and unconquered in the face of a brutal enemy, should without fail also concern himself not only about his rifle, but also, equally, with the spiritual condition, the spiritual armament of the defenders of the Socialist Fatherland.[64]

Gorbachev, who was a military rocket engineer, saw the Scientific and Technological Revolution as an "inexhaustible" source of topics for literary exploration. One of the areas that he deemed worthy of additional literary study was the interaction of the members of the teams that serve the new weapons complexes such as the missile systems so familiar to him. When serving a system like this, an engineer, a technician and a private soldier are all colleagues, each of whom does his part to make the system function. It is the relationships between them that need to be further explored in military fiction. Team-served weapons were reshaping the traditional hierarchical relationship of the Armed Forces, creating very interesting conflicts for authors to explore.

Gorbachev's shopping list of topics for military fiction to explore was:

- the romance and heroism of the service,
- the unity of the Army and the people,
- the personality of the professional officer as a part of an advanced Socialist society,
- the high ideals, convictions and morals of servicemen and
- their readiness to perform feats of valor.

V. Kozhevnikov, Secretary of the Directorate of the Writers' Union of the USSR and Boris Leonov, the premier literary critic of military fiction, both addressed the need for authors to more fully examine racial friction in the services.[65] The viewpoint for writers to take in their examination of this topic was that, despite their differences, the various nationalities serving in the Forces are joined by their common duty to serve the Motherland and loyalty to the ideals of socialism. This was later also tied to the need for more coverage of the internationalism of the Warsaw Pact Forces.

Ivan Kozlov and Aleksandr Belyaev[66] raised the old topic of who should write about the contemporary military: professional authors from outside, with only superficial knowledge of what life there is like, or writers serving in the Forces. Kozlov's opinion was that only those who made the military their life could write about it properly. Only they could provide the audience with the details of the lives of the defenders of the Motherland that it wanted.

Even though this was a conference on contemporary military literature, Leonov and several others managed to introduce the topic of the war to the conference. They did this by tying the war to the definition of Soviet patriotism. Only by making the serving soldiers of today the successors to the traditions of heroism of the war could literature insure the loyalty of the younger generation.

In his speech, Army General Epishev, the chief of the MPD, reinforced the ideological points made by Mikhalkov and N. Gorbachev, concentrating on the power of the written word in the battle for men's minds.[67] He clearly stated the criterion by which the Party judged the value of works of literature as "its ideological thrust, the author's position as a member of the Party, which makes the work an event, that will make its influence felt in the inculcation of the people."[68]

His shopping list of topics for authors to investigate in their works about the military included

- *kollektivism* as the negation of egotism and self-centeredness,
- duty to the Motherland, to the people and one's own conscience,
- social responsibility of serving one's country,
- strict regulation of life in the ranks,
- high moral and physical demands of the service.

He also called upon the participants to join the battle of competing ideologies and help counter the effects of disinformation aimed at the youth of the USSR from the West, which encouraged them to be apolitical, skeptical, materialistic believers in the generation gap.

One of the primary tasks of the creative intellectual elite was, in Epishev's view, inculcating young people with social goals for the greater good, ideological conviction and a desire to be an active participant of society. He prophetically stated that the course of economic growth and the sociopolitical development of Soviet society depended on victory on this front. He was right. It did. They lost.

In general, all three of the speakers were pleased with the way in which the genre was developing. This was the high-water mark for the genre, before the invasion of Afghanistan and the forces of glasnost and perestroika began to affect the political infrastructure of the military.

ROUNDTABLE DISCUSSIONS IN KIEV, 1978

In late February, *Literary Gazette* and the Ukrainian Writers' Union held a two-day roundtable discussion of military fiction in Kiev. Ivan Kozlov defined the character traits of the hero of Soviet military fiction as something that was new to the literary scene when the character of the Soviet soldier first appeared in works about the Civil War in the twenties. This character "makes a conscious decision to go off to do battle for the good of the working people, is ready for self-sacrifice, is spiritually rich, is a true citizen and patriot."[69] These traits were reaffirmed not just in military fiction about the war, but also in real life, boasts Kozlov.

Kozlov focuses primarily on a trait that had not received any noticeable attention at previous meetings and conferences: the humanism of the Soviet soldier. He sees this as one of the most valuable qualities in a soldier, whether it is in his relationship to a buddy at the front or to civilians, or to children and orphans. Even though military fiction about the war had always treated this topic well, said Kozlov, his major concern was with repulsing the attacks on the genre from the USSR's enemies abroad, who were trying to negate the concept of humanity in war in general, saying that Soviet soldiers were just as brutal as the Nazis.

This theme had received very interesting treatment in V. Sobko's *Guarantee of Peace* about the immediate postwar period in Germany and would be picked up again, as the war in Afghanistan began to enter military fiction, in Nikolaj Burbyga's *The Pacification Detachment*. It was not until 1990, when the bonds of socialist-realism had already broken down, that a work of fiction about the immediate postwar period was published, which provided a glimpse of the not-so-humanistic side of the Soviet soldier in conquered Germany: Boris Bakhtin's *The Sergeant and the Frau*.

Nikolaj Gorbachev expounded on the problems of character development in the midst of the Scientific and Technological Revolution. In order to show the true heroism of a character's action, an author has to "develop the entire complex of moral, psychological and ethical characteristics of the hero, his ideological conviction and engagement as a citizen."[70] In the days of the cavalry, when men on horseback charged each other with sabres drawn, or in more modern times, when fighter pilots fought it out one-on-one, it was easy for an author to develop the psychology of a character together with the action. Gorbachev felt that the interaction of man and machine had made this harder by moving the dynamics of the story from the exterior to the interior plane, creating what he called "mental dynamism." For Gorbachev, the challenge was to fully develop his characters, using this new literary process.[71]

Mikhail Kvlividze, a Georgian poet, took a stance that was somewhat at odds with the MPD's view of literature. "Literature cannot give answers. It asks questions. Ready answers can only be provided by bad literature."[72] He softened the harshness of his statement by adding that the questions asked by literature should be so phrased as to predetermine the answer to them in some degree, but that is still not the approach favored by the MPD.

Literature that asks questions without providing ready answers to them is one that makes the audience think about what they have read and is, therefore, at odds with the ready answers of socialist-realism that is so dear to the hearts of the military command and political hierarchy that interfaced with the writers' unions.

WORKSHOP, 1981

In June 1981, the magazine *Literaturnaya ucheba* [Literary Studies], the journal of literary criticism and political sociology of the Writers' Union of the USSR and the Central Committee of the Comsomol, together with the MPD, held a five-day workshop for emerging writers serving in the military. In his speech on the opening day of the workshop, the deputy chief of the MPD, Colonel General A. D. Lizichev, called on the participants to produce more military fiction on the modern military. He offered a number of worthy topics for the authors to develop, when responding to his call to literary arms:

- the development of the character of the military commander from platoon leader to regimental commander,
- the development of cohesion in the *kollektiv* of modern, complex weapon systems served by teams instead of a single individual,
- the growing role of discipline and sense of duty,
- the family life of officers serving in remote garrisons.

The development of the character of the commander in military fiction was the oldest of the four on Lizichev's list. It had been a perennial on the MPD's list since the formation of LOKAF and had produced a number of works of interest such as Kuleshov's *The White Wind*, Kambulov's *Faithfulness* and Ivanov's *The Mountain Pass*.

The changing interpersonal relationships between officers, enlisted men (EM) and civilian technicians in the Scientific and Technological Revolution had a long history. It had first been raised at the First All-Union Conference on Military Fiction in 1955. Nikolaj Gorbachev's trilogy is perhaps the best example of a work on this topic.

Discipline had a long history on the MPD's wish list. It too first appeared in 1955 and had gained prominence as the years went by. Duty had a history almost as long, first appearing in the Central Committee Resolution of 1967. The increasing attention given both these topics on the MPD's shopping list points to a growing problem in these areas as Soviet society changed in the seventies and eighties. There was hardly a work of military fiction without an AWOL (Absent Without Leave) episode in it.

The family life of officers in remote garrisons was a completely new topic on the MPD's shopping list. It had long been a topic for exploration in military fiction, appearing in such works as Pronyakin's

Court of Honor (1974) and Biryukov's *Only Three Days* (1975), which had both shown that there was not much family life there.

In their concluding remarks the leaders of the workshop noted that the participants were indeed knowledgeable about the specifics of modern military life and that they had some interesting ideas and material to present, but, for the most part, they still lacked the professional skills and techniques to fully develop the personalities of their characters or the events that they take part in.[73]

SESSION OF THE DIRECTORATE OF THE WRITERS' UNION, 1982

The second perestroika of Soviet literature began at the 1982 session of the Directorate of the Writers' Union of the USSR to discuss Union operations in Leningrad. The first perestroika of Soviet literature had been the creation of the Writers' Union in 1932 on the basis of a Central Committee Resolution entitled "On the perestroika of the Creative Literary Organizations." In his speech to the session, A. Chepurov, the First Secretary of the Directorate of the Leningrad branch of the Writers' Union, quoted CPSU General Secretary Brezhnev:

> "In essence," said Leonid Il'ich Brezhnev, "we are talking about perestroika"—yes, that's right. It was not a slip of the tongue, precisely perestroika—"of many of the sectors and spheres of ideological work. The content has to become more up-to-date, and the methods have to meet the demands and requirements of the Soviet people. ... All ideological inculcation has to be conducted in a lively and interesting manner, without cliched phrases and the standard assortment of ready-made formulas."[74]

Chepurov had taken these words to heart for the Leningrad chapter of the Writers' Union and this session of the national directorate was being publicized to share his initiative.

COMMISSION PLENUM, 1982

The CMF of the national Writers' Union held its plenary session for 1982 in the Frunze Central Officers' Club in Moscow together with the MPD. It was dedicated to the topic of "the modern Soviet military in literature."

In his speech to the plenum, V. Karpov, a conservative chronicler of the war, stated that the man in the army greatcoat had become one of the main characters of Soviet literature with good reason, not, as those hostile to the Socialist system say, because we are a warlike people, but because we have had to defend our choice to build Communism in our country.

In his speech, the deputy chief of the MPD, Colonel General A. D. Lizichev pointed to the reasons for continued efforts on the part of writers to inculcate young people with a dedication to the Socialist Motherland and the great cause of Communism.

> Since the end of the war a new generation has grown up. A generation that does not know what war is. For them peace is the natural state of affairs. Some of them even think that preserving and strengthening the peace does not require any or almost no effort. This often gives birth to a pacifist, carefree attitude, to underestimating the reality of the military threat. This is not permissible. Literature is called upon to say its influential word about this.[75]

THE THIRD PLENUM OF THE DIRECTORATE OF THE WRITERS' UNION OF THE RSFSR, 1984

The Third Plenum of the Directorate of the Writers' Union of the RSFSR was held on 22 February 1984. The tone for the plenum was set by the message of greetings sent from the participants to General Secretary Chernenko:

> We recognize that literary activity is one of the most important areas of ideological work. Literature has always served the party of Lenin and has been on the front line of the struggle for the victory of the ideas of Communism. ... Let the word become a powerful weapon in the battle for the coming of peace for humanity, for our country without war.[76]

It was noted that the heroic-patriotic axis of Russian literature had concentrated primarily on the exploration of the Great Patriotic War. Even though the war was long over, it continued to live in the memory of the people who had lived through it, and it had the quality of a racial memory in those born after the war. Vladimir Karpov offered another image of the connection of the war with the present. For him "the connection between history and the present was like the connection between the roots, the trunk and the crown of a tree. The roots and the crown cannot exist one without the other."[77]

Daniil Granin compared the memory of the war in the West with that in the USSR.

> They want to get rid of the memory of it, to get over it, obviously, because it is not connected with the same number of

casualties, with the same sadness, with the same sorrow and pain of the millions of people that it is in our country. ... They have forgotten about the war. We still remember and we cannot forget. We would like to forget, but we cannot. For us the suffering and the pain and our anger are directed against the threat of a new war.[78]

Reporting on the plenum was very strident. It was full of the vocabulary of the ideological battle that was being waged with America and the West on the propaganda front. It almost totally ignored all the other issues that had been very much a part of the discussions of the genre earlier.

In general the plenum was pleased with the amount of military fiction on the war that was being published in the literary journals at the time. The CMF was praised for its activity, especially for its close contacts with the MPD. The plenum did, however, criticize works of military fiction on the contemporary military for not always rising to the level of the importance and the seriousness of the topic. The CMF was tasked to raise the ideological and creative level of works on the modern-day military by attracting more talented writers to the topic.

MEETING WITH THE LEADERS OF THE CREATIVE UNIONS, 1986

On 3 June 1986 the MPD held a meeting with the leaders of the creative unions and prominent writers and artists working on military topics. The goal of the meeting was to discuss the future role of literature, the arts and the mass media in the patriotic inculcation of Soviet young people and Soviet soldiers. Chief of the MPD, Army General A. D. Lizichev, saw the present situation of "widespread societal change, sharpening ideological struggle, and heightening military threat" as requiring new and energetic steps.[79] In times like these, he found, it was hard to overstate the role of the creative arts and mass media in accomplishing this task. Citing the new edition of the Party program, Lizichev reminded the participants that "a major task of ideological inculcation remains military-patriotic inculcation, the creation of a readiness to defend the Socialist Fatherland, to give it all your energies, and, if it becomes necessary, your life."[80]

Lizichev took pride in listing the successes of the MPD's joint efforts with the creative unions. Writers, journalists, artists, playwrights and screenwriters were being sent on TDYs to Field Training Exercises (FTX) and to Afghanistan. A number of unnamed central and provincial periodicals were devoting more space to the patriotic and international inculcation of Soviet soldiers. The MPD was ready to support any useful initiatives for improving work in this area.

Despite these successes, Lizichev felt that there were still a number of areas in which things could improve. One of these was the artistic exploitation of the heroism of Soviet history. In Lizichev's opinion, the Great Patriotic War remained an "inexhaustible" source of material on the bravery and heroism of the Soviet people. Quoting Aleksej Tolstoy, Lizichev was sure that the war would remain the starting point for all art for hundreds of years.

The Minister of Defense, S. L. Sokolov, echoed Lizichev's view of the "inexhaustible" nature of the war as a source for new works of literature to teach young people the meaning of heroism. This was especially important, he felt, in view of the fact that over 60 percent of the population of the USSR had been born after May 1945.

Lizichev went on to criticize some recent works for their elements of abstract pacifism. Their emphasis on the losses and hardships of the war at the expense of heroism were not the right way to approach the topic. As far as Lizichev was concerned, there can only be one truth about the war: "that is the truth of Victory, the truth of heroism and of the steadfastness that the Soviet people displayed in the years of their greatest trial."[81] Sokolov backed him up by saying that books, films and plays with this kind of tendentious treatment of the war should not be allowed into print. They are detrimental to the inculcation of young people and soldiers of the USSR.

The next topic on Lizichev's list was the contemporary military. He noted that this topic was seldom taken up by big-name writers and artists. It was, in his opinion, the changes in the new military, brought on by the introduction of the latest achievements of science and technology, the rising intellectual and cultural niveau of the men in uniform, that offer writers and artists a broad range of topics to explore, including

- increasing the social responsibility of military men for doing their duty,
- service under conditions of a growing threat of war,
- diligence and unilateral command,
- the individual and the military *kollektiv*,
- intellect and the military system,
- morals and war,
- the military family.

Works on these topics should make every effort to show the growing role of the Soviet Armed Forces as a defender of the Socialist Fatherland, and the heroism that is found every day in the military service. They should raise the prestige of being a professional military man, and attempt to get young people to want to become officers. They should also do more to promote *kollektivism*, internationalism, racial harmony and the brotherhood in arms of the armies of the Socialist Commonwealth.

As a background against which to paint the artistic development of these themes, Lizichev suggested operational duties at PVO and rocket sites, long-range naval patrols, service in Afghanistan and the Chernobyl disaster.

In answer to the question that he often received, Lizichev said that the negative elements in military life could not be entirely whitewashed. The presentation of these events, however, had to be tempered, to show the main lines of social development in the Armed Forces. The education of young people should not be solely on the basis of negative examples.

The First Secretary of the Writers' Union, G. Markov, reinforced Lizichev's calls for more works on the contemporary military, but noted that a few TDYs to units and ships were not sufficient basis for deep understanding of the processes that shaped life in the present-day military. Because of that, it was necessary to look for writers among those already serving in the ranks and to help them develop as authors. He felt that working on a military newspaper was the best place for young writers to gain the insight and skills that they needed to become authors.

Marshal Sokolov added his call for works on the contemporary military to Lizichev's and Markov's. In addition to the items on Lizichev's shopping list, Sokolov also asked for works portraying

- faithfulness to one's military duty, military oath, the unit's combat streamer,
- discipline,
- the Armed Forces as a school of citizenship, bravery and patriotism,
- the role of the modern commander, political officer, staff officer, engineer, and specialist,
- the role of warrant officers and sergeants.

He wanted literary portraits of people in these positions that could serve as shining examples to be emulated.

He too pointed out the differences in the soldiers of today when compared to those of as little as twenty to thirty years ago. While there were many positive differences, there were a number of negative ones as well. They had less experience at life, were less steeled by their participation in the labor force and less physically prepared than their predecessors. These were things that caused them problems when they had to serve in the Armed Forces, and writers needed to present a true picture of life and the service that would help young people adjust better to it.

CONFERENCE OF THE LEADERSHIP OF THE MILITARY PRESS, 1989

In 1989, in the face of the impending reduction in force (RIF), which was projected to reduce the numerical strength of the Armed Forces by several million men, and under the glasnost gun, the chief of the MPD, Army General A. D. Lizichev, called a conference of the leadership of the military press in Moscow on March 3. In view of the rapidly changing political landscape of glasnost and perestroika, the MPD apparently chose to ignore the strategic arm of the print media, the literary press, with its long reaction time between concept and publication, and to concentrate on the tactical issues of the role of the periodic press, with its much shorter lead time from concept to publication.

The importance that the MPD placed on improving the coverage of military-patriotic activities in the press was stressed by the personal appearance of the Minister of Defense, Army General Dmitrij T. Yazov. Many of the topics that General Yazov ordered the press to cover during his speech[82], already had long standing on the list of topics to be covered in military fiction:

- sacred duty to defend the Socialist Fatherland,
- mastering military technology,
- discipline,
- interracial harmony,
- *kollektivism*,
- pride of service,
- officers' ethics,
- initiative,
- the traditions of World War II.

Other items on his list reflected the tactical situation of dealing with glasnost and perestroika that was at hand, such as

- the move from low-efficiency, wasteful methods to high-efficiency, economical ones, accenting quality,
- the RIF and its impact on combat readiness,
- the elections.

While recognizing the fact of perestroika and glasnost, Yazov tried to keep the press under Party control by continuing to set guidelines for press coverage of perestroika. He charged the conference participants with presenting "hard facts" rather than taking glasnost as a license for journalistic gullibility, superficial judgments, bias and sensationalism. He wanted the press to provide answers for any issues that they raised about perestroika in the military such as

- the all-volunteer military,
- the formation of home-town-based National Guard units,
- the reduction of a draftee's tour of duty to one year,

all of which he opposed.

In his view, the duty of the press was to collect information, digest it and then to distribute the essence of what the reporter had learned in the process. When working with readers' letters, which had become a major force under glasnost, the press needed to bring the issues raised by the author of the letter to a conclusion and thereby maintain control of the issue rather than just throw out an open-ended question and let the discussion go off on its own. Yazov was, in essence, trying to control the change inherent in perestroika, rather than be controlled by it. He reminded the participants of Lenin's tenet that a newspaper should be not only an active supporter and public relations man for the *kollektiv*" but also "the *kollektiv*'s organizer." It was their duty as loyal members of the Party and convinced Communists to advance the Party's ideas on perestroika and show that the origin for perestroika was the Party itself. His view was that each newspaper and magazine earned its position as an authoritative source of information among its readers by "the clarity of its ideological position, its sharp, current affairs coverage, its consequent, firm implementation of the Party's policies and the policies of perestroika."

The first item on Yazov's list to receive detailed treatment was improving the quality of training. He attacked stagnation, inertia, cliche and mediocrity in the training cycle, all of which were topics that had seen widespread treatment in military literature, in such works as Vozovikov's award-winning *His Father's Son* and Bogatov's *Rise to Your Own Level*. He called on the press to make sure that each officer and soldier was aware of his duties and obligations, as defined by the regulations and by their own consciences, and would carry out the tasks assigned to them, guided by the regulations and their consciences so as to achieve the best possible end result. All this was nothing new, but support for them at this level was.

Yazov accused the press of stilted, superficial, unenthusiastic coverage of these topics and urged them to correct the problem. His suggestion for doing this was to take a closer look at the experience of the older generation of military journalists, especially those who had covered World War II. Their example was worthy of emulation.

The war itself continued to be a source of tremendous spiritual potential and should not be forgotten in their coverage of the military. The example of the bravery and heroism of the war and the presentation of today's soldiers as the successors to upholding those traditions remained, as always, a welcome topic in the military press. Of course, Yazov wanted that coverage to be objective (a code word for "from the Party's point of view"), rather than from some other, subjective, point of view.

Next on Yazov's list was discipline, which "has been and remains one of the most important topics for the press." His critique of the coverage of this topic was much the same as for the coverage of training. He wanted the press to delineate concrete suggestions that could be followed by unit commanders to address this problem.

His comments on discipline, however, put a new light on this topic. Obviously under pressure from a growing number of press reports and works of military fiction such as Polyakov 's *One Hundred Days till the Order* (1988), Yazov called specifically for the press to attack the disciplinary problem of *dedovshchina*—the tyranny of the longer serving soldiers over the new draftees—something that had not been explicitly stated before in the order placed by the MPD with the writers' organizations for military literature. The issue of race relations also received a much broader coverage than had previously been the case, indicating a growing problem in that area that had only received cursory attention in military fiction. This issue was very likely fallout from Afghanistan, where Russian soldiers came into close contact with soldiers from the Central Asian republics and the Afghan Army.

Yazov's speech was followed six months later by an editorial in *Red Star* entitled "The Political Organs and the Press."[83] This editorial is important because it was an admission that the MPD no longer had a monopoly on what the Soviet fighting man reads. Glasnost had permitted opinions, different from those long espoused by the Party, to appear in the press and in literature. Perestroika had done away with the days when "some political organs simply decided to remove newspapers and journals, which expressed a point of view different from that which is generally accepted " (another code word for the Party's view), from day rooms and libraries.

Gone were the days when the annual periodical subscription campaign had been conducted by political officers in "press gang" fashion and subscriptions to *Pravda, Izvestiya* and *Red Star* were mandatory. In 1989, subscriptions to these papers had become voluntary and subscription rates were down dramatically. As of the end of August, only 26 percent of the previous year's subscribers had renewed their subscriptions to *Pravda*; 32 percent to *Izvestiya* and 28 percent to *Red Star*. Even though the MPD did not realize it at the time, the editorial's admission that "no one has the right to dictate to a person what he has to read" was, in essence, the signal of the MPD's surrender in the battle for men's minds that LOKAF and Soviet military fiction had been created to win.

ALL-UNION ASSOCIATION OF MILITARY FICTION WRITERS, 1991

Still not aware that it had lost the battle, the MPD participated in the formation of the All-Union Association of Military Fiction Writers in March 1991. The MPD joined together with the national Writers' Union; the Writers' Unions of the RFSFR, Ukraine, Belorussia, Kazakhstan and Uzbekistan; the Ministry of Defense; the Main Political Directorates of the KGB; the Ministries of the Interior (police), the Navy and the Fishing Industry; the Central Committee of the Comsomol; and DOSAAF to support this new initiative in military fiction.

Col. (ret.) Yu. A. Vinogradov, secretary of the Russian Writers' Union, was named president of the All-Union Association. The appointment of a Russian writer is not surprising, because the Russian Writers' Union had always been in the vanguard of the genre of military fiction. The association had been formed, according to Vinogradov,[84] because the attitude of the official literary organizations and publishing houses toward works of military fiction had become rather "cold." This had prompted those concerned to establish the association, which was to be the new center within the Writers' Union of the USSR to promote the genre.

The association's support from the publishing industry was to come from the Military Publishing House [Voenizdat], the "Patriot" and "Granitsa" [The Border], "Otechestvo" [Fatherland], "Muzhestvo" [Bravery], and "Veteran" Publishing Houses, the Commercial Naval Publishing House (KIML) and from three periodicals: *Sovetskij voin* [Soviet Warrior], the journal of the MPD; *Pogranichniki* [Border Guard Troops], the journal of the border guard troops; and *Na boevom postu* [On Guard], the journal of the Moscow PVO District.

Their initial publishing plans called for the publication of two series under the general titles of "Military Adventures" and "Naval Adventures." They also intended to publish a series containing works which had been awarded literary prizes. In cooperation with the Military Publishing House, they further planned to publish a new "Officer's Library," similar to the one that had been published before the war.

In creating the association, Vinogradov and the genre's other supporters were simply following a trend observed throughout Soviet society at that time to rename existing organizations to improve their public image. The Commission of the national Writers' Union on Military Fiction, the successor organization to LOKAF, had been essentially restructured with a new name that contained the Western word "association" rather than the Slavic word *ob"edinenie*, which had been the "O" in LOKAF. The association's political ideology remained the same as LOKAF's: "patriotism, true internationalism, and service to the Fatherland."

The association's goals and programs also remained the same as the goals of military fiction had been under the control of the Commission on Military Fiction:

- the production and publication of works of military fiction,
- encouraging and aiding young authors still serving in the Forces to write,
- holding writing workshops for young authors still serving in the Forces,
- sending authors on creative TDYs to visit units and ships,
- creating a yearly prize for the most important work in the genre,
- subsidized publication of collections of military poetry expected to have low print runs,
- the creation of the association's own literary monthly journal and its own socio-political weekly.

Even as the MPD continued to fight a delaying action, by forming this new association, Mikhail Gorbachev issued a decree on the dissolution of the political organs in the Armed Forces at the end of August 1991.[85] The removal of the MPD from the coalition that supported the genre marked the end of the era of *Soviet* military fiction.

NOTES

1. Quoted in Viktor Andreevich Chalmaev, *Otbleski plameni* [Reflections of a Flame] Moscow: Military Publishing House, 1978, p. 14.

2. The now-classic work of the Civil War, which relates the tale of Vasilij Ivanovich Chapaev, commander of the twenty-fifth Rifle Division, which fought against Kolchak.

3. Gen. Lt. A. Kopytin, "Naravne s boevym zapasom: VOENIZDATu 50 let" [At the Same Priority as Ammunition: The Fiftieth Anniversary of VOENIZDAT], *Red Star*, 22 October 1969, p. 4.

4. "Ko vsem sovetskim pisatelyam" [To All Soviet Writers], *Pravda*, No. 172, 24 June 1930, p. 7; and "Krasnaya armiya zhdet svoego pisatelya" [The Red Army Awaits its Writer], *Literaturnaya gazeta* [Literary Gazette], 26 June 1930. For a list of participants, see the Appendix at the end of this book.

5. *Chetvertyj s"ezd pisatelej SSSR: Stenograficheskij otchet* [Fourth Congress of the Writers' Union of the USSR: Stenographic Record] Moscow: Sovetskij pisatel' Publishing House, 1967, p. 272.

6. "Boevoj otryad na fronte literatury" [Combat Detachment on the Literary Front], *Literary Gazette*, 5 August 1930.

7. Ibid.

8. "Pervij plenum tsentral'nogo soveta LOKAF" [The First Plenum of the Central Soviet of LOKAF], *Literary Gazette*, 9 April 1931.

9. Gen. Lt. A. Kopytin, "Kniga na sluzhbe vospitaniya voinov" [Books Serving to Educate Soldiers], *Kommunist vooruzhennykh sil* [Armed Forces Communist], No. 20, 1969, p. 32.

10. 1st Capt. V. Ust'yantsev, "Naravne s ognepripasami" [At the Same Priority as Ammunition], *Sovetskij voin* [Soviet Warrior], No. 19, 1979, p. 32; and Gen. Lt. A.

Kopytin, "Naravne s boevym zapasom."

11. Pavel Ivanovich Berezov, *Pisateli i oborona* [Writers and Defense], Moscow: Moskovskoe tovarishchestvo pisatelej [Moscow Association of Writers], 1933, p. 9.

12. "Sozdat' ob"edinenie pisatelej krasnoj armii" [Create an Association of Writers of the Red Army], *Literary Gazette*, 30 June 1930.

13. *Literaturnaya Ehntsiklopediya* [Literary Encyclopedia], A. V. Lunacharskij, chief editor, Moscow: Nauchno-issledovatel'skij institut literatury i isskustva [The Scientific Research Institute for Literature and the Arts], 1932, vol. 6, p. 554; reprinted by the American Council of Learned Societies in Russian Series No. 25, Edwards Brothers, 1949.

14. Pavel Ivanovich Berezov, *Writers and Defense*, Moscow: Moscow Association of Writers, 1933, pp. 15 & 195.

15. *Literary Encyclopedia*, vol. 6, p. 556.

16. "The First Plenum of the Central Soviet of LOKAF."

17. *Literary Encyclopedia*, vol. 6, p. 556.

18. *Vos'moj s"ezd pisatelej SSSR: Stenograficheskij otchet* [Eighth Congress of Writers of the USSR: Stenographic Record], Moscow: Sovetskij pisatel' Publishing House, 1988, p. 477.

19. Boris Leonov, *Utverzhdenie: geroiko-patroticheckaya tema v russkoj i sovetskoj literature* [Affirmation: the Heroic-Patriotic Motif in Russian and Soviet Literature], Moscow: Khudozhestvennaya literatura [Creative Fiction] Publishing House, 1988, p. 332.

20. "To All Soviet Writers," *Pravda*; and "The Red Army Awaits its Writer."

21. "The First Plenum of the Central Soviet of LOKAF."

22. Ibid.

23. *Oruzhiem slova* [Armed with Words], V. Kosolapov, L. Lazarov and V. Piskunov compilers. Moscow: Khudozhestvennaya literatura Publishing House, 1978, p. 23.

24. *Pervyj vsesoyuznyj s"ezd sovetskikh pisatelej 1934: Stenograficheskij otchet* [First All-Union Congress of Soviet Writers: Stenographic record], Moscow: State Publishing House for Literature, 1934, p. 515; reprint, Moscow: Sovetskij pisatel' Publishing House, 1990.

25. A. A. Surkov, "O sostoyanii i zadachakh sovetskoj literatury" [On the State and Tasks of Soviet Literature], published in *Vtoroj s"ezd sovetskikh pisatelej: Stenograficheskij otchet* [The Second All-Union Congress of Soviet Writers: Stenographic Record], Moscow: Sovetskij pisatel' Publishing House, 1956, p. 31.

26. *The Second All-Union Congress of Soviet Writers: Stenographic Record*, p. 275

27. Ibid, p. 276.

28. "Vse-soyuznoe soveshchanie po voenno-khudozhestvennoj literature" [All-Union Conference on Military Fiction], *Literary Gazette*, 2 June 1955.

29. Ibid.

30. S. Golubov, "Nekotorye problemy voenno-khudozhestvennoj prozy" [Some Problems of Prose in Military Fiction], *Literary Gazette*, 31 May 1955.

31. "All-Union Conference on Military Fiction," *Literary Gazette*, 2 June, 1955.

32. Mikhail Alekseev, "Volnuyushchaya tema" [An Exciting Topic], *Red Star*, 27 May 1955.

33. *Soldatskaya sud'ba* [A Soldier's Fate], Yu. Lopusov and Nikolaj K. Starshinov compilers. Moscow: Molodaya gvardiya Publishing House, 1985.

34. "Da zdravstvuet Sovetskaya Armiya!" [Long Live the Soviet Armed Forces!] (editorial), *Literary Gazette*, 21 February 1948, p. 1.

35. "All-Union Conference on Military Fiction," *Literary Gazette*, 2 June, 1955.

36. Lt. V. Yarchuk, "Slovo k pisatelyam" [A Word to Writers], *Red Star*, 27 May 1955, p. 3.

37. S. Shatilov, "Bol'shaya, blagorodnaya tema" [A Great, Honorable Topic], *Literary Gazette*, 28 May 1955, p. 2.

38. Alekseev, "An Exciting Topic."

39. "All-Union Conference on Military Fiction."

40. Ibid.

41. Alekseev, "An Exciting Topic."

42. Marshal R. Ya. Malinovskij, "Vospevat' geroicheskoe" [Praise the Heroic], *Sovetskaya kul'tura*, 11 February 1964.

43. Ibid.

44. "Praise the Heroic," *Red Star*, 9 February 1964 p. 2.

45. Malinovskij, "Praise the Heroic."

46. Ibid.

47. Ibid.

48. The resolution was issued on 21 January 1967.

49. The articles in *Red Star* are: S. K. Kurkotkin, "Byt vojsk i boegotovnost' (k nachalu raboty vsearmejskogo soveshchaniya po uluchsheniyu byta vojsk)" [Troop Living Conditions and Combat Readiness (A Foreword to the All-service Conference on Improving Troop Living Conditions)], 26 November 1985; "Bytu voinov - zabotu i vnimanie" [Concern and Attention for Soldiers' Living Conditions] (Editorial), 14 July 1984; "Bytu vojsk - neoslabnoe vnimanie" [Unweakened Attention for Troop Living Conditions] (Editorial), 28 July 1983; "Bytu voinov - neoslabnoe vnimanie" [Unweakened Attention for Troop Living Conditions] (Editorial), 14 May 1981.

50. *Fourth Congress of Writers of the USSR: Stenographic Record*, pp. 272-273.

51. Ibid., p. 160.

52. Quoted in "Kruglyj stol: vospitat' patriota" [Roundtable: Raising a Patriot], *Literaturnoe obozrenie* [Literary Review], No. 2, 1978, p. 16.

53. "O doblesti, o podvigakh, o slave" [About Valor, about Feats of Arms, about Glory], *Literaturnaya Rossiya*, 14 March 1969.

54. DOSAAF is an organization similar to junior ROTC, which provides military training to students in high school.

55. "Sluzhenie rodine" [Serving the Motherland], *Literary Gazette*, 19 March 1969, p. 2.

56. E. Boltin, "Volnuyushchie stranitsy letopisi Velikoj Otechestvennoj Vojny" [Exciting Pages of the Chronicle of the Great Patriotic War], *Kommunist*, No. 2, 1969, p. 127.

57. "Serving the Motherland."

58. "Sozdat' knigi dostojny velikomu podvigu!" [Create Books Worthy of the Great Feat of Arms!], *Literaturnaya Rossiya*, 21 March 1969, pp. 3-4.

59. "Serving the Motherland."

60. Ibid.

61. Ibid.

62. Sergej Mikhalkov, "Na strazhe mira" [Guarding the Peace], *Literaturnaya Rossiya*, 9 December 1977; and A. Yakhontov, *Radi zhizni na zemle* [For Life on Earth], *Literary Gazette*, 28 December 1977, p. 4.

63. Mikhalkov, "Guarding the Peace."

64. Irina Bogatko and Vladimir Bondarenko, "Literatura o cheloveke s ruzh'em" [Literature about the Man with a Gun]. *Literaturnaya Rossiya*, 16 December 1977, pp. 4-5.

65. Yakhontov, "For Life on Earth."

66. Ibid.

67. Bogatko and Bondarenko, "Literature about the Man with a Gun" and Yakhontov, "For Life on Earth."

68. "Vysokoe prizvanie voennykh pisatelej" [The Great Calling of Military Writers], *Red Star*, 11 December 1977, p. 2.

69. N. Vysotskaya and K. Grigor'ev, "Radi zhizni na zemle: kruglyj stol Literaturnoj gazety i Soyuza pisatelej Ukrainy" [For Life on Earth: a Roundtable Discussion Hosted by Literary Gazette and the Writers' Union of Ukraine], *Literary Gazette*, 22 February 1978, pp. 1, 4.

70. Ibid.

71. Nikolaj Gorbachev, "O podvige, ob armii" [On Feats of Valor, On the Military], *Sovetskaya Rossiya*, 25 February 1978.

72. Vysotskaya and Grigor'ev, "For Life on Earth."

73. Lt. Col. Yu. Velichenko, "Seminar molodykh pisatelej" [Workshop of Young Writers], *Red Star*, 18 June 1981; and "Seminar molodykh avtorov, pishushchykh na voenno-patrioticheskuyu temu" [Workshop of Young Authors, Writing on Military-Patriotic Themes], *Literaturnaya ucheba* [Literary Studies], No. 1, 1982, pp. 40-41.

74. "Po veleniyu vremeni: V sekretariate pravleniya SP SSSR" [As Dictated by the Times: In the Directorate of the Writers' Union of the USSR], *Literary Gazette*, 12 May 1982, pp. 1 & 6.

75. "Sovetskomu voinu posvyashchaetsya" [Dedicated to the Soviet Soldier], *Literary Gazette*, 24 March 1982.

76. "Pisateli v bor'be za mir" [Writers in the Struggle for Peace], *Literary Gazette*, 2 March, 1984, pp. 2-3.

77. Ibid.

78. Ibid.

79. "Vospevat' ratnyj trud, slavit' voinskij podvig" [Praise the Labor of the Forces, Glorify Military Feats of Arms], *Red Star*, 6 June 1986, pp. 2-3.

80. Ibid.

81. Ibid.

82. D. T. Yazov, "Byt' na ostrie perestrojki" [Be on the Cutting Edge of Perestroika], *Red Star*, 7 March 1989.

83. "Politorgany i pechat'" [The Political Organs and the Press], *Red Star*, 2 September 1989, p. 1.

84. Maj. I. Yadykin, "Poehziya podviga i dolga" [The Poetry of Feats of Arms and Duty], *Red Star*, 2 April 1991, p. 4.

85. "Ob uprazdnenii voenno-politicheskikh organov v Vooruzhennykh Silakh SSSR, vojskakh Komiteta gosudarstvennoj bezopasnosti SSSR, vnutrennikh vojskakh Ministerstva vnutrennikh del i zheleznodorozhnykh vojskakh: Ukaz Prezidenta SSSR (M.S. Gorbachev)" [On the Dissolution of the Military-political Organs of the Armed Forces of the USSR, of the Troops of the Committee on State Security, of the Internal Troops of the Ministry of the Interior, of the Railroad Troops: Decree of the President of the USSR (M. S. Gorbachev)], *Red Star*, 31 August 1991.

2

The Aftermath of the War

It is easier to make war than to make peace.

Georges Clemenceau

Soviet military fiction in the postwar period can be said to begin with Vadim Sobko's novel, *The Guarantee of Peace*. The action of the novel begins the day after the German surrender, on 10 May 1945, in the town of Dornau, near Dresden. The work is a model propaganda piece that tells the story of the military commandant of Dornau as he and his staff help the Germans in the Soviet Zone of Occupation build a democratic Germany that will be the Guarantee of peace in Europe. (Sobko, 6 & 112)

Land reform, the nationalization of industry and the formation of the Socialist Unity Party of Germany (SED) are painted in the standard colors of Soviet propaganda of the period, which is certainly one of the reasons that Sobko's book was awarded the Stalin prize for literature (third class) in 1950. Sobko's novel is of interest, not for these cliches of Cold War propaganda, which make up the bulk of the work, but for its study of the relationship between the conqueror and the conquered. The goal of this subthread of the novel was to adjust the reader's perceptions of Germany and the Germans.

This was a very important propaganda task in the postwar period, in which the viewpoint of the commandant's translator, Valya, was undoubtedly more than commonplace. Sobko shows the reader how Valya felt about the Germans in a scene in which she submits a request for reassignment. Earlier that day, while talking to a German in a nearby village, she learned that he had fought on the Eastern front in the city of Belev, which is her hometown. She is furious about this and cannot stand to deal with the Germans as if nothing had happened,

when this man could very well have been the one who killed her
father. (Sobko, 73)

This opinion is seconded by Maj. Savchenko, who, while preparing
to go to the premiere of a Soviet play in the newly reopened city
theater, comments:

> Life is an amazing thing! Just think that a year ago today we
> were still fighting for Berlin. Remember how tired, how
> covered with dust and how angry we were! The Brigade was
> preparing its last strike and everyone lived with only one
> thought—to finish off the enemy. A year later and I'm sitting
> with the Brigade Chief of Technical Services [now the town
> commandant] and the Instructor from the Political Department
> [now the commendatura's political officer]. We're in dress
> uniform and preparing to ... Damnation! Can you imagine
> saying this a year ago? We're sitting in Dornau and preparing
> to go to a concert in the town theater, to which the Germans are
> invited. Just remember that they attacked us in 1941. (Sobko,
> 196)

Sobko's commandant, Col. Chajka, is the voice of reason. He
counters both his subordinates' arguments with: "there are Germans and
there are Germans." (Sobko, 196) This is the base of the dichotomy that
Sobko presents, in which there are two distinct character types of
Germans:

- the "bad" Germans, represented by the unrepentant former
  Nazis, now minions of the Americans and the British—that
  is "theirs," and
- the "good" Germans, who hated Hitler and who realize that
  they were liberated from Fascism by the Soviets—that is
  "ours."

The novel's chief "bad" German is SS Sturmbahnfuehrer Kurt
Zander, former head of the Dornau Gestapo. Just before the Russians
arrived, he destroyed all Gestapo archives and left for Munich in the
American Zone, where he and many of his former colleagues were
recruited by the Americans for espionage in the Soviet Zone. (Sobko, 26)
When he returns to Dornau, Zander brings a message of hope to those of
his ilk who remained behind. The Americans and the British support
their ideals. In the Western Zones, which the "bad" Germans view as
the promised land, "democratization, denazification and
demilitarization are not in favor" (Sobko, 128) and the Potsdam
agreements are mentioned as little as possible.

Zander has generous funding and orders for the bad Germans. The orders include making death threats to progressive Soviet sympathizers, sabotaging factories and administrative programs, continuing to spread Joseph Goebbels' rumor that the "Russians" are going to deport everyone to Siberia, and turning members of the Soviet military community against each other. In the end, however, the enemies of the new Germany are rounded up by the commendatura staff and East Germany is made safe for the Soviet brand of democracy.

The "good" Germans are made up of former concentration camp inmates, who had been imprisoned for their Communist sympathies; German veterans of the Civil War in Spain, who had fled to the Soviet Union afterward; German POWs, who were won over by their warm-hearted captors; the working class, which was won over by the nationalization of industry; the rural populace, which was won over by land reform; and the intelligentsia, which was won over by the words and deeds of the Russian town commandant and his staff.

As he develops the character of each of the representatives of these groups, Sobko tries to show them in the best light for his target audience. Sobko gives the good Germans a compliment by having one of the bad Germans complain that he has "the impression that the Germans have lost their senses and are starting to show sympathy for the Bolsheviks." (Sobko, 127) This kind of character reference for the good Germans is especially effective in a society, such as the USSR, where government-controlled sources of information suffer from a credibility gap. It was common practice, throughout the Cold War, to cite Western sources whenever they supported the Soviet point of view, because Western sources had a higher credibility quotient.

The underlying goal of all the commendatura's efforts in Dornau is to win the peace by reshaping Germany into a peace-loving country on the Soviet model. (Sobko, 111-112) As commandant Chajka puts it: "We entered into Germany in battle and we are going to leave Democratic Germany as friends." (Sobko, 196) In military fiction, winning the peace means reshaping the way readers conceive of Germany, changing their perception from one of war and Fascism to one of peace and Communism.

Sobko's star German actress, Edith Hartman, states Sobko's goal succinctly when she says: "The word 'German' was spoken like a curse all over the world and now it has to take on a new sound and a new meaning." (Sobko, 207) Life in Germany, as it is presented in Sobko's book, is the basis for that new meaning. As the novel draws to a close, Sobko has Capt. Sokolov's wife sum up what has happened in the Soviet zone of occupation during her tour in Germany:

We have changed a lot here in Germany. We work, bustle around, worry, do bunches of things, carry out orders and directives, and somehow we stop noticing what is happening to us ourselves. But then, one fine day, you realize how much you have achieved. After all, when you come right down to it, you're opening people's eyes to peace and setting them out on the road to happiness. (Sobko, 274-275)

Aleksej Kireev's novella *Flows the River Elbe*, which was awarded a Ministry of Defense Certificate of Encouragement in 1972, picks up the story of the Soviets in Germany in 1951, where Sobko's story leaves off. Kireev's town commandant, Col. Karev, sounds a lot like Sobko's Col. Chajka, when he talks about his job:

"Yesterday you hated the Germans fiercely, beat them into submission, and now you have to look 'em in the eyes, and straight in the eyes at that, holding eye contact." [Karev] thought about it, turning it over in his mind, "that's the way it should be, isn't it: not all Germans are the enemy." (Kireev, 286)

Kireev preserves Sobko's two character types for his Germans, but adds an interesting twist to each of them. The bad Germans have been joined by second-generation White Russian emigrés and the good Germans have become good enough to become wives for junior Soviet officers.

The bad Germans in Kireev's novella are represented by Kurt Romacher and his ilk, who are waging a two-pronged attack on East Germany. The first prong is directed against the East German equivalent of the Soviet young pioneers, the Free German Youth (FDJ). The second prong is directed against the Soviet troops in the Group of Soviet Forces Germany (GSFG).

As the story opens, Romacher is bragging that they just completed an operation in which they dressed up as Soviet soldiers and broke up several bars in the town. As a result of this incident, the local commander placed the town off limits to all officers and men, except in organized groups. This is a restriction that continued well into modern times and was not just limited to GSFG. It shows up again in Stepanov's novella *At the Brandenburg Gate*, which was published in 1973, and in Yurij Petukhov's ...*Two Springs from Now* about life in the Southern Group of Forces (Hungary), which was published in 1983.

The goal of all Romacher's operations is to spread unrest among the Soviet troops and dissatisfaction with the government among the FDJ. Their primary tactic is the distribution of leaflets in areas where each target audience is to be found. The content of the leaflets for each group is aimed specifically at them. The FDJ gets the true confessions of a young East German, who has crossed over to the West, and the troops get leaflets warning of the impending restriction on leaves and passes, which is a severe blow to morale.

Romacher is assisted by Kol'ka "Koka" Sidorokin, a second-generation White Russian emigré living in the East. Sidorokin is driven by his father's deathbed directive to "take revenge on them [the Bolsheviks] however you can. Subvert them. A tooth for a tooth." (Kireev, 125)

The inclusion of Sidorokin is most likely an indirect attack at the activities of the People's Labor Union [Narodnyj trudovoj soyuz] (NTS), which was very active against the USSR from its base of operations in West Germany. The description of the leaflet campaign directed against the East (Kireev, 201 & 207-228) is consistent with NTS tactics. NTS had an extensive printing operation that was even successful in producing authentic-looking retranslations into Russian of Khrushchev's secret speech at the XX Party Congress and passing them off as the real thing inside the Soviet Union. The connection to NTS is further strengthened when Kireev gives the name of one of the publications being spread as *Posev*, which was the organ of NTS. Romacher defends this tactic against Koka's doubts regarding its effectiveness with the analogy of drops of water falling on granite. If they are frequent enough and fall from high enough, they can eventually break it down. (Kireev, 127)

The introduction of German war brides gives the good Germans an increased legitimacy as members of the Socialist family of states as the East Bloc solidified in the fifties. Kireev describes two Russian-German marriages that Col. Karev has helped to make possible. He hints that this is a much more widespread phenomenon than just two marriages, when Col. Karev tells one of the prospective grooms that he is not the first, and probably will not be the last, to come to see him with a request to get married.

Both the grooms are young lieutenants serving in GSFG. Both the brides are from good German families. The father of the first bride is a Communist and a factory worker. Her mother works in a confectionery factory. She herself is a salesgirl. All in all, a solid working-class family.

The story of the second bride and groom is the main plot in the book. Their relationship is so involved that it would make a good soap opera. The bride's mother is a war widow, teacher and supporter of the new order. Her husband was killed on the Russian front, but is depicted as a victim of Fascism, who fought the Russians only because the Nazis forced him to. In the closing days of the war, she and her young daughter are befriended by a Russian soldier, who turns out to be the prospective groom's father. He is killed in a firefight right before their eyes and they have tended his grave as carefully all these years as if it had been their own husband and father. The prospective groom learns of this, quite appropriately for this genre, at a political rally. His mother is pleased that her husband's grave has been found and sends her thanks to the bride's mother via her son.

The plot is even further complicated by the fact that, in the beginning of the story, the prospective bride loves a German boy, the defector, who is the hero of Romacher's leaflet for the FDJ. He is, however, later forced down over their hometown while flying a spy mission. In the end, the bride sees the error of her ways and agrees to marry the gallant young Russian lieutenant.

As if this were not enough, the bride's mother is in love with Koka, the second-generation White Russian emigré, who is a member of Romacher's ring of saboteurs. Koka is killed by the ring and the mother is wounded after he recants his evil past for the love of this good woman. The moral of the story is, of course, that political correctness goes hand in hand with international love and marriage.

The initial comment to both the requests for approval of an international marriage is one of disapproval on both sides. On the German side, the prospective bride is asked by one of her co-workers why she is interested in a Russian. "As if there aren't any of our boys ... a Russian is here today, gone tomorrow." (Kireev, 152) This is echoed on the Russian side by one of the Russian enlisted bit players, who says that it's alright to fall in love with a German girl, "but it's better to fall in love with one of ours." (Kireev, 134)

The grooms, even though they were too young to participate directly in the war, both have a reason to hate Germans, because they both lost their fathers in the war. Their selection of German girls for brides, however, shows that they are prepared to accept that the Germans as a people are not responsible for their fathers' deaths. Official sanction for the marriages by Col. Karev likewise shows official sanction for the German people as a whole to become members of the Socialist family of nations as well.

The other groups of forces undoubtedly also produced a number of mixed marriages, but these were not reflected in military fiction. The issue is only just barely skirted in Afghanistan by Valerij Povolyaev in his novella "H" Hour, in which both the intended bride and groom are killed in a firefight before the bureaucratic approval process can get any farther than the groom's platoon leader.

Viktor Stepanov continues the story of the relationship between the Russians and the Germans in his novella At the Brandenburg Gate. There are no bad Germans in the East at all in Stepanov's novella. The threat is entirely from the West. The action begins in 1970, when the Regional Committee (RAJKOM) awards a respected war veteran, Semen Kashtanov, a trip to Berlin as a reward for his services to the people. In the course of the story, Stepanov plays Kashtanov's wartime memories of Berlin off against the realities that he comes into contact with on his trip to show the reader the new Germany.

For Kashtanov "the war did not end in '45, or 10 years or 15 years later." (Stepanov, 1973, 82) He is constantly reminded of the war by the piece of stainless steel in his back that holds his spine together where it was damaged by German fire fifteen days before the end of the war at the Brandenburg Gate. Kashtanov is not an isolated character type in military fiction. 1st Sgt. Rybalko in Nikolaj Kambulov's *The Corporal of the Guard Has Not Come Yet*, which plays in the 1960s, is even more emphatic in his rejection of the end of the war:

> Has it really ended?! I still haven't slept a single night with the feeling that the war is over. ... No, the war isn't over, this is a breathing spell, a temporary lull. The enemy is tricky, they are tightening up their rear, replenishing their ammunition supplies, gathering their forces. ... Read what they write [in the newspapers]. Look, Western Germany is rearming. It's forming a Navy. The Nazi generals are demanding nuclear weapons. (Kambulov, 1970, 151)

In the early stages of the story, Stepanov builds on Kashtanov's negative feelings about Berlin. This was the city that had drawn young Sgt. Kashtanov "like a magnet" across Russia for four years from Volokolamsk to the Brandenburg Gate. A city that he would have "crawled thousands of kilometers across the snow to reach" (Stepanov, 1973, 82); a city that was "damned for all eternity"; and that had "earned the hatred and retribution of all the peoples of the world." (Stepanov, 1973, 87) When he returns there twenty-five years later, everything has changed. It is now a modern city that has risen from the ashes and ruins of war.

Kashtanov is helped in resolving his feelings about Berlin and the Germans by his son, Pvt. Sergej Kashtanov, who is serving in GSFG, and by Kashtanov's old commander, then Lt., now Col. Prokhorov, who is also now Sergej's commander. Stepanov needs both these characters to combat the older Kashtanov's hatred of the Germans. He needs Col. Prokhorov to respond to the argument that was very common with the wartime generation of Russians that "for those who did not see it, none of that [the war] ever happened." (Stepanov, 1973, 88) Col. Prokhorov did see it and that makes his opinion credible to Kashtanov senior. Stepanov needs Sergej to serve as the older Kashtanov's guide to the present, to help him see the realities of contemporary Germany better.

The change in the German people is explained by Col. Prokhorov : "The GDR, I'll tell you, is not the same country that we entered in '45. Not only are the houses new, the people have grown as well. A whole generation has sprung up in the time since then." (Stepanov, 1973, 91)

Kashtanov can understand how the younger generation of Germans can be different than the ones he fought, but he is still not sure how he should feel about the generation of his contemporaries.

Col. Prokhorov offers his old friend the argument that the Germans, who fought against the Soviets, were subjected to the pressure of Hitler's and Goebbels' propaganda. This reasoning works with Kashtanov to some extent. He concedes that members of the German working class might have been tricked into "defending their fatherland," but what about the diehards who mowed down half of their platoon just fifteen days before the end of the war, when it was obvious that they were finished? Why didn't they surrender?

Col. Prokhorov is hard-pressed to answer this question and the conversation draws to a close with Prokhorov not having convinced Kashtanov entirely. Col. Prokhorov can see that his old friend understands the problem on an intellectual level, but the hate that Kashtanov has left over from the war is seated deep in his consciousness and is just as much a part of him as the piece of stainless steel holding his back together.

This enduring nature of Kashtanov's hatred of the Germans is highlighted in a flashback to the end of the war. Col. Prokhorov recalls the incident in which a German machine gun nest killed half their platoon just days before the final victory. As they buried their dead, Kashtanov swore that he "would never forgive ... ever." (Stepanov, 1973, 107) Stepanov returns to the image of the dead calling for revenge again to underscore just how strong it is. He evokes Kashtanov's memory of voiceless calls for revenge issuing from the thousands of graves topped by red stars that lined the road to Berlin for the reader to share in his sense of righteous hatred. As far as Kashtanov was concerned, "Those Germans could not be forgiven." (Stepanov, 1973, 129)

This sentiment is echoed on a much more personal basis in Valerij Biryukov's *Only Three Days*, in which he evokes the main character's memory of the death of his wife and unborn child at the hands of the Germans as the source of the "implacable hatred" that drove him to overcome his fear in battle and to fight on for victory. To him "every battle, in which even a few Nazis were killed, was his homage to the dead." (Biryukov, 72)

For the postwar generation of soldiers in military fiction, homage to the dead took on a less lethal character. In Yurij Pronyakin's *Court of Honor*, which plays in the sixties, it has become "the sacred duty of the living to the fallen, the obligation of the postwar generation to the generation that lived through the war" (Pronyakin, 67) to serve conscientiously as a defender of the Motherland. The Germans were still the enemy from the war, but the implacable hatred had disappeared.

The episodes with the younger Kashtanov paint a picture of the Germans as they are twenty-five years after the end of the war. Stepanov begins with Sergej's notion of Germans as it had been shaped during his formative years by his father's continued outbursts of "damn German!" when his wound bothered him and by the movies that Sergej had seen about the war. By the time Sergej was drafted, his notion of Germans was "a generalization of unjustified evil, that had carried out a surprise attack on his entire country, on every family in June of 1941." (Stepanov, 1973, 119)

Sergej's first face-to-face contact with a real German was in GSFG. Col. Prokhorov had arranged a visit from the neighboring German People's Army (NVA) unit. Sergej had not expected to see that German soldiers looked just like Russian soldiers. They do, except that the uniforms were a bit different. Try as he might, however, Sergej could not find anything in the face of his first German acquaintance that matched the threatening images of Germans inherited from his father and from the war movies he had seen in his youth. He could not imagine the young man sitting next to him taking aim at him. This young German was his friend. (Stepanov, 1973, 120)

Stepanov continues to develop this image as he describes a multinational Warsaw Pact exercise "Comrades-in-Arms," in which the Germans are fighting side by side with the Bulgarians, Hungarians, Poles, Romanians, Russians, and Czechs. (Stepanov, 1973, 95)

Stepanov ties the joint exercise into the senior Kashtanov's experience during the war by having the exercise take place in exactly the same place that Prokhorov and Kashtanov lost half their platoon to the German machine gun nest in 1945.

Stepanov neatly folds time back on itself as the young Kashtanov fights his way across the same piece of ground and begins to think about his father's hate for the Germans. In considering it, he finally begins to feel the impact of the losses that the Soviet Union suffered during the war. He sees that the price paid by the Soviets for victory was not just the 20 million lives lost in combat. That loss was compounded by the millions of children, who were not born of the dead, who did not have a chance to become fathers.

During the exercise, Sergej becomes friends with a young NVA soldier named Kurt Steinhart. This eventually leads to a visit for both Kashtanovs to the Steinhart home. The home appeals to the senior Kashtanov. He finds a solid respectable average worker's home, without any chic. (Stepanov, 1973, 139) When Kurt takes off his uniform blouse, the senior Kashtanov thought for a minute that this wasn't some German named Kurt, but just the neighbor boy back home. He even considers for a moment what a fine couple young miss Steinhart and Sergej make, but then recants of the thought almost as soon as he has it: "there are enough of our girls in Ivanov." (Stepanov, 1973, 140)

After his week's stay in Germany, Kashtanov senior begins to look at Germany and the Germans in a different light. He has seen them in an exercise, fighting over the same piece of ground that cost the lives of half his platoon twenty-five years ago. He has visited them at home and has come to realize that not every German was a fanatic supporter of Hitler. As he comes to know them better, he comprehends the psychological pressure that they must have been under to fight for Hitler. (Stepanov, 1973, 129) He also comes to understand that things change with the passage of time. (Stepanov, 1973, 140) "The result of victory was not just in how many casualties the enemy suffered, but also in the style of life that rises up out of the ashes and grows tomorrow, a year later, decades later, centuries later." (Stepanov, 1973, 144) These revelations help him to put aside his hate for the Germans and even to become friends with the family he met.

By the time Stanislav Gribanov published his short story *I Am Going on a Sortie* (1985), it was no longer necessary to comment on the relationship between the Soviets and the Germans. The East Germans had already been accepted as a part of the Socialist family of nations. The reason that Lt. Olenin is serving in GSFG is "to defend the skies of the new Germany, the friendly industrial and agricultural workers' Republic" (Gribanov, 107) from the enemy across the border that forms the dividing line between two different worlds.

This is the new front line of the Cold War, where everything seems peaceful, but yet there are "cannons sticking out of the fairy-tale woods that are enveloped by mist at the horizon" (Gribanov, 107) and they are aimed at the Soviet fliers who are there to keep the peace. Every sortie can turn into a combat mission, which is why all the regiment's pilots are holders of the highest flight qualifications.

The war inevitably does come into the story, as one of the young pilots looks for his father's grave near their garrison. He is assisted in his search by the Germanic-Soviet Friendship Society. The Soviets have succeeded in giving the word "German" a new face. Instead of using the Slavic word for German, *Nemets*, they use the Latin root, German, as the name of the Friendship Society. At the same time, other works of contemporary military fiction had also begun to avoid the use of the word German (*Nemets*) as a word synonymous with the enemy. The enemy is called the "Nazis" or "Fascists," not the Germans.

The very day that the news of the location of his father's grave reaches the unit, the young pilot sacrifices his life to save the lives of the peaceful German populace. His aircraft crashed due to a mechanical fault, but he rode it down rather than eject and allow it to crash into a nearby town. This ties the sacrifice of the father and the son for the German people together. The father died to free them from Fascism and the son to protect them from a deadly accident.

Sobko's, Kireev's and Stepanov's works are all aimed at calming the hatred that the Soviet soldiers and officers felt for the Germans, and winning acceptance for the Germans into the Socialist Commonwealth of Nations. Soviet military philosophy, however, calls for hatred of the enemy to be a part of a Soviet officer's *weltanschauung*.

In his novella *Recruits*, Viktor Filatov explains why this is so. It is to overcome not only the concrete enemy on the battlefield, but also the ethereal enemy inside every soldier. "You will be your own worst enemy," says Filatov in a long philosophical aside. "Your timidity and lack of self-discipline, your inability to use your hate for the enemy to suppress all other feelings in yourself except for one—the desire to rip out the enemy's throat." (Filatov, 1978, 162) These will combine to keep a soldier from digging his foxhole deep enough, from storming up a hill despite the pouring rain and the slippery mud that makes it hard for him to cross an especially dangerous sector.

Aleksandr Kuleshov picks up on this theme in his novel *The White Wind*. His main character, Lt. Levashov, expresses it quite well:

> A soldier has to hate the enemy. And it is does not matter that he cannot say specifically who the enemy is at this given moment. But you're not going to tell me that bombs aren't falling, shells aren't bursting and innocent, peaceful people aren't dying anywhere on the Earth? Then aren't the ones who are responsible for those deaths the enemies of mankind? Maybe they haven't attacked your country yet, but they are always ready to do so. (Kuleshov, 1977a, 271)

The hatred for the Germans had to be refocused to the new enemies of the Cold War. Sobko, Kireev and Stepanov all attempted to do just that in their novels. In these novels the focus of that hatred is shifted to the Americans, either indirectly as supporters of the bad Germans or directly as the source of the threat that the Soviet military has to face. Stepanov's new enemy smells of napalm. "This is not some abstract 'enemy,' you can write the word without quotation marks. The name and the disposition of the enemy's troops are not in secret documents in safes. His predatory face looks out from the international news columns of the papers everyday." (Stepanov, 1973, 95) The allusion to America in Stepanov's and Kuleshov's descriptions of the enemy is more than clear to the target audience.

In military fiction about Afghanistan, the focus becomes even sharper. Afghan military fiction definitely paints an evil picture of the mujahedeen, but behind practically every mujahedeen band there is a foreign advisor. They are the source of all the money that keeps the mujahedeen going. In his *Echo of the Mountains of Afghanistan*, Kim Selikhov even goes so far as to cite some pseudo-statistics on how much money has been committed to subversive activities in Afghanistan by the Western Powers. According to Selikhov's hero, Capt. Khabib, "the White House has generously allocated millions of dollars … in 1984 … England counted out 18 million pounds sterling, the Federal Republic of Germany 60 million DM and Japan several million yen." (Selikhov, 138)

Nikolaj Ivanov's foreign advisors in his novellas *The Mountain Pass* and *Storm over Gindukush Mountain* are Americans. Ivanov calls them "the gentlemen from over the ocean" (Ivanov, 1987, 55 & 58; Ivanov, 1986, 24), which is an unmistakable reference to America that has been in use since the Cold War. (Sobko, 279)

In *Storm over Gindukush Mountain*, Delavarkhan, the mujahedeen leader thinks to himself that "the gentlemen from over the ocean" really know how to conduct operations to achieve a political effect. "They've had a lot of experience in this line of work." (Ivanov, 1986, 24) Not only that, Delavarkhan finds that political operations pay much better than normal killings. His current political operation is to steal some Soviet uniforms and weapons and then to carry out some atrocities, using them so as to turn the populace against the real Soviets. This is a much more violent form of what Romacher was doing in Kireev's novel.

This is the only reference to foreigners in *Storm over Gindukush Mountain*, but in his novella *The Mountain Pass*, Ivanov brings a foreigner on stage. His name is Rould and he is from "overseas" in "the States." Khavar, the mujahedeen leader, in *The Mountain Pass*, is much less pleased with the instructions he gets from "the gentlemen from over the ocean" than Delavarkhan. Khavar considers "dumping political operations … where and when to make a raid, how and whom to kill—he knew all that without any instructions." (Ivanov, 1987, 55) As for the money, he could make five times as much knocking off a store than they will give him in Pakistan.

It is clear from Ivanov's description that Khavar is completely under Rould's control. In his narrative, Khavar continuously turns to Rould for approval of his actions while making an oration to the populace of a vill that his group has just "liberated." (Ivanov, 1987, 36-37) Ivanov then backs this up by letting the reader in on Rould's thoughts about Khavar, showing that Rould considers Khavar to have been a very good student, who has learned his lessons well.

Rould, however, unlike the Soviets, is only a fair-weather friend for the mujahedeen. When the group finds itself in a difficult situation, Rould sneaks off, abandoning Khavar and his group to their fate. Ivanov underscores the poor relationship between the mujahedeen and their foreign advisor in Khavar's statement to his deputy, when Khavar finds out that Rould has slipped out the back door on them: "Mark my words, in the end they'll betray our struggle just as contemptibly" (Ivanov, 1987, 58), as Rould did when he left the group to its own fate.

In Prokhanov's short story, *The Grey-headed Soldier*, it is the Englishman Staf who is clearly in charge of the mujahedeen group. The group leader, Akhmatkhan, does not come across as a leader, but rather as a translator of the Englishman's orders, because, while Staf's Russian is near native, he cannot speak Pushtu. Morozov, the Soviet soldier captured by the group, clearly sees Staf as "the master of his [Morozov's] fate." (Prokhanov, 1987, 359) Everything that was taking place in the camp was just a show for Morozov's benefit and Staf was the director of the show.

Kim Selikhov leaves no doubt in the least who the foreign backers of the mujahedeen are in his novella *Echo of the Mountains of Afghanistan*. The plot of Selikhov's novella centers around the search for a newly active mujahedeen leader Pir Baba-khan, who turns out to be none other than Lt. Col. Martin Lewis of the Central Intelligence Agency (CIA). Lewis apparently speaks Pushtu so well that he is able to pass for a native, which keeps his true identity hidden until almost the end of the story.

Selikhov recounts the atrocities committed by Pir Baba-khan, a.k.a. Lt. Col. Lewis, in great detail. Not only does Lewis cold-bloodedly murder innocent civilians, he plants booby traps in children's toys and plans to poison the water supply for all of Kabul with chemical warfare agents cooked up in a secret American military lab in California. (Selikhov, 81)

Selikhov's crowning touch for Lewis' abominably treacherous personality is Lewis' idea to form a "Brigade of Children", which is to be named "Death to the Unfaithful", a name which finds a certain resonance with the Cold War "Death to Spies" (*Smersh: Smert' shpionam*) operation of James Bond fame. The brigade's mission will be to plant mines, poison water supplies and gun down the unfaithful. (Selikhov, 130) Selikhov deftly grounds the idea for the brigade in the prototype of all evil in military fiction in the postwar period, the Hitlerjugend from the Third Reich. (Selikhov, 126) Selikhov's socialist-realist happy ending is that Afghan security forces triumph and Lewis is captured, never to be seen or heard from again.

Just as the Americans worked through the mujahedeen rather than confronting the Soviets directly in Afghanistan, they were preparing to do the same thing in postwar Germany. Sobko's book has several references to the Americans and British preparing to rearm the Germans in their sectors for use as "cannon fodder" in the impending "war" against the Soviets. (Sobko, 78 & 140)

The vision of Soviet troops in postwar Germany presented by Sobko, Kireev, Stepanov and Gribanov is one of gallant knights in shining armor. This is appropriate for socialist-realist military fiction, but it glosses over the dark side of the Soviet occupation of the Eastern Zone of Germany. Boris Bakhtin wrote a short story about this side of the occupation in 1976, but it was not published until long after his death (1981), following the fall of socialist-realist censorship in 1990.

The Sergeant and the Frau is written as a flashback to the first day after the end of the war, the same day that Sobko's novel starts. It describes how a sergeant from the Soviet Army of occupation is quartered in the house of a German woman, who Bakhtin only references as the "Frau." Initially Bakhtin develops the sergeant's hatred of the Germans and contrasts the living conditions of the conquered to those of the victors. It is spring, everything is green. The Frau's house is clean and pretty. There is a carpet with a hunting scene on the wall. There is plenty of everything. There is a table with a handmade tablecloth, a china service, a bottle stand with a music box in it that plays while you pour from the bottle, meat with a sauce, home-baked pastries, five types of cheese and a stein of beer. There is even hot running water. In general, everything is completely civilized. (Bakhtin, 316-318) The sergeant compares this to a village in the USSR, where people are living in dugouts, often without windows, surrounded by bomb craters and lit by kerosene lamps, when you can get kerosene, that is. This is because the Germans burned the villages as they retreated, destroying everything.

In what appears to be a private version of the war reparations the Soviets extracted from the East Germans, the sergeant fantasizes about taking the *Frau* back to the USSR to have her wait on his family and guests. He does not get a chance to realize his private war reparations plan, however, because while the sergeant is sleeping with her, in a drunken state of paranoia, he imagines that she has a knife under her pillow and is going to kill him with it. When she reaches under the pillow for a handkerchief, he kills her with a single shot, even though he later admits that he could have easily overpowered her, if she had indeed had a knife.

When he confesses all to the military prosecutor, the prosecutor chastises him for "shielding a fascist," and threatens to send him to the Gulag, if he mentions the word "handkerchief" again. The official story will be that she did have a knife. The sergeant is simply put on a train back to the USSR as a guard, and is discharged as soon as he gets back. It is easy to see why this story could not be published under the strictures of socialist-realism controlled military fiction, where it would have tarnished the armor of Sobko's, Kireev's and Stepanov's knights of GSFG.

As Bakhtin's story draws to a close and the sergeant's interlocutor in the flashback comes on stage, Bakhtin closes the loop that he opened in the beginning of the story about the sergeant not being able to understand the Frau or she him. The sergeant tells his companion prophetically: "it will be a long time and a lot of blood will be spilled before we learn how to explain something to each other." (Bakhtin, 324) With the interlocutor in the foreground, the comment is directed both backward in time to the Frau and forward to the present-day reader. The year 1990 was probably sooner than Bakhtin expected and the revolution that brought about the changes that let his story be published was, undoubtedly, much less bloody than he expected.

Sobko's commandant Chajka would probably have been just as surprised at the answer to his question: "I wonder what Germany will be like when the orders are issued that let us leave here? What will Dornau look like and what will the locals be like?" (Sobko, 111) I doubt that he ever envisioned the reunification of Germany on the Western model that took place after the fall of the wall in November 1989.

3

The Changing of the Guard

The time factor ... rules the profession of arms. There is perhaps none where the dicta of the man in office are accepted with such an uncritical deference, or where the termination of an active career brings a quicker descent into careless disregard. Little wonder that many are so affected by the sudden transition as to cling pathetically to the trimmings of the past.

Captain Sir Basil Liddell Hart
Thoughts on War, 1944

The late fifties and the early sixties were a turbulent time for the Soviet military. There was a reduction in force (RIF) under way, and the Scientific and Technological Revolution was causing considerable change in both doctrine and armaments. This was also the time that the first of the generation of World War II officers began to retire from the service. These were all events that produced profound changes in the Soviet military and they left their mark in Soviet military fiction as well.

The Soviet military went through a series of four RIFs between 1955 and 1961. The last of the series was announced by the Supreme Soviet on 15 January 1961. This was to have reduced the Soviet military, which had already been reduced from 5,763,000 to a total of 3,623,000 men, by another third.[1]

Nikolaj Gorbachev gives a hint at the origins of the RIF in his novel *The Battle*, which describes the birth pangs of the Soviet antimissile program in the late fifties. According to Gorbachev's story, it was at a session of the Council of Ministers during which a letter to the Central Committee from certain "prominent marshals" on the necessity of building an anti-ballistic-missile-missile [ABM] system was to be discussed. The conclusion of the marshals' letter was that such a system was necessitated by the "stormy development and stockpiling of strategic rockets in several of the countries of the aggressive blocks of NATO, SEATO and CENTO." (Gorbachev, 1977, 230)

In his introductory remarks, the chairman of the session noted that this line of reasoning leads to the idea that "the development of rockets brings the value of the Air Force and surface Navy of the future into question." It appeared to the chairman that this problem and the discussion of the development of an ABM system were connected, and, therefore, "offered an opportunity for a serious change in the numerical strength of the Army." (Gorbachev, 1977, 230)

A "heated and explosive" debate followed in which extremists called for going exclusively to ABM systems, and those with a more conservative view defended the strategic Air Forces and surface Navy. In his description of the defense rendered by the four-star admiral for the Navy at the session, Gorbachev hints at the reason for the Navy's poor showing in the RIF that followed.

The admiral's "calm, uninspired and almost indifferent" presentation (Gorbachev, 1977, 230) could hardly have won him much support among those present at the session. The description of the session of the Council of Ministers ends with no decision being taken on the RIF, but with an approval for the development of an ABM system, which is the main plot of the novel.

The characters in Gorbachev's novel were not overly concerned about the RIF, because their jobs to develop the new ABM system were secure. The characters in Nikolaj Kambulov's two-volume novel *Faithfulness*, however, were. In the first volume, *The Corporal of the Guard Has Not Come Yet*, which plays in 1960, Kambulov presents the RIF as a two-part problem for Soviet commanders: (1) to keep the troops from developing a Short-timer's attitude, and (2) to decide which officers would go and which would stay. (Kambulov, 1970, 6 & 8)

The problem of who to keep on active duty and who to discharge was a major one for Soviet commanders. "Cadre are the strength of the Army, we shouldn't discharge those [people] that we need," says Col. Gromov, the commander of an artillery regiment in *The Corporal of the Guard Has Not Come Yet*. (Kambulov, 1970, 257) Kambulov's picture of the problem presents personnel officers as the bad guys and unit commanders as the good guys. When Kambulov's Gen. Zakharov, the division commander, asks his chief of personnel for help in making a decision about the RIF, all the personnel chief's input was based on what he called the "three whales"[2]:

- statement of personal history [*anketa*];
- officer efficiency report [*attestatsiya*] written by the officer's commander with input from the political officer; and
- 201 file [*posluzhnoj spisok*]. (Kambulov, 1970, 11)

Zakharov chides his chief of personnel for such a formalist approach to peoples' careers (Kambulov, 1970, 169) and in the end forces him to abandon it. (Kambulov, 1970, 199)

As Zakharov demonstrates, files are a poor substitute for personal knowledge of one's subordinates. According to the personnel chief's "three-whale" measure, Col. Sizov, the Chief of Staff, is a prime candidate for the RIF. "His education is not at the level of modern requirements" (Kambulov, 1970, 169), says the personnel chief of Col. Sizov, meaning that Sizov had not been to the Command and General Staff College (CGSC), a requirement that was being heavily pushed at that time.

Gen. Zakharov, however, meets with Sizov personally and finds him to be an intelligent, thinking officer, who keeps up with the current literature in his field. (Kambulov, 1970, 173) Instead of releasing Sizov in the RIF, Zakharov arranges for him to be moved to a staff position in the military district headquarters, where Sizov can put his talents to use. It is Sizov's success in his new job that convinces the personnel chief that Zakharov was right all along, and makes him change his approach to the RIF.

Not everyone got to stay on active duty, however. In *The Corporal of the Guard Has Not Come Yet*, it is a regimental commander, Col. Vodolazov, a fifty-year-old war veteran with twenty-five years of service. His decision to retire is based, ostensibly, on his failing health. Not only was he wounded three times during the war, but he is suffering from heart trouble as well. In his Disposition Form (DF) requesting retirement, addressed to Gen. Zakharov he writes:

> I thought about this a long time before I submitted my request to you, comrade general. Do not think that I have decided to retire because someone insulted me or encroached upon my rights. No, I have simply come to the firm conclusion that my service in the Army has reached its normal, natural end. I am fifty years old. I was wounded three times. I do not have the energy or the fire anymore that a military man needs to carry out his duties with dignity, and I do not know how to serve only halfheartedly. (Kambulov, 1970, 9)

Even though his DF is well-written, the colonel has doubts about his decision. Is it really the pain in his chest or the knowledge there is a RIF under way that prompted him to submit his retirement papers?

"Even one-on-one with himself, Vodolazov couldn't answer that question," says Kambulov, dodging the issue. (Kambulov, 1970, 26)

Having made the decision, however, it is not in Vodolazov's character to turn back, and he does get out. Interestingly enough, as soon as Vodolazov leaves the service, he takes on a job every bit as demanding as that of a regimental commander—chairman of a collective farm. This turn of events makes it look like Kambulov was somewhat more inclined to think that it was the RIF rather than the pain in his chest that prompted Vodolazov to retire, but that he did not want to come right out and say so.

Against the background of the RIF, Vodolazov's fellow officers and his division commander also have their doubts about the sincerity of his request. Is he running away from the threat of the RIF, or is he really ill? The Chief of Staff for Artillery, Col. Grosulov says that if this was three or four years ago, he would recommend that Zakharov call Col. Vodolazov to his office and insist that Vodolazov withdraw his DF, because good commanders are hard to find. Now, however, Col. Grosulov is prepared to let Col. Vodolazov retire. (Kambulov, 1970, 10) The same initial reluctance to let good people out of the service is echoed by Col. Surgin's evaluation of his chances of retirement in 1957 in Yurij Strekhnin's novel, *I Bequeath You*. "They probably wouldn't have let me out, even if I requested it, even though there was a RIF going on at the time." (Strekhnin, 1977, 170)

Quite probably the RIF was indeed viewed by many officers as a convenient excuse to leave the service, and one of the concerns of Vodolazov's fellow officers was that his retirement might be misinterpreted by the younger officers in the division, who were also facing the RIF, like Lt. Uzlov. He submitted his request for discharge, because

> sooner or later, as you well know, comrade colonel, some officers will be discharged to the reserves. I have decided to take that step now, while I am twenty-three years old, when I have every chance of getting into college, getting a degree, and then with a good specialty, being able to successfully work in the national economy. (Kambulov, 1970, 40)

His resolve to be discharged is strengthened by an item in a newspaper of the day with a front-page picture of a young man in a uniform blouse without epaulets and the caption: "Reserve Lt. Il'ya Rozov. He is in a good mood, because he has just been accepted to MGU [Moscow State University]." (Kambulov, 1970, 70)

Uzlov's fellow officers find it hard to understand his decision. They remind him that he is a communist, but to no avail. (Kambulov, 1970, 73) Then they begin to search for the real reason behind his request, which emerges as his dissatisfaction with a make-work job with no responsibilities. A perceptive new commander recognizes the problem and provides him with a platoon to command. This produces the required socialist-realist happy ending, in which Uzlov stays on to serve his country and later even becomes a regimental commander himself.

Lev Snegirev's main character in his novella *Thaw in Midwinter*, however, does leave the service. Snegirev's story of Sr. Lt. Pavel Levchuk plays in the late fifties. Levchuk was too young to participate in the war, having finished high school only in 1944. As soon as he graduated, the draft board sent him to the junior officers armored academy instead of to the front. In 1955, in the first of the RIFs, he was still a platoon leader at age twenty-seven, which Snegirev plainly points out is much too long in grade at that level. (Snegirev, 15)

The RIF finally catches up to Levchuk and he is discharged. The draft board, reversing its normal role during the RIF, sends him to be a quality controller in a furniture factory. Snegirev's story reads almost like a socialist-realist remake of Dudintsev's *Not by Bread Alone* and foreshadows the adventures of Afghan vet Ivan Pospekhin in Polyanskij's *Afghan Syndrome*.

In the civilian world, Levchuk has problems with the factory director, whose management style is very reminiscent of Stalin's. Director Krygin, like Stalin, was of the opinion that "things go better when people work not due to the force of their conscience, but out of fear." (Snegirev, 28) Levchuk, because of his military training, is very conscientious and refuses to put his quality control stamp on what he considers to be "defective products," just to fulfill the production quota. (Snegirev, 22) It is the clash of these two philosophies that is at the heart of the conflict in the novella.

Snegirev's story is much more positive than either Dudintsev's or Polyanskij's. In the end, Levchuk triumphs over the bureaucracy and is able to implement his ideas to benefit the national economy. He eventually rises to the rank of plant director, which gives the story a happy, socialist-realist ending.

Kambulov's description of first sergeant Rybalko, who represents the ultraconservative elements in the Army in *The Corporal of the Guard Has Not Come Yet*, is the model for the literary retirees in other works of military fiction to follow. He is incensed at Col. Vodolazov's retirement. He and Vodolazov are the same age. He was wounded just like Vodolazov. He, however, intends to stay on active duty in spite of his age and his wounds, and thinks that the colonel should too, because of what Rybalko sees as the relentless fascist threat. He is sure that every time we disband another regiment, that there is joy "over the ocean." (Kambulov, 1970, 228)

His view of the threat is supported on the one hand by the glimpse that Kambulov gives the reader of the newspapers of the day with headlines like:

NATO Maneuvers

West Berlin—A City on the Front Line

American Military Instructors in Laos (Kambulov, 1970, 23)

and articles that cover West German rearmament and demands by "Nazi Generals" for nuclear weapons. (Kambulov, 1970, 151 & 282) On the other hand, Rybalko's view is rejected by the characters who interact with him in the novel. They call him a "hawk" and dismiss his view as out of date. (Kambulov, 1970, 29 & 151)

Rybalko is the personification of the Old Guard, who equates the number of troops on active duty with the level of the Soviet Union's military strength. Their views are summed up in the expression: "bullets are dumb, a bayonet is the thing!" (Kambulov, 1970, 173) Rybalko feels that "a rocket, of course, is a fine, threatening thing, but a cannon, when you get in close, is easier to handle . ... Rockets be damned! A man is stronger than any atom!" (Kambulov, 1970, 228-229) Rybalko and the character type he represents did not understand that the introduction of nuclear armed missiles had changed the accepted military concept of distance. (Kambulov, 1970, 5) Close-in was no longer in bayonet range.

In the end, Rybalko is won over by the new technology and comes to understand the new meaning of distance, when the unit is air transported over a distance that

> a few years ago would have taken days, weeks or maybe even months to cover. ... Now I see clearly [says Rybalko] that I was somewhat mistaken. ... They were reducing the Army. ... I suffered a lot because of that, but I didn't see that our firepower and technological strength were growing day by day. ... [now] I am reassured. (Kambulov, 1970, 290)

Even though Rybalko was reassured, the Party was not. It reversed its decision to reduce conventional forces and put an end to the RIF in June 1961, because "the NATO bosses have increased their provocations in Berlin." (Kambulov, 1970, 259) In the end, age, ill health brought on by the war and the press of technological change combine to finally push first sergeant Rybalko into retirement two years after Col. Vodolazov in *The Rocket's Thunder*, the second part of Kambulov's two-volume novel *Faithfulness*. Faithful right up to the end of his career, Rybalko continues to serve with dedication, going out into the field to support a Field Training Exercise (FTX), when he could have just sat around at post and waited for his orders.

In the mid-seventies, the problem of the retirement of the last of the officers with actual combat experience from World War II came to a head. Thirty years after the Great Victory of 1945, those who had taken part in the Great Patriotic War[3] were leaving the service and the Soviet military was losing its direct, daily contact with the war. As Col. Korsunov in Anatolij Polyanskij's novel *The Right to Take Risks* complained: "There are only a few individuals left in the ranks: a few staff officers, a dozen or so warrant officers, and even they will be retiring soon. The generation of the war is leaving. ... Even the regimental and many of the division commanders never smelled gun powder." (Polyanskij, 1978, 95-96)

The problem presented by the departure of officers with front-line, wartime experience was threefold:

- the weakening of the propaganda effect of the war;
- the loss of commanders with actual combat experience; and
- the Old Guard's perception that the new generation of officers were too inexperienced to take on their commands.

In the mid-seventies, the Great Patriotic War was still a symbol of the martyrdom of the Soviet people, united in their defense of the Motherland, and was the answer to the question of why the Soviet economy was not what it should be. The need to prevent another such war and to overcome the devastation that was wreaked on the Soviet Union by the last war were constantly cited as the reasons why the Soviet people had to continue to make sacrifices in the name of heavy industry and defense. The war was a powerful propaganda tool and the Party had every intention of maintaining it as such.

The simplest and most effective way of keeping the "memory" of the war fresh, even in those who were not yet born when it ended, is through contact with veterans of the war, who have had it impressed upon them that they have a duty to impart their experiences to the younger generation. As these veterans retired and left the ranks of the Soviet Armed Forces, other, younger officers had to take up their task of keeping the memory of the war alive. This situation was far from satisfying, because even if the younger officer has studied his part as a keeper of the faith to perfection, "when events are described by someone who actually took part in them, they produce a completely different impression" (Polyanskij, 1978, 235) than when they are secondhand. To keep a more direct contact with the war, veterans were encouraged to return to units in which they served or in which their sons were serving, to talk with the troops about their wartime experiences. (Rybin, 1984, 208 & 242; Kuleshov, 1977a, 230; Pishchulin, 1976, 13)

As the ABM project, which is the central element of Gorbachev's novel, draws to a successful close, Marshal Yanov states Gorbachev's law of renewal:

> New times come and new people appear. ... That is an
> unappealable law that no one has any power over. ... You need
> to accept it, assist it any way you can, not hinder it and get in
> its way. ... You need to look at it, not from the personal,
> individualistic point of view, but from the wider, farther-
> reaching point of view of humanity and history. That's where
> your new faith, your comfort, your strength and your life should
> be. There's a time for everything. You know that. You know it
> well. That means you should be worthy of your time and your
> destiny. (Gorbachev, 1977, 342)

This view is a good socialist-realist one, in that it shows a Marxist
realization of necessity. It is intended to counter the feeling more
commonly expressed by literary retirees that when front-line veterans
retire, they take with them "the most valuable front-line experience
paid for in blood" (Polyanskij, 1978, 96), a sentiment that is to be
repeated fifteen years later by the generation of officers who served in
Afghanistan, as the system rejects the lessons of Afghanistan and even
forces some Afghan vets out of the service.

Anatolij Rybin expands on the value of actual combat experience in
his novel *The Boundary Line*. When a new thirty-two-year-old
regimental commander is introduced to the division commander and his
staff, they comment that it won't be long before all the division officers
will have been born after the end of the war. Rybin sees this as the
natural order of things, but has the division commander, Gen. Maj.
Mel'nikov, express the concern that the experience of those who fought
the war needs to be preserved in the forces. It is much too valuable to let
it be lost entirely. The division political officer ends the conversation
on a positive note with the comment that it is the attitude to combat
experience that is the important thing here: "for some it is only a
memory, but for some it is the essence of the matter, the dialectic."
(Rybin, 1984, 8) What Rybin wants to preserve is the distilled essence
of the lessons learned in the war, not just the memoirs of the World War
II veterans which were beginning to come out in large numbers at that
time as a part of the MPD's effort to keep the memory of the war alive
among the populace.

Lt. Dmitrij Blinov, in Viktor Bogatov's *Rise to Your Own Level*,
echoes Rybin's view of what constitutes the essence of the experience of
the war. When Blinov conducts a training class, he uses the history of
the war, citing "tactical examples of platoon and company actions in
combat against the Nazi aggressors" as a basis for his lectures to
achieve "the maximum effect." (Bogatov, 143)

As is to be expected in a society ruled by a gerontocracy like the

Soviet Union in the seventies, the main fear expressed by retiring officers in works of military fiction is that the new generation of officers, who will replace them, is too young and inexperienced. If the older officers of military fiction had their way, they would, like Rybalko, remain on active duty for the good of the cause that they have served so long. Like Rybalko, however, they are being forced to retire by their ill health, most often following a heart attack brought about by overwork. Their concern is: will the new commander "have enough *experience* to continue what I have begun? That's the problem, where do you get experience? The major is so *young!*" (Biryukov, 1975, 13, *emphasis* added)

This view of younger officers is repeated over and over again in various works of military fiction. "We've got a new young commander, just out of CGSC ... At least I've got the *experience*, thank God!" (Polyanskij, 1978, 10, *emphasis* added) "Chalov is a *young* officer. He doesn't have enough *experience*, you know that. He might miss something. A regiment is not the same as a company." (Polyanskij, 1978, 76, *emphasis* added)

Interestingly enough, *young* Col. Chalov applies the same criterion to his evaluation of his subordinates: "He's a *young* officer. A little *inexperienced*, but he's got a good fitness report." (Polyanskij, 1978, 108, *emphasis* added)

Yu. F. Strekhnin's novel, *I Bequeath You*, which was selected to receive a Ministry of Defense literary certificate of appreciation in 1974, is the next novel to deal with retirement. The action takes place in 1968, just before the Soviet invasion of Czechoslovakia. It relates the story of how fifty-five-year-old Col. A. K. Surgin, the chief of a motor rifle division's Political Department, reacts to a heart attack and impending retirement in his twenty-fifth year of service.

By that time, serving officers with combat experience had already become a rarity. As the division commander remarks to Col. Surgin: "Retirement is looming on the horizon for you and me. ... Pretty soon you won't be able to find a division commander who saw [action] in the war, not to mention anybody more junior." (Strekhnin, 1977, 243) Strekhnin, however, like Gorbachev's Marshal Yanov, views this as a natural process.

> [It's] the law of renewal, and there's nothing you can do about it. It's a good law, especially in our rapidly changing age. It's a fact that old generals don't win new wars. ... They'll send some sharp young officer with a new CGSC pin to replace me. He'll look around quickly and begin doing excellent work (Strekhnin, 1977, 5),

which is just what Col. Surgin's successor does.

Col. Surgin, just like first sergeant Rybalko, is not ready to retire. There is a big FTX coming up. The international situation is worsening. If he had not had a heart attack, he would not be thinking about retirement, because when he is at work he feels "very needed by people." He considers knowing that you are needed "a vital element of life" (Strekhnin, 1977, 6) that has become "a spiritual necessity" for him. (Strekhnin, 1977, 178) Now that he has suffered a heart attack, he is faced with the dilemma that he needs to take it easy and relax or they will forcibly retire him, but if he takes it easy and relaxes, he cannot do the job that he loves.

In his novella of the Air Force in the late fifties, *The Zampolit*, Anatolij Sul'yanov shows that there was another option for officers like Surgin: Use your pull to stay on active duty.

> One of the older officers suffered a stroke, which left him with a partially paralyzed right arm and leg. The doctors did everything that they could. They treated him in the hospital for a long time. He went to a sanitorium. He rested. He got better. He started to walk. The doctors warned, however, no stress, no nervous exertion! He had enough time for a pension, an apartment. They offered him retirement. If you only knew what a flurry of activity this recently recovered man began! Letters, telegrams, and grievances flew off to the center. And what do you think? There was a phone call from up above and the patient was cured. He was not one of the strongest workers and even less so after his illness, but now he's on active duty and he's torturing himself and others. He's become capricious and short-tempered and doesn't go out to visit the line units any more than is necessary. With the help of influential people, he even got promoted.

Sul'yanov comes down firmly against this option, however. "It's disgusting, offensive. We need to take decisive action against this evil, and by that I mean Favoritism." (Sul'yanov, 1982, 116)

It is interesting here to take a look at what the author considers the reasons for Col. Surgin's poor health. They are the job, which he does not want to leave, and his wartime service, both of which combine to make him a needed and experienced political officer, but at the same time are the cause of his ill health. (Strekhnin, 1977, 110) Col. Surgin had the chance to take a staff job, which would have been less of a strain on him and allowed him to remain in the service longer, but he felt that

> for a military man, if he's managed to get used to the people and develop a camaraderie with them, a regiment, a battalion,

> a company, ... any military *kollektiv*, where the main work
> that an Army exists for takes place, whether in peacetime or in
> wartime, that *kollektiv* will always be a family for every one
> of its members. A staff or Political Department, on the other
> hand, despite my deep respect for them and in spite of my
> comprehension of their necessity, will always only be
> organizations, because the main member of the military
> family—the soldier—is missing. He's only a guest there.
> (Strekhnin, 1977, 140)

It is this reasoning that prompted Surgin to decide to stay at the working level, where the physical demand is greater, but where he considered that his contribution to the main task of the Army would also be greater. As the novel closes, Col. Surgin leaves the question of turning over his duties to the younger generation open. He does not retire, but gets ready to move out with his unit to Czechoslovakia. He leaves it to the main characters of later works to hand over their duties to younger men.

The main characters in these later works follow the pattern of Col. Surgin. They are about fifty years old. They had a chance to move on to staff work that they passed up. They do not want to retire, but unlike Col. Surgin, they are not sure that "some sharp young officer with a new CGSC pin" will be up to the job that the hero of the story is about to hand over to him.

Anatolij Polyanskij's novel, *The Right to Take Risks*, describes the last six months of service of the chief of the Political Department of an airborne division, Col. A. S. Korsunov. The action of the novel takes place in the mid-seventies. Col. Korsunov began his service as a seventeen-year-old private at the end of the war. He is now forty-seven years old. As the story begins, he is leaving the office of the general who has told him that he will have to retire because of his heart attack.

If it had not been for his heart attack, Col. Korsunov would have stayed in the service. He likes his present job, and gave up a chance to take a staff position as the general's deputy to keep it. He wanted to keep on working with people and not sit "in an office behind a big desk." (Polyanskij, 1978, 9)

In his meeting with the general, he manages to convince him to let him stay on duty for six more months to get the division ready for an FTX, because "our commander is new, a young officer, just out of CGSC. The division is getting in new draftees. Who better to get them ready for combat [the FTX] than me, the chief of the Political Department?! At least I've got the experience, thank God!" (Polyanskij, 1978, 10) This is the central point around which most main characters' hesitation to retire revolves: the perceived lack of experience of the younger generation of officers. It is discussed again and again throughout the novel.

The division commander is ten years younger than Col. Korsunov and the regimental commander is twenty his junior. "You're too young, Vyacheslav Aleksandrovich [says Korsunov], ... twenty-eight ... is that really an age for a regimental commander who has hundreds of people under his command plus equipment like this?! Just the motor pool alone is worth millions of rubles." (Polyanskij, 1978, 19)

Early on, the author hints that things will not be as bad as Col. Korsunov fears. "No, everything is OK. Inexperience is excusable and correctable. There just needs to be a will and a desire to get to the heart of the matter," says one of the junior officers about a subordinate. (Polyanskij, 1978, 81) As the novel reaches its happy, socialist-realist ending, the division's participation in the FTX has been successful. Thirteen of the fifteen gold watches for outstanding performance during the FTX that were awarded by the minister went to members of Korsunov's unit. Col. Korsunov is happy that his efforts over the past six months have not been wasted and he rides off symbolically into a sunrise, suggesting the beginning of a new era.

In his novella, *Only Three Days*, Valerij Biryukov describes the last three days of service of the commander of an artillery battalion, Guards Lt. Col. A. A. Savel'ev. Savel'ev is over fifty years old. He has to retire, as did the officers mentioned previously, because of the heart attack he had six months before the story begins. Just like Col. Surgin, the war is the reason that his health is not what it should be. "The war ruined the health of war veterans like us, but we cannot find the time to treat our ills, and that's wrong!" (Biryukov, 1975, 45), says the division commander on the eve of Savel'ev's retirement.

What are Lt. Col. Savel'ev's concerns as he prepares to turn over his battalion to Maj. Antonenko, who has just graduated from CGSC? The same as his other literary counterparts: how his younger, inexperienced replacement will handle the battalion that has been his for almost fifteen years.

Lt. Col. Savel'ev is faced with an impending change in his battalion's armament. Even though he knew down deep that his health was not the main reason that he had to retire, he did not want to admit it to himself. He reasons that he is not running from change; he could have mastered the new equipment if it hadn't been for his heart attack.

"The equipment is only secondary," continued reasoning Savel'ev stubbornly, leaving out the very "something" that Antonenko surpassed him in, but which he very much did not want to admit. "The main thing is people. Will Antonenko have enough *experience* to continue what I have started?

That's it. Where's he going to get the *experience*? The major is so awfully *young!*" (Biryukov, 1975, 13, *emphasis* added)

Luckily for Lt. Col. Savel'ev, the battalion gets a move-out order to participate in an FTX, and the division commander to whom the battalion is subordinate decides to postpone the change of command until after the FTX so that Maj. Antonenko can study Savel'ev's command technique. The division commander shares Savel'ev's concern about the major's inexperience in working with people and cautions the major that

It'll be well worth your while to learn from him. Savel'ev knows how to work with people, and that is a great art that comes with time. That's why I am repeating myself: look around, don't shoot from the hip, don't be in a hurry to change things, if something suddenly seems strange to you in the battalion.

At the same time, however, the division commander also recognizes Lt. Col. Savel'ev's shortcomings with respect to the new technology, and praises him for having had the courage to admit that he has grown old and to make the decision to retire. (Biryukov, 1975, 26)

For the remainder of the story the author follows the change in the major's attitude over the three days of the FTX under the tutelage of Savel'ev. The result is a good socialist-realist happy ending. Now the major, armed with both the knowledge of modern technology that the CGSC gave him and the art of working with people that he acquired from Savel'ev, is prepared to fulfill the division commander's prophetic words: "the young are destined to go farther," which show up in a number of the other retirement stories as well. (Biryukov,1975, 26; Polyanskij, 1978, 233)

Lev Snegirev's short story *The Tanks Take Up a Defensive Position*, presents a positive view of a young officer learning from the older generation. The contrasting characters in Snegirev's story are Lt. Col. Bukov, a thirty-year veteran, and Capt. Lopatin, a young company commander. Bukov is the umpire assigned to Lopatin's company for an FTX. Snegirev establishes the contrast between the two in his scene where they reconnoiter the area where Lopatin's company will take up a defensive position. Lopatin moves quickly and assertively through the woods, while Bukov follows him, out of breath and barely able to keep up. Snegirev contrasts the physical superiority of the younger officer to the superior knowledge of the older officer by showing that Lopatin's tactical decision is questionable and that he cannot tell a bomb crater from one from an artillery round.

When Bukov challenges Lopatin's tactical decision as

unimaginative and warns him not to count on the notional enemy being more stupid than he is, Lopatin cuts him off sharply with the rebuff that "I am responsible for the company. During combat you won't be next to me to prompt me with the correct decision. You may give me "D" at the exercise critique, but I won't change the defensive area." (Snegirev, 106)

Bukov does not react to this rebuke, but sighs and steps aside while the young captain marks the positions for his tanks on his map overlay. He is disturbed by the thought that after almost thirty years of service, he is about to leave the military and Lopatin is representative of those who will replace him.

> There's no argument that today's young officers are educated and energetic, with a sense of initiative that is so necessary to a commander. But who gave them that aplomb, that indisputable confidence in their own strengths and capabilities? After all, he, Bukov, didn't have any of that, but had to learn both the sweetness of victory and the bitterness of failure on his own during the war. (Snegirev, 106)

Snegirev resolves the conflict to socialist-realist satisfaction by having the captain change his mind and establish a new defensive position, when he is confronted by a local resident, who actually fought over this piece of ground during the war. Bukov is relieved at the change in Lopatin's decision, even though his new boots, a simile that Snegirev had built up for Bukov's relationship with Lopatin, still were somewhat tight.

In his short story *Magnetic Deviation*, Yurij Pronyakin takes a further look at the self-confidence of the new generation of officers. Young Sr. Lt. Opalin, the commander of a SCUD launch vehicle, is betrayed by overconfidence in his own abilities. Opalin's crew has just beat the standard time for positioning the rocket for launch by three minutes and he is enjoying a feeling of success, when the umpire informs him that his aiming data is off by 010. He had been so fixated on beating the standard time that he had neglected to recheck the aiming data. This is, in essence, the same mistake made by Zen'kovich's Lt. Peresypkin in preparing a radar station for operations. He did not check a subunit that was on the checklist, because they had checked it the week before and he needed the extra time to get a problem unit up and running and still finish within the allotted time for the preoperations checkout.

In the end, Opalin realizes his mistake. He forgot to take the magnetic deviation into consideration when plotting the firing angle. On the next timed exercise, he takes his time and checks everything, eliciting worries that he will not make it to the launch control panel in time for a good score. His more cautious approach is successful and he gets a score of "excellent." As he leaves, the umpire gives Opalin this piece of sage advice: "Confidence in yourself is a good quality, but only in conjunction with a check on yourself, otherwise your confidence might pull you off to one side like the magnetic deviation." (Pronyakin, 1974, 237)

All three of these stories, Pronyakin's, Zen'kovich's and Snegirev's, are successful as socialist-realist pieces of military fiction, because they show the young officers learning from their mistakes and growing into better officers because of them in accordance with the Marxist dialectic.

There is not much life after retirement in military fiction. Marshal D. N. Yanov in Nikolaj Gorbachev's *The Battle*, which plays in the early sixties, provides a good character portrait of the turmoil that retirement brings to the lives of dedicated, single-minded officers. In the course of the novel, Marshal Yanov gives way to the forces of technological change and retires. The story opens as he first begins to think about retirement, when the commander in chief (of Rocket Troops) questions him about his health. The making of the decision to retire then plays as a subthread of the plot throughout the novel.

The marshal is over sixty, and his heart has begun to act up. He has been widowed for two years, and the death of his wife was a heavy blow to him. Following her death, he began to spend more and more time at the office, which, of course, compounded the problem of his poor health.

Gorbachev's description of Yanov's decision to retire concentrates on the heavy emotional charge surrounding the decision. Yanov goes through several versions of his DF requesting retirement before he quits trying to convey the emotion involved in a decision to end his forty-four-year career, which was driven by a strong sense of duty. Finally, he settles on the laconic, bureaucratic formulation: "I request that I be relieved of the position I occupy, because age and the high demands brought about by technical progress, especially in the last few years, do not permit me to carry out the duties placed upon me in the proper fashion." (Gorbachev, 1977, 327)

After he has made his decision and turned in his DF, "he feels a strange sense of loss. He feels as if this step marks an end to everything: his duties, constant concerns, thoughts, aspirations, even life itself. He's like a fish thrown up on the shore by an unexpected wave, with no way back to its natural element." (Gorbachev, 1977, 331) For him, retirement is, as Gorbachev says that the wags put it, a transfer to the "heavenly group," that is, where the only road leads to Heaven. (Gorbachev, 1977, 327) Yanov had never thought about retirement. He had sort of expected that he would keep working until he simply ceased to exist.

Sergej Lutskij's short story, *At Home in the Unit*, presents a poignant vignette from the life of Col. (ret.) Aleksandrov. The colonel has been retired for six months and moved away from his old unit. On the pretext of going to get a document that can only be picked up in person, he visits his old unit just one last time and revels in the chance to participate in the morning muster formation. He is pleased to find that he is still remembered in the unit and enjoys a tour of the unit area. During his visit, he comes to realize that even if no one in the unit remembered him, the things that he had set the foundations for and dedicated his life to would continue to live and grow, and in that he saw the promise of eternal life.

Fedor Khalturin wrote two versions of a retirement short story that is very similar to Lutskij's. One version is called *The Man and the Howitzer* and the other *The Song*. The core of the two versions is the same. It is the first day of retirement of an artillery battalion commander, who had commanded the unit for almost eight years. The day's events are much like those in *At Home in the Unit*. The retiree goes back to his unit one last time, seeing old friends and acquaintances and recalling his accomplishments.

The two versions are, however, diametrically opposed in their approach to retirement. The main accent in the first version, *The Man and the Howitzer* (1977) is on the war. Nikolaj Il'ich Kopytov is the last serving war veteran in his regiment. Looking at the young officers of his battalion on this day, he "realizes, perhaps for the first time in his life, with a sharp, merciless directness, that he is almost fifty years old and those four war wounds did not leave his health untouched." (Khalturin, 1977, 21)

The story ends with a flashback to his war experiences as he sits by the side of his 122-millimeter howitzer and looks at the markings on the gun plate that record the number of kills made with it. As he prepares to leave for the last time, he looks forward to the future, but he "knows that his heart will always be in his own regiment." (Khalturin, 1977, 26)

In *The Song* (1980), the accent is more positive. There is no mention of the war. Lt. Col. Sergej Fedorovich Lopatin looks at the young officers of his battalion and "realizes, perhaps for the first time in his life, with a sharp, merciless directness, that he is almost fifty years old and *it is past time for him to give up his place to younger men.*" (Khalturin, 1980, 7, *emphasis* added) The phrase after the "and" in this quote is the key difference in the two versions. Lopatin is remarking about the changing of the guard. Kopytov is lamenting the end of an era.

The focus in *The Song* is on the decision of where to go and what to do after Lopatin retires. After his last day in the unit, he has still not decided. It is only when he hears a song on the radio about the grove back home that he decides. He will go back to his home village in Siberia and become a junior ROTC instructor at the school.

This version of the story ends, not with his heart remaining where he has served all these years, but with it firmly attached to the place where he spent his youth. His wife, having heard the song too, understands what his decision is before he can tell her. She is ready "to go with him where his heart leads." (Khalturin, 1980, 21)

Vladimir Kozlov presents a vignette about a recently retired, postwar-generation lieutenant colonel, who is still living in his old apartment that echoes the feelings of the World War II generation of officers in the seventies. Lt. Col. Aleksandr Eipiana has been retired for only two weeks following a thirty-year career and the alert bell is still connected in his apartment. When it goes off late at night, despite his wife's protestations about his poor health and that he is retired now, he gets up and goes in to the unit to see if they really do need him. As he walks to the unit to answer the call, in his mind's eye he can see his wife standing at the window proudly following him with her eyes. He is sure that she will wait up for him to come home just like she has done all the years of his career.

Kozlov's story is just a brief character sketch, but the character type is repeated often enough in military fiction that it is almost a cliche. Col. (ret.) Vodolazov, like Lt. Col. (ret.) Eipiana, does not adjust well to the idea of retirement. When someone calls him a retiree, he becomes quite upset. He insists that he is reserve colonel Vodolazov, not a retiree. Being in the reserve means that he can still be called up to active duty if needed. Instead of moving to Voronezh, where there are lots of retirees, he takes a job near his old unit as the head of the local collective farm. People like Col. (ret.) Vodolazov, Nikolaj Kopytov and Lt. Col. (ret.) Eipiana are the people who have the most trouble adjusting to retired life because their careers have been their entire existence and they cannot let go and move on to something else. They are members of Gorbachev's "heavenly group."

NOTES

1. *Mala Encyklopedia Wojskowa*, Vol. III, MON, Warsaw: 1971, p. 639.

2. A reference to the mythological belief that the Earth rests on the backs of three whales swimming in the sea of the cosmos.

3. The "Lesser" Patriotic War was the one fought against Napoleon in 1812.

4

The Hero of Our Times

One cannot think that blind bravery gives victory over the enemy.
                    Field Marshal Prince Aleksandr V. Suvorov (1729-1800)

In the post-World War II period, a significant item on the MPD's shopping list of topics for military fiction was to show that life in the military was still full of thrills and excitement. These stories were to be directed at the draft-age audience of young men as a very subtle part of the Soviet military's recruiting campaign for the service academies and indoctrination campaign for basic service soldiers. Young men of that age all want a chance to be "the hero of our times." The MPD wanted to show them that the service was the place to do that.

In his short story *Two at Night*, Nikolaj Zen'kovich shows exactly what the target audience for a hero-of-our-times story looks like in his character sketch of Pvt. Efimchik. Efimchik dreams of becoming a hero. He has a whole library of books about heroes and feats of heroism. He has been in the service for only about six months and has not had a chance to do anything heroic, but he is waiting "persistently" for the right occasion to present itself. While he is waiting, "he reads everything that had to do with heroes and feats of heroism again and again, absorbing details and specifics about them like a sponge." (Zen'kovich, 11)

This is exactly the effect that the MPD was seeking to produce with its own made-to-order stories. The goal of military literature was to nurture the desire of young men like Pvt. Efimchik to be heroes and to counter the perception common in the postwar period that life in the postwar military was just drill and ceremonies (D&C) or playing at war. Young men who think like Efimchik are much easier to deal with as conscripts or to recruit for the service academies. If life in the service looks like it is "where the action is," then the recruiter's and drill instructor's tasks are a lot easier.

Anatolij Polyanskij effectively demonstrates both what the problem is and where the MPD thinks that the solution rests in his novel *The Right to Take Risks*, which plays in the mid-seventies. When one of his sergeants complains to Col. Korsunov, the chief of the Political Department of Polyanskij's airborne division, that he does not want to stay in the Army after his basic service is finished, because "I'm not interested, the scope of activities is too limited and the conditions, you know yourself ..." (Polyanskij, 1978, 36), Korsunov thinks to himself that they need to do more to get qualified specialists like the sergeant to stay in. He sees the solution as playing on the romantic desire of young men like the sergeant to be challenged and to achieve.

> Who at twenty-something is not attracted by the romance, the self-sacrifice, of a noble goal? That's what we need to emphasize in our presentations. ... Young men are going to the BAM,[1] the KAMaz[2] and other big construction projects. How is the idea of defending the Fatherland any less inspiring, particularly in our branch of service: the Airborne—the synonym of bravery? (Polyanskij, 1978, 37)

In his *Court of Honor*, Yurij Pronyakin shows how the desire to be a hero, common in young men of draft age, was reinforced in the fifties and sixties through the pressure placed on them by the World War II generation. This is most clearly seen in a speech by Pfc. Dashkov, the Secretary of the Comsomol organization in Pronyakin's antiaircraft rocket (PVO) battalion, at a monument to the war dead. "We haven't done anything heroic in our lives, and maybe we won't. These are not the times for that sort of thing, but we have to be worthy of the heroes of the war in everything we do." (Pronyakin, 1974, 67 & 176)

Dashkov's speech serves to underscore the tension between Pronyakin's PVO battalion commander, Maj. Ul'yantsev, and his father, which was brought about by this pressure. Pronyakin sets the stage for the conflict in his description of the senior Ul'yantsev's return from the war. He was so decorated that "he blinded his son with the gleam and deafened him with the jingling of his medals and decorations." When young Maj. Ul'yantsev comes home on leave, his father immediately asks him why he does not have medals or decorations. His father had just read a long list of awards in *Red Star*[3] the other day and did not see his son's name there. He pours salt on the wound, inflicted by his first question, by adding "or aren't you serving the way the others are, son?" Maj. Ul'yantsev's response to this question is a question to his father: "Did you just serve for the decorations?" (Pronyakin, 1974, 91) This is the central point in Pronyakin's defense of the postwar generation of officers from this kind of pressure.

Pronyakin returns to this issue again, later in the novella, when Maj. Ul'yantsev's battalion is getting ready to engage an aerial border violator. As the moment nears to give the order to fire, Ul'yantsev thinks about why he is in the service. For him it is not the medals and the decorations that are the reason he chooses to serve his country in uniform. Serving for the medals and decorations is just "romantic naivete." He does not need medals as long as he can prevent the reoccurrence of events like those of 22 June 1941[4] that were a turning point in the lives of millions of people. (Pronyakin, 1974, 176) Awards and decorations, of course, follow the successful engagement of the border violator, but Pronyakin wanted to show that they were not the motivation for the novella's cast of characters, but rather the reward for doing their duty well in exceptional circumstances.

In *Court of Honor*, Pronyakin does a good job of showing life in the PVO, the front line of the sixties, as a combination of the mundane and the heroic. After the elation of a successful live fire exercise, when the unit returned to garrison from the range, Pfc. Dashkov began to notice that some of the soldiers, himself included, did not have the same drive that they did at the range. While Pronyakin notes that this was "no special reason to sound the alarm. They were carrying out their duties well enough" (Pronyakin, 1974, 69), this is exactly the problem that Pronyakin is addressing for the MPD: how to get more than just "well enough" out of the troops faced with normal, day-to-day duties.

On the one hand, he has characters like young Pvt. Mikhail Timoshin, who is not unlike the type of the reader that Pronyakin and the MPD want to influence.

> When Mikhail first started his service, the military seemed full of excitement and heroism. As his service progressed, however, his enthusiasm began to fade and the service started to seem like an endless series of training exercises, demanding so much exertion that all his muscles ached. Mikhail saw that it was really like the "Old-timers"[5] said: "The service is work and an enlisted man [EM] is not a guest ..." Eventually the thought formed in Mikhail's consciousness that for an EM, the service is an endless hard job, not allowing you to relax for a minute. (Pronyakin, 1974, 74)

Timoshin's thought is countered by Maj. Yurenev, the battalion political officer, who, speaking at a Comsomol meeting before a live fire exercise, says: "doesn't service in the Army, with all its tension and harsh surprises, demand, well, if not heroism in the strict sense of the word, then at least a certain fortitude, boldness and decisiveness?" (Pronyakin, 1974, 67)

Pronyakin has Yurenev continue this train of thought by suggesting that the everyday can be exciting too, "by making it a spiritual necessity ... to learn all the fine points of your duties, earn a higher skill level rating, become an honor student, master a second specialty." (Pronyakin, 1974, 69) In essence, Yurenev's cure of the problem is to make the troops into workaholics, who live for their jobs.

While the cure undoubtedly would work, if it could be implemented, Viktor Bogatov shows what happens when something like this is suggested to the troops in his *Rise to Your Own Level*. When Lt. Blinov proposes that the members of his platoon learn a second specialty, "he was surprised that the troops were not enthusiastic" about his proposal. (Bogatov, 38) In fact, there was no reaction from the platoon at all until Pvt. Skobelev is asked directly what he thinks about the idea. Skobelev's response is as close to hostile as an EM can be expected to be in answering an officer in a work of socialist-realism. "What can I say? I'm squared away on that score. I can handle the weapons on the BMP[6] and everything else. That means that my job is to wait for my discharge." (Bogatov, 38) Skobelev's only real interest is in who can be excused from physical training (PT) and D&C. When he asks Blinov who qualifies for that, this does give the troops something to get excited about. They even give up a free Sunday to practice for the test, the results of which will determine who is to be excused.

Yurenev himself seems to be as much in need of his own advice as Timoshin. Pronyakin shows that Yurenev's attitude to the service has changed too. As his career progressed, his "feeling of excitement from serving as a PVO officer began to dim." (Pronyakin, 1974, 45) Pronyakin has to go to some lengths to counter the effect of this insight into Yurenev's character. He has to work hard to show that Yurenev is a dedicated and competent officer, who carried out his duties to the satisfaction of his superiors.

Pronyakin could have avoided the problem by simply making Yurenev a gung-ho, do-or-die officer, like Col. Korsunov, but by showing that Yurenev had to overcome the same problems that Timoshin had, Pronyakin makes Yurenev's advice more acceptable to the audience, and, most likely, Yurenev more true to life.

Pronyakin is successful in showing that heroism in peacetime is being ready to accomplish the heroic, because you never know when or if the opportunity to do so will come. Pronyakin's characters do get their opportunity as the novella draws to a close. It is here that Pronyakin demonstrates that the threat to the Soviet Union is real and that its military men are heroes, not in the sense of heroism as it was displayed during World War II, but in a new sense, defined by the times of the postwar period as they engage and shoot down an aerial border violator. This is exactly the approach needed to respond to the MPD's requirement to show basic service soldiers that they too have an important function to fulfill, even if it seems that most of the time they do not.

Responding to the MPD's requirement while writing about heroism in the peacetime military is a hard task. It is easy to show how a character can be a hero against the backdrop of war or warlike scenes similar to Pronyakin's description of the engagement of the border violator. For scenes set in peacetime, however, the author has to work a little harder to produce situations for the characters to display their courage. Quite often authors of postwar military fiction bring the war into their stories to highlight peacetime situations where the character can be a hero.

Evgenij Ivankov does this by stressing the continuity between the heroics of wartime and the heroics of peacetime in his short story *First Sergeant Koshkarev*, published in 1962. He begins by establishing the first sergeant's wartime bravery in a flashback and then goes on to show that, even in peacetime, the first sergeant can still be a hero, by describing how he rescues a young mother and her baby from a truck that careens off the road after its drunken driver falls asleep at the wheel.

Col. Mikhail Sviridov uses the inverse of this approach in his short story *Believe Rusakov*. The heroic highlight of this story is the description of the rescue of the passengers on a bus that was hit by a truck. Not only Pvt. Rusakov, but also his whole platoon is involved in the rescue, braving the fire that broke out after the collision. Sviridov's story, however, plays in the early eighties, and his tie-in to combat is not to World War II, but to Afghanistan. Sviridov is not drawing on the war as a source of heroism, but rather is projecting the heroism of the rescue forward to the war in Afghanistan, where they need the help of heroes like Rusakov.

Telling the story of the Explosive Ordinance Disposal (EOD) teams, which were cleaning up the lethal litter left behind by the war, is an especially good approach for bringing the war into postwar fiction. For the heroes in V. Demidov's *We Leave Last ... The Diary of an EOD Man* (1967), Dmitrij Azov's *What Color Is Earth?* (1980), and Yurij Il'inskij's *Blast at Dawn* (1982), the war really is not over yet, because they are still putting their lives on the line every day to clean up after it.

Lev Snegirev's short story *The Road*, which plays in 1970, is a particularly interesting example of this approach, because it shows the reader the development of a conscious decision to accept the lethal risk presented by the situation and to measure up to the bravery displayed by the World War II generation of military men. Jr.-Lt. Kolesnik is the officer assigned to accompany a truckload of unexploded munitions from where they were found, to a location sixty kilometers away, where they could be safely detonated.

At first glance, the mission has only a slight potential for danger and bravery. Road conditions are good. Traffic on the road has been halted. There should be no problems, but Snegirev thickens the plot by unexpectedly adding a blinding blizzard that makes road conditions treacherous. Not only is the road slick, but it has been so completely covered with snow that the driver cannot see where the road ends and the ditch at its side begins. Sliding off the road into the ditch means almost certain death and now Jr.-Lt. Kolesnik is put to the test.

Snegirev surprisingly reverses the expected traits of the story's two characters. It is Kolesnik who freezes into inaction and the driver, Pvt. Malygin, who comes up with the solution to the problem. It remains for Kolesnik to discover the inner courage to implement Malygin's suggestion. Kolesnik eventually finds the fortitude to do what needs to be done in the memory of a war movie he had seen when he was a kid. In this movie, a column was crossing thin ice to bring food to a besieged town. To complete their mission, the people in the column were risking certain death in the freezing water, if the ice broke underneath them. With this image in mind, Kolesnik gets out of the vehicle and walks through the blizzard ahead of the truck, showing the driver where the road is and leading them to their final destination.

Snegirev's role reversal, while effective as a literary device in Western military fiction, did require a bit of justification to make it work in socialist-realism. Snegirev's explanation of the source of Kolesnik's indecision is that Kolesnik is a product of the Reserve Officers' Training Corps (ROTC) program and not a service academy graduate. The service is not his life's career. He is only completing his obligatory stint on active duty after college before going back to the civilian world. Malygin's solution to the problem is really not his own idea, but the story of what his platoon leader, who is a career officer, did once before in a similar situation. Snegirev is, therefore, not really playing an officer off against an EM, but is playing an ROTC officer off against a career officer (once removed), which makes his approach acceptable in socialist-realism.

Vyacheslav Vsevolodov uses a variation of the EOD approach to bravery in his short story *Nine Grams of Lead*, which plays in a small garrison dispensary in 1986. In his story he not only brings World War II on stage, but the war in Afghanistan as well. Together they inspire Lt. (Med.) Bol'shakov to screw his courage to the sticking point and accept a risk to save the life of a patient.

The nine grams of lead are a German bullet in the shoulder of the patient that Bol'shakov has to treat. The man has just been struck by a vehicle and in addition to his other injuries, a bullet left in his shoulder from World War II has been dislodged and has started to move so that now it must be removed to save his life. Bol'shakov is the only doctor at the dispensary, but he is not a surgeon. The dispensary is the only medical facility around. There are plans to build a civilian hospital in the town, but that is in the future and the operation needs to be performed now. At present, the only surgeon anywhere nearby is the commander of the dispensary, who is off on a tour of the subordinate aid stations and cannot get back in time to do the operation. Even though his inaction may be as deadly as his action, Bol'shakov is afraid to accept the risk of an operation for which he has no training, because that also means accepting responsibility for the patient's life.

The patient, Ivan Petrovich, is himself another source of the war in the story. He served as a front-line surgeon during World War II and relates to Bol'shakov how the war forced him to attempt even the most hopeless operations. He once even operated on a wounded soldier in the mud using a pocketknife without an anesthetic, because it was the only way to save the man's life. "Most of them [the wounded] died, but even if it was only possible to save one out of ten, that justified any risk" (Vsevolodov, 344), says Ivan Petrovich, who then offers to let Bol'shakov operate on him with just a local anesthetic so that he can advise Bol'shakov during the operation.

He makes the offer, because he senses that Bol'shakov is "young and intelligent, even though inexperienced," and his advice can help Bol'shakov overcome his inexperience. Ivan Petrovich also sees that Bol'shakov's hesitation to undertake the operation stems from a shortcoming of his training at the university.

> They didn't teach you the main thing—they didn't teach you how to take risks! You don't know how to dare, or if you like, how to aspire and consequently, discovering something new is beyond your grasp. Taking a risk means accepting the responsibility for the correctness of your judgement, your knowledge, intuition, if nothing else. (Vsevolodov, 344)

Vsevolodov tips the scales, already loaded with the bullet that needs to come out and with Ivan Petrovich's story about the operation in the field with a pocketknife and no anesthetic, by adding a newspaper article about an operation on a soldier wounded in Afghanistan. To give more weight to this article, Vsevolodov has both the authority figures in the story, the dispensary commander and Ivan Petrovich, give Bol'shakov this article to read. It praises the bravery of the surgeon, who operated on a soldier to remove an unexploded rifle grenade round from his shoulder. This situation put the surgeon's life on the line along with the patient's. If anything went wrong, they would not only lose the patient, but the surgeon—at best—would lose his hands as well. The article pushes Bol'shakov over the edge of his indecision to accept the risk and to perform the operation on Ivan Petrovich.

In Anatolij Polyanskij's *The Right to Take Risks*, Col. Korsunov thinks about what gives someone the right to take a risk.

> Sticking your neck out, counting on good luck is not useful and even harmful. But if someone faces danger, risks his life consciously, in the name of the greater goal, then he not only needs to have personal bravery, but also to be convinced of the righteousness of the cause that he serves, to have a developed sense of responsibility and, of course, to know what he is doing. ... The only people who have a right to play with fire are the ones who are most prepared to keep the danger of a conflagration to a minimum. (Polyanskij, 163)

Aleksandr Kuleshov also uses the EOD approach in his novel *The White Wind*, but he adds a few other situations for his hero of our times to test his heroic mettle as well. Lt. Yurij Levashov, the political officer in Kuleshov's airborne company, gets to show how much bravery goes into service in the postwar military in a number of ways:

- leading the EOD team that removes an old German explosive charge from a power generation station (Kuleshov, 1977a, 303), for which he gets a medal;
- leading a fire fighting detail to safety after they are cut off by a wildfire in a peat bog, just like a wartime commander leading his troops out of encirclement (Kuleshov, 1977a, 296), which also gets him a medal;
- rescuing a paratrooper, whose chute candled, by grabbing the trooper's chute and taking them both down on his own canopy, which, though it does not get him a medal, does earn him the respect of his men. (Kuleshov, 1977a, 162)

Kuleshov ices the cake for the MPD, when he has Col. Surov of the Political Department announce to young Lt. Levashov that he will be getting a medal. Surov makes it very plain that modern-day military service still has a place for acts of bravery: "They give awards for soldierly bravery, that's what for. What are you so surprised about? You say that there's no war. You're right, there's not. But there is military[7] service. In peacetime, just as in wartime, the service isn't easy, and there's always room for bravery in it." (Kuleshov, 1977a, 348)

The most typical feats of bravery in postwar military fiction, not involving the war, are fighting fires or saving people from drowning. In *The White Wind*, a young lieutenant in Levashov's company bravely rescues a soldier from a frozen river. (Kuleshov, 1977a, 128) In Viktor Bogatov's *Rise to Your Own Level* the same feat is repeated again.

(Bogatov, 117) In Anatolij Polyanskij's *Morning Starts at Midnight*, the victim is rescued from a pool of quicksand in a swamp instead of a river. (Polyanskij, 1984, 159) A peat bog fire in *The White Wind* earns the EM medals for their bravery. (Kuleshov, 1977a, 259) Capt. Snegur is awarded a medal for parachuting into a forest fire to rescue the children at a Young Pioneer camp. (Polyanskij, 1978, 134) Pfc. Tsyganok earns an engraved personalized watch for rescuing the cattle from a burning barn at a collective farm in Nikolaj Kambulov's two-volume novel *Faithfulness*. (Kambulov, 1970a, 226; also Kambulov, 1970b, 27 & 72)

In *Court of Honor*, Pronyakin makes light of this kind of heroism in the dialog between Pvt. Timoshin and his girlfriend. She teases Timoshin by asking him if he has had the opportunity to put out a fire and rescue children trapped in one, or to save someone from drowning. In having her do so, Pronyakin is demonstrating what a cliche this type of heroic episode had already become in military fiction by the early seventies, when the novella was written. Pronyakin's novella avoids this kind of heroism altogether, and sticks to the heroism of waiting for the chance to defend one's country and being able to act when the time comes.

The clash of man against the elements is also overworked as a background for characters to display their courage. This scenario is represented by such works as Georgij Sviridov's *Victory Does Not Come Easy* (1969); Nikolaj Asanov's *The Disaster Is Cancelled* (1968), which relates the story of the Tashkent earthquake in 1966; Nikolaj Zen'kovich's short story *Two in the Night* (1983), in which Pvt. Efimchik gets to display his courage in a raging blizzard, and Evgenij Besschetnikov's novel *The Snows Are Melting* (1986), in which a unit of combat engineers helps the local populace during the flooding that follows a spring thaw. Even Anatolij Polyanskij produced a short story in this vein on the bravery of the soldiers on Sakhalin as they helped the local populace, following the destruction caused by typhoon "Phyllis". It was called, simply enough, *Typhoon*.

Mikhail Godenko took an interesting approach to heroism in his novel *Eternal Fire*, which was published in 1987. Ostensibly, the novel is about a reactor accident on the prototype of the first Soviet nuclear submarine. The date that the novel was published and some problems with Godenko's historical time line suggest that the novel was really about the reactor accident at Chernobyl (1985) rather than solely about what has been a common enough event in Soviet nuclear naval history.[8] The icebreaker *Lenin*, which served as the test bed for the prototype seagoing reactor, suffered a major reactor accident in 1966 that left the ship too hot to board for several years.[9] The Indians, who lease two "Charlie" class Soviet nuclear submarines, refer to them as the "Chernobyl" class instead because of all their reactor problems.[10]

The first Soviet nuclear submarine was the *Leninskij Komsomolets*, which was commissioned on 8 April 1958.[11] Godenko, however, cites Yurij Gagarin as one of the heroes, who has died for his country like Lt. Gorchilov, the main character of *Eternal Fire*. Gagarin died in 1968. Godenko also cites Namibia as one of the political hot spots in the world at the time of his story. Namibia did not become a state until 1968.

Another factor that points to Chernobyl as the source of Godenko's inspiration for this story is that Godenko is Ukrainian. Not only his name, but also a major character in the book and a healthy peppering of Ukrainian words underscore the fact. Chernobyl is located in the Ukraine, just north of Kiev.

Godenko's goal in the novel is to examine the heroism and valor of the men, who had to face the invisible threat of nuclear radiation. The accident and the fear of his characters as they face it are held in the background. His focus is on the "internal dynamism" of the accident. His main concern is to show why the characters acted rather than what they did. The accident is described in broad strokes: a break in the coolant circulating system that threatens the boat with a core meltdown. The description of the action is scant: the reactor officer and two EM from his section enter the containment and repair the fault.

The reactor officer, Lt. Gorchilov, whose name evokes an image of sorrow,[12] does not hesitate. The narrator doubts that Gorchilov has had the time to weigh his decision to enter the containment. "There is no time to think at moments like these." On the other hand, the narrator notes that this was not an unconscious decision. He is sure that Gorchilov has thought a lot about how he would behave in a tight spot and his decision now was really already made and was only waiting for the event to which it was the answer, so that it could be expressed as a concrete action.

Gorchilov was

> puzzled that the did not feel any fear. After all, not long ago even the thought of being irradiated made his face tighten with cold. Now, when he had opened the containment and stepped into a zone of intense radiation, the feeling of fear had disappeared. Why? Maybe from the unexpectedness, from the shock? Maybe abstract conjectures, when there is nothing concrete to do, when one is not concentrating, when one does not have a goal, demagnetize you, give rein to unnecessary reflexes, get you worked up over nothing? When it is not occupied with something, all the power of your imagination goes into creating a feeling of apprehension and fear, into forcing a living organism to be cautious. But, when there is a real threat and not a made-up one, when your mind and your efforts are focused on

the goal of getting yourself out of the way of danger and getting others out, when you understand that you alone are responsible for everyone, that they are counting on you, waiting for you to take action, when the captain of the boat consults you and has his hopes pinned on you and you are busy trying not to let him down, trying not to seem weak and indecisive to him and the others, then fear retreats, or rather you don't have time for fear. You just don't think about it. (Godenko, 66-67)

Godenko returns to this idea again as Gorchilov is lying in hospital after the accident, exploring Gorchilov's feelings about his imminent death. The description is a very Marxist one. There is nothing after death. Gorchilov is, however, calm in the face of the termination of his existence, because he recognizes that he acted for the greater common good. (Godenko, 147) His only regrets are for what he did not get to do with his life: to marry the girl of his dreams (Godenko, 149) and to have children. (Godenko, 144)

Gorchilov himself has a strangely un-Marxist concept of death. He felt that his body had died long ago, but that his mind and his feelings were still alive, functioning and not at all afraid of death. Maybe it was this separation of the spirit and the flesh that gave rise to the fable that the spirit leaves the body to go to other spheres, to other dimensions? There is an expression: "the soul says good-bye to the body." The body is mortal. The soul is immortal. (Godenko, 148)

Maybe it was possible for someone, who was dying, to leave his personal observations and feelings for the living.

Gorchilov cannot leave his soul with the living like Mr. Spock of Star Trek did after a similar feat of bravery during a reactor accident, but he will not be forgotten. His name will be on the roster of the fleet forever. He will be awarded an Order of Lenin. Godenko develops the Marxist concept of eternal life in a dream sequence, in which the captain of the boat, Capt. III Mostov, imagines that he is having a conversation with Gorchilov.

"Congratulations, engineer."
"For what?" said Aleksej with innocent surprise.
"For your Order of Lenin."
"Thank you, comrade captain third class. Only I wasn't thinking about it. What does a medal matter? I won't be the better or the worse for it. I am what I am and what I'm not ..."
"Don't talk like that. A medal is an indication of society's relationship to you."

"Will it save me? Save us?" he said, pointing to his wardmates.

"It will."

"From death?"

"From being forgotten. It is more for those, who are left behind, so that in their hour of danger, they won't throw up their hands, so that they won't feel alone, so that they'll know that people will think about them, remember them, consider that their extra effort was not in vain." (Godenko, 165-166)

Another common scenario, which allows the author to demonstrate the heroism of his characters, is a Field Training Exercise. On an FTX, however, everything is simulated and an act of simulated bravery, which results in the "hero" being notionally "killed" by an umpire, is invariably followed by the question "What would he have done in real combat? Would he have risked certain death?" (Kuleshov, 1977a, 344) The socialist-realist answer to this question is usually the same: "Of course, people are ready to perform acts of self-sacrifice to save their comrades, in the name of victory over the enemy." (Polyanskij, 1978, 193)

The frequency with which this question is treated in military fiction points to a rather widespread doubt of the exercise "hero's" motivation for his act of bravery. The commander does not, and cannot know why the "hero" was prepared to "die". Maybe he was only tired or lazy and wanted to "goldbrick, get to be one of the 'dead,' so that he could get out of an exhausting foray." (Kuleshov, 1977a, 187) "No doubt about it, they were goldbricking, said somebody else with assurance. Bakhtin only talks a good hero." (Rybin, 1984, 122)

On an exercise, those who are pronounced "dead" by the umpires are removed to a rear area, where there is food and a chance to rest (Kuleshov, 1977a, 172), while the "living" continue to carry out the assigned mission. Before the exercise is over, they will probably have exhausted all their rations, and they will surely not have a chance to rest before it is finished either. For the exercise "living," "every word [from the mouth of the commander] condemns people to the devil's own labor, and demands unimaginable exertions from them." (Polyanskij, 1978, 197)

In Aleksandr Kuleshov's The White Wind, as soon as the main goldbrick in the novel learned that the "war" is over for the exercise "dead," he began courting a simulated "death," for its obvious advantages over real "life" on the FTX. His behavior is, however, justly unmasked, in good socialist-realist style, in an Operational News Leaflet, the unit's field newspaper published by the political officer's team. (Kuleshov, 1977a, 172)

Kuleshov tries to balance the goldbrick's simulated, exercise "death" of convenience with a simulated, altruistic exercise "death" in a scene from the end of the exercise. The altruistic exercise "death" is that of a frogman, who "detonates" a floating mine before it can get to the bridge that his unit is crossing. This time the act of self-sacrifice is viewed as a result of the soldier's high moral character, but Kuleshov does not offer any real reason for believing the frogman over the "goldbrick." He just notes that "someone had his doubts and even joked about it. Someone shrugged his shoulders: 'it's hard to say.' The majority, however, including Levashov, had no doubts. Zotov [the frogman] would undoubtedly have risked certain death for his comrades. They believed in the high moral character of their soldiers." (Kuleshov, 1977a, 344)

Kuleshov does make an attempt to redeem the exercise "dead" in a scene at the end of the exercise. As the paratroopers of *The White Wind* wade out of a river on to the bank, the tents are pitched, fires are blazing and a field kitchen stands, steaming tastily. This had all been set up for them by the exercise "dead", who "glanced *guiltily* at their exhausted comrades." (Kuleshov, 1977a, 179, *emphasis* added) If Kuleshov had been consistent in his treatment of the problem, only the story's goldbrick should have glanced "guiltily" at his comrades, because all the other exercise "dead" would have been those who had acted heroically for the greater good of the unit during the exercise. They would have had no reason to feel guilty for what they did, because their "sacrifice" would have helped the unit complete its mission.

Stanislav Babaev builds on the exercise scenario as a means for displaying heroism by seeming to take the simulation out of it in his novella *Conflict*. He presents a story in which it at first appears that one of the company commanders, Capt. Kuklin, has bravely sacrificed his life to save others by throwing himself on a loose, live grenade at a firing range. Babaev then, however, begins to cast doubt on Kuklin's motivation and finally negates the feat of bravery altogether, by revealing that it was only just a practice grenade and that Kuklin was not killed—the message from the range had been garbled in transmission.

The deputy regimental duty officer, Lt. Kozintsev, who took the message, is the first to cast doubt on Kuklin's heroism. He cannot believe that Kuklin was capable of sacrificing himself for another person. Somebody else maybe, but not Kuklin. The seeds of doubt, planted by Kozintsev's remarks, cause Kuklin's battalion political officer, Sr.-Lt. Rykov, to examine Kuklin's character in detail. Babaev makes it clear that Kuklin is not a people-person and that he has very few, if indeed any, friends in the unit. He has the "unfortunate gift of offending people." (Babaev, 168) This "gift" is the result of his being an excellent technical specialist, who has a low threshold of impatience with those who are less skilled or experienced. This character trait has held back his career and kept him in a company-grade position long after he should have been promoted to a battalion-level job.

Babaev continues to detail the problems in Kuklin's career and personal life until it seems that Kuklin's act of bravery might have actually been a suicide attempt instead. It is at this point that he reveals that Kuklin is alive. After that there is even less belief in Kuklin's bravery and self-sacrifice among the other characters in the novella. Everyone is sure that Kuklin could have told a live grenade from a practice one and that he threw himself on the grenade only for the effect, knowing that there was no danger.

Only Rykov believes that Kuklin really thought that it was a live grenade and goes to bat for him with the regimental commander, Lt. Col. Sabura. He wants to get Sabura's help so that together they can help Kuklin rise above his personality problems. The regimental commander is unimpressed by Kuklin's "feat of bravery" in quotes. He says that "even if it was a live grenade, you are not supposed to fall on it. Not fall on it! Throw it off to the side and far away if you are an officer. And that's not a feat of bravery, that's an obligation, duty. ... It's all the more unforgivable for Kuklin, with all his experience." (Babaev, 193)

Aleksandr Gorlov supports Sabura's viewpoint about how to deal with a loose, live grenade in his short story *The Measure of Bravery*. Gorlov's main character, Col. Troshin, does exactly what Sabura says that Kuklin should have done when he saw the soldier drop the grenade at the range. He picks it up and throws it away, knocking the soldier to the ground at the same time. (Gorlov, 7)

Sabura continues to polemicize with Rykov that he is as well aware as Rykov is that "Kuklin knows his stuff like the palm of his hand and that he has an iron character," but that is not all it takes to be victorious on the battlefield. "It's not enough to know tactics, know how to shoot, to fight. ... It's not enough to be decisive, brave and sharp-witted. That's not enough! You have to be a real man, with a heart and it has to ache." (Babaev, 193)

Rykov counters that this incident proves that Kuklin does have a heart and that when the time came, he did act like a real man. This has to be rewarded now, if they are to save Kuklin as an officer and help him rise to the level of his capabilities. Sabura finally agrees with Rykov and shows him an order that he signed a month ago to promote Kuklin to battalion Chief of Staff, but which he had been holding on his desk, because he was not fully convinced that he had made the right decision. Rykov has at last convinced him that it is time to recognize Kuklin and the order will go forward now.

The point of Babaev's story is not only to criticize Kuklin for his antipeople attitude, but also to criticize the system for not helping

Kuklin earlier. Real people-oriented officers should have taken action to help Kuklin long ago. Babaev skillfully avoids the socialist-realist quagmire of assigning guilt for this problem by giving both Sabura and Rykov an alibi. Rykov is blameless, because he has been on the job for only three months. Lt. Col. Sabura is off the hook, because he had already recognized Kuklin's potential and was just waiting for the right moment to act.

Nikolaj Zen'kovich continues the examination of the effect of not being a people-person on an officer's career in his short story, *The Training Incident*. In it he tells the tale of why Lt. Ol'khovoj is given a command in preference to his friend and apparent co-equal, Lt. Peresypkin. They are both honor graduates from the junior officer's PVO academy. Both arrived in the unit at the same time. They share a room in the bachelor officers' quarters (BOQ). They were even born on the same day. All external measures of success are essentially the same for each of them. Zen'kovich initially gives Peresypkin a slight lead over Ol'khovoj in a conversation between the company and regimental commanders. When asked for his recommendation about which of the two should get the job, Capt. Saul'skij tells the regimental commander that "Peresypkin's crew is, perhaps, the best in the company. Peresypkin is the most promising of the junior officers." (Zen'kovich, 141)

Nevertheless, Saul'skij has reservations about Peresypkin as a candidate for the job. It is the subtle difference in their styles of people management that is the deciding factor in the selection. Peresypkin is exactly what his name implies[13]: an excellent technician taken to the extreme. He is "too abrupt with his subordinates ... the service is his whole life." (Zen'kovich, 140) In his view "today's officer is a technician from head to toe, businesslike, a man of few words, who knows how to save his own and other's time." (Zen'kovich, 138) He sees meetings and developing relationships with people as a waste of time. He only wants to define the problem, "build up a decisive superiority of forces on the decisive sector" (Zen'kovich, 137) and take action. As Peresypkin likes to say, "an officer serves, on the average, fifteen and a half million minutes. Therefore, one should treasure his valuable time." (Zen'kovich, 141)

Ol'khovoj, on the other hand, is not quite as good a technician as his roommate, but he is a better people-person. It is this trait that earns him the nod for the position, because, as the regimental commander puts it: "Ol'khovoj's success with his crew rests on a more solid foundation" (Zen'kovich, 142) than Peresypkin's. "Today's commander is a multifaceted personality," says Saul'skij, "first and foremost, he's a student of human nature. He not only knows the technology, but people as well." (Zen'kovich, 146-147)

After the announcement of the appointment, Peresypkin submits a

DF requesting reassignment, because he has trouble playing second fiddle to Ol'khovoj. Zen'kovich produces the required socialist-realist happy ending by having Capt. Saul'skij talk Peresypkin into taking his DF back so that they can keep him in the company and help him grow as a person and an officer, just as Col. Sabura and Rykov planned to do with Kuklin. Saul'skij defines their goal as putting Peresypkin's people skills into dialectical balance with his technical knowledge. "A commander can only count on success when that is the case." (Zen'kovich, 147)

Zen'kovich's approach to this happy ending, however, is somewhat unusual in military fiction. Nowhere in the story is there a political officer to be seen. The kind of people insight demonstrated by the company commander is usually reserved for the political officer, and may be the reason that Zen'kovich's work was published only in a provincial press instead of in the central military press, Voenizdat.

When military fiction returned to a real shooting war in Afghanistan, there were plenty of opportunities for authors to display the heroic mettle of their characters. The war in Afghanistan was an FTX writ large minus the simulation. In Afghanistan, the dead did not come back at the end of the exercise to serve a hot meal to those who had lived through the action; they got sent home in body bags. Babaev's and Zen'kovich's accent on officers being people-oriented combined with this to engender a different point of view from which to evaluate a character's heroism. What Pronyakin termed the "romantic naivete" of serving just for medals and decorations became "reckless bravery" in the mountains of Afghanistan. As Sgt. Knyazev puts it in Valerij Povolyaev's *"H" Hour*, from his vantage point in Afghanistan, "the age of romanticism is over." (Povolyaev, 158)

Nikolaj Ivanov explores this issue in his novella *The Mountain Pass*. As Sr.-Lt. Trunin prepares to turn over his detachment area to a new commander, Trunin thinks to himself that this brand new junior lieutenant (so new that he still has his shiny dress insignia on in a combat area) has a lot of things to learn. Trunin hopes that his replacement's obvious courage and daring will not make him risk his subordinates when the situation does not call for it. (Ivanov, 1987, 15)

His fear is of what Valerij Povolyaev's narrator calls "reckless bravery" in Povolyaev's novella, *"H" Hour*. This kind of courage and daring is useless in combat. This is because recklessly brave people are, like Gorchilov, not conscious of the reality of the danger that they are in. They are detached from the danger, as if they were watching an exciting adventure movie and not actually taking part in the action. This calls forth a sort of childish excitement in them that is out of place on the battlefield.

Lev Snegirev echoes this point of view in his short story *Thaw at Midwinter*, when Lt. Levchuk is talking about a game he used to play as a boy that could have gotten him killed. "Do you really imagine that boys think about that [the possibility of being killed]?" (Snegirev, 10) A "brave fool," as Povolyaev's narrator calls them, who does not think about the danger, is just going to get himself killed and that is a law of nature. In the narrator's opinion, what a combat commander needs is people, who, while recognizing the danger, are able to act despite of it, without acting stupidly, even in the most complex of situations. (Povolyaev, 194)

Vyacheslav Vsevolodov offers a good description of what this process looked like at the front in World War II, in his conversation between Ivan Petrovich and Bol'shakov.

> We knew how not to think about our lives. In general, assumptions like this one are false at their roots. A soldier thinks about death, death you understand, when he's in the trenches, because he is death's minion. He carries death to the enemy and like any minion, he tries to do his job as well as possible. But a soldier, therefore, has to risk his own life too. All the time, without a break, always. And something that follows you all the time becomes normal, natural and unnoticed after a while. And the life of your friend, your foxhole mate, the guy from the same county you're from, becomes much more valuable. ... It's not instinct and intellect that rule a man. When a soldier faces hostile fire, he is taking a risk, but it is a conscious decision, understanding that he might die, but otherwise, victory is impossible. (Vsevolodov, 345)

Kuleshov is more of a fatalist with regard to a soldier's relationship with death. In his *The Nighttime Sun*, the narrator says that soldiers in combat, whether they are charging the enemy with a loud "hurrah" or sneaking up on him, "are not supposed to think about the fact that this may be the last thing that they do on earth. ... A soldier should not think about death, but about his military luck, which, just to spite death, will keep him alive until victory." (Kuleshov, 1981, 306)

The modern, nuclear battlefield, however, continues Kuleshov's narrator, requires not only new protective equipment and measures, but also "new nerves, new self-control and an even higher morale." (Kuleshov, 1981, 306)

Helping soldiers to overcome their fear in combat is a part of a leader's job. Kuleshov's political officer in *The White Wind*, Lt. Levashov, recalls the lesson at the academy on this topic as:

> War, being a continuous and serious threat to life, is, of course, a most natural stimulus for fear. "Bear in mind," said the colonel,

"that there is nothing shameful in the feeling of fear in and of itself. Fear is the psychological reaction of a person to the advent of a danger to himself. It becomes shameful, when a person is not in a condition to overcome that reaction. The personal example of the commander is the main means used to help soldiers overcome fear." (Kuleshov, 1977a, 109)

A leader's personal example in combat can be a strong motivating force. It is not without reason that the motto of the U.S. Infantry Officers' School is "Follow me!" When, however, it is the follow-me example of Sr.-Lt. Plotnikov, the acting political officer of a recon company in Vladimir Vozovikov's *The River Cannot Be Silent*, who, as the situation becomes critical, "resorts to the ultimate means at his disposal: to stand up tall in front of a line of infantry men and draw them behind you to death or victory, not being yet aware of what you are going to do, but prepared to take the most desperate steps" (Vozovikov, 73), people get killed.

Ivanov's concern is that a brave fool is not only going to get himself killed, but also that he will take a few others with him when he goes. In his novella *"Al'kor" Goes Out of Action*, he presents an episode in which 1st Sgt. Starchuk chides Sr.-Lt. Voronov, as the lieutenant prepares to rush into combat. Starchuk notes that, while it is true that Afghanistan will give you stars, he wants to make sure that they are not stars for Voronov's shoulders (promotion) and his chest (medals) at the expense of stars placed on others' graves. (Ivanov, 1990, 223)

As the story develops in *The Mountain Pass*, Trunin's replacement does get himself killed through a foolhardy action, but before the change of command can take place. At the end of the story, when Trunin has finally turned over his command and is leaving the detachment area, he thinks again to himself that this new commander has more promise than the last one, but that he still does not have enough experience (Ivanov, 1987, 69)—combat and field experience that can only be picked up a small piece at a time. (Ivanov, 1987, 15)

This shift in the view of what is heroism is a dramatic change in perspective for Soviet society, which placed the good of the collective whole above that of the individual. Perhaps, if there had been more Lt. Trunins and 1st Sgt. Starchuks and a few less Sr.-Lt. Plotnikovs around during World War II, the Soviet Union might not have suffered 20 million casualties.

NOTES

1. The Bajkal-Amur section of the Trans-Siberian Express rail line.
2. The Kama River Truck Plant.
3. The central Soviet military newspaper.

4. The day that Nazi Germany invaded the Soviet Union.

5. Draftees in their last year of service.

6. BMP is the designator for the Soviet-produced combat infantry vehicle.

7. Kuleshov is playing on the homonymy of the Russian adjective for military (*voennyj*), which is the same as the adjective for war (*voennyj<vojna* [war]).

8. Norman Polmar and Thomas B. Allen, *Rickover*, New York: Simon and Schuster, 1982, p. 557.

9. Ibid., p. 558; and Viking Oliver Eriksen, *Sunken Nuclear Submarines: A Threat to the Environment,* Oslo: Norwegian University Press, 1989, p. 67.

10. Ibid., p. 68.

11. Jan Breemer, *Soviet Submarines: Design, Development and Tactics*, Coulsdon , U.K.: Jane's Information Group, 1989, p. 101.

12. The Russian word *gore* means grief, sorrow, woe.

13. The Russian verb *peresypat'*, from which his name is derived, means to sprinkle too much of something somewhere, as in sprinkle too much salt on your food.

5

Use Your Initiative, *But* Follow Orders!

It's the orders you disobey that make you famous.

Douglas MacArthur [1]

The perception of junior officers as inexperienced is one part of a major problem for the Soviet Armed Forces. Certainly younger officers make mistakes due to their inexperience, but that is part and parcel of the process of gaining experience. As Lt. Col. Yuzovets in Il'ya Mikson's novella *Officers* says, "the acquisition of practical experience takes time, time, time." (Mikson, 15) The heart of the problem for the Soviet military is its attitude to mistakes. The blame for every mistake has to be assigned to someone.

Stalin concentrated all power in his own hands, but ran the purges to be able to assign the blame for his mistakes to others. The collective leadership that followed spread decision making across a group of people to avoid individual responsibility for the consequences of bad decisions. In the military, however, guilt is always assigned to the commander as standard operating procedure.

In his novella *The Zampolit* [The Deputy Commander for Political Affairs, the Political Officer], Anatolij Sul'yanov shows that the unwritten policy of holding the commander responsible for everything that happens in his unit was taken to the extreme in some instances. At a Comsomol meeting that has been called to review a mistake made by a flight mechanic, which almost resulted in a crash, the squadron political officer questions what he sees as the new tendency to punish the commanders more often than the guilty. "If an EM does something bad, three commanders get a reprimand. When an aircraft with a mechanical defect is certified flight worthy by someone like that rosy-cheeked flight mechanic there, they punish everyone up to and including the regimental commander" for his mistake. (Sul'yanov, 1982, 111)

Vladimir Vozovikov shows the same policy is in effect in the armored troops. In his novella *His Father's Son*, Lt. Ermakov warns Pvt. Razinkov during a training exercise that, if Razinkov ever forgets and leaves his fingers on the rim of an unsecured hatch while the tank is in motion, Razinkov will lose his fingers and become an invalid and his commander will probably face a court martial. (Vozovikov, 33)

Boris Nikolskij shows what kind of effect this policy can have on an officer's career. Lt. Chereshnya is thinking about his troops and

> how much the results of this training exercise and the upcoming IG [2] inspection mean to him personally. The paperwork for his promotion has been on the division commander's desk for some time now. His admission to CGSC depends in turn on that promotion and his career advancement. The papers would probably have been signed and in Moscow long ago, if Chepurnov[3] had not let him down. What on earth made him go AWOL? So he could see a new movie. At least that is what he said the next day. ... Of course, Chepurnov went off to the guardhouse right away, but in addition to that the lieutenant caught a lot of heat too. For his poor conduct of indoctrination work. (Nikolskij, 1983, 108-109)

In his novel *The White Wind*, Aleksandr Kuleshov briefly relates how a division commander was relieved of his command because of an incident in one of his subordinate units. He is held responsible even though he had nothing to do with the incident, because

> he was responsible for the overall atmosphere in the division, for every officer's, sergeant's and EM's attitude toward his job, for the fact that they were not demanding enough in one of his units. The general also had to answer for not being able to foresee the dangers that his people would be subjected to on the exercise, what kinds of difficulties they would face in their jobs, the lack of comfort in the bivouac, the unexpected nature of the missions. For the fact that he did not foresee how his junior leaders at all levels would react under this circumstance or that. (Kuleshov, 1977a, 131)

If the commander is ultimately the one who will be blamed for everything that happens in his unit, then it is human nature for him to want to control everything that happens as closely as possible, so that if there are mistakes to be blamed for, then at least they are his own. This results in a command style that centralizes command authority at the highest possible level, which in turn deprives junior officers of an opportunity to become more experienced, by preventing them from gradually taking on more and more complex tasks. This in turn perpetuates the perception of junior officers as inexperienced, which makes senior officers less willing to trust subordinates to get the job done right, which closes a vicious circle of distrust.

As Lt. Levashov, the political officer of an airborne company in Kuleshov's *The White Wind*, recalls the removal of the division commander, his conclusion is that the general "is primarily guilty of depending on others." (Kuleshov, 1977a, 132) He sees the solution to this problem in the words of his academy commandant: "It is better to give an order that may seem self-obvious to your subordinates rather than to not give an order for an action that they will not take without a command." (Kuleshov, 1977a, 132) This is the train of thought that is the basis of the axiom that has become so much a part of the Soviet military mind-set that it has taken on the status of a proverb: Trust, but verify!4 which appears in work after work of military fiction. (Kuleshov, 1977a, 109, 132, 167, 214; Komissarov, 110, 174, 177; Rybin,1984, 114, 131, 155, 161, 233; Biryukov, 1975, 24, 30-32)

The treatment that this issue receives in military fiction shows that the problem has been recognized and that an attempt is being made to come to grips with it. Its longevity as a topic of concern, however, points to a limited success in dealing with it.

Vladimir Vozovikov demonstrates what can happen to junior officers trying to grow into leaders under this system in his novella *His Father's Son*. Even Vozovikov's maverick independent thinker Lt. Ermakov hesitates in indecision, when he loses contact with battalion and regiment following a simulated nuclear strike. Without radio contact with them, he feels very much alone. In desperation, he calls the exercise umpire and asks him what he should do next. The umpire just throws the ball back in his court.

> I was just about to ask you the same question. ... You wanted independence. You've got it. You've got more than you could even have dreamed about a half hour ago. Don't you have anything to say? Independence is easy when you can feel the breath of battalion, regiment and division on the back of your neck. (Vozovikov, 1977, 69)

Ermakov recovers nicely and goes on to lead his troops on a successful foray behind "enemy" lines. Vozovikov underscores Ermakov's take-charge attitude by comparing him to Sr. Lt. Linev. Linev was the most senior platoon leader and as such should have taken command of the company when the umpires notionally "killed" the real company commander. Vozovikov shows Ermakov waiting

interminably for Linev to take up the command and take action before
the tactical clock inexorably runs out. Finally, when he cannot stand
Linev's inaction any longer, Ermakov assumes command himself. This
was the right decision as far as Vozovikov was concerned, because
Ermakov then leads the company on to victory and glory, following the
nuclear strike that really puts him on his own.

From their interaction with the other characters in the novella,
Ermakov was clearly a nonconformist and Linev a conformist member of
the organization. The most logical extension of Vozovikov's story line
is to ask what would have happened if Linev had been in charge of the
company following the nuclear strike instead of Ermakov. Would he
have been able to take independent action that would lead the
company on to success?

The task of military literature is to support the official point of
view that initiative on the part of junior officers is welcome, in an
effort to change the existing state of affairs. The initiative displayed
by junior officers in works of military fiction is, therefore, always
presented in a positive light. In military fiction, at least, their new
ideas and approaches to problems are almost always crowned with
success. The number of authors who provide similar scenarios clearly
points to a widespread problem that covers the period from the late
sixties through Afghanistan.

The common reaction to a subordinate's initiative is the accusation
"you acted of your own will." It is hurled at the guilty party like a
curse in a raised voice. In Russian this is a single word[5] that is closely
related to the Russian term for AWOL[6]—being Absent Without Leave
(permission). From this point of view, acting of one's own will is
tantamount to violating, if not a written military regulation, then at
least an unwritten military code of ethics. It is this concept of
initiative as wrongdoing that is at the heart of the Soviet military's
inflexible command structure.

In his *Nighttime Check*, Anatolij Kuz'michev shows just how rigid
the prohibition against questioning orders can be in the Soviet
military. In a flashback, Lt. Ignat'ev recalls how he had complained to
his company commander about being overworked so that he could get
out of doing a demonstration. His commander, Capt. Lyal'ko, had tried
to make a joke out of it. If he had not done so, recalls Ignat'ev, "it would
have been a scandalous violation of the elementary requirements of the
regulations not to discuss an order once it has been given, but to carry it
out and precisely, unquestioningly and on time." (Kuz'michev, 1982,
219) Kuz'michev underscores *unquestioningly* as the way that orders are
to be carried out a bit later in the story (Kuz'michev, 1982, 225), but
leaves out "precisely" and "on time." This would appear to indicate
that *unquestioningly* is the most important of the three qualities
needed for the execution of an order.

Kuz'michev makes a subtle distinction later toward the end of the novel, when Lt. Ignat'ev is talking with his father, Gen. Ignat'ev. The general is on the PVO IG staff and is well up-to-date on the developments in the area of training requirements that are of concern to his son. He is pleased to note that there are lots of suggestions coming in from line units on how to improve training. "People are not just blindly and obediently following instructions from above. They are showing an interest, a desire to improve the cause that each of them serves." (Kuz'michev, 1982, 240) The distinction that Kuz'michev is making is in the general's choice of the word *instructions*. Instructions can be discussed and improved upon, but orders, once they are given, are inviolate.

"To give orders and to demand the execution of orders by our subordinates is our, let's say, duty," says the battalion political officer to a brand-new company political officer, just out of the academy in A. Egorov's *Step onto the Line of Fire*. He cautions his charge, however, that orders will be carried out more quickly and more precisely if his subordinates are conscientious. The main thing in the work of a political officer he concludes, therefore, is "to teach a conscientious attitude" to their subordinates. (A. Egorov, 59)

In his *Rise to Your Own Level*, Viktor Bogatov supports Gen. Ignat'ev's stance on personal initiative, but shows how hard it is to push new ideas through the system. In a discussion between Lt. Blinov and his battalion political officer, Maj. Brovin, Blinov says:

> It has become customary when someone proposes something more or less unusual, to ask him what the precedent for this is. If there is no precedent, then disapprove it, just because it is not in the regs. In any case, it's not in the regs, yet. Try to come up with something new or invent something under those conditions. (Bogatov, 80)

Bogatov reinforces this statement at the conclusion of a Party Bureau session when Brovin says almost the same thing. It is the "specifics of life in the Army that oblige us to be somewhat reserved with regard to Blinov's experiment." (Bogatov, 153)

Blinov's contention is that there is no place for orders that attempt to micromanage an operation on the modern battlefield, which is characterized by a fluid situation due to the use of modern weapons and tactics. There simply is not time to ask permission from higher headquarters (HQs) before taking action. The time lost in that process can spell the difference between success and failure of the operation. Junior officers need to have the latitude to carry out their orders creatively, and not "to the letter, with no deviations." (Mamontov, 1983, 205) As Lt. Krasnov says in Mikson's *Officers*, "Without

initiative, you cannot carry out an order the way it should be done."
(Mikson, 8)

Blinov's opinion, however, meets with strong resistance from among
his peers and superiors at a session of the Party Bureau for his unit.
They question just what it is that makes Blinov an expert on the
psychological preparation of troops for combat on the modern
battlefield. More senior officers and higher levels of the command
structure are concerned with that problem. What business has Blinov of
thinking that he knows better than they do?

Leonid Konovalov answers this question in his short story *The Long
Night*. It is the tale of what happens in a company when its strong
commander, who always kept his officers on the go, is promoted and
transferred. When Ustimenko was in charge, Lt. Zhmyshchin always
complained that he had too much to do. When Ustimenko's
replacement, a young officer, who has never been a company commander
before, takes over, Zhmyshchin complains that life in the company is
boring. Things have come to a standstill. When Ustimenko was in
charge he always had a thousand and one things to do. Under
Ustimenko, the company had been one of the best in the division. Under
Ryndin, the new commander, it is one of the worst.

The first-person narrator reproaches Zhmyshchin for not taking
the initiative to improve things. Zhmyshchin chaffs under his friend's
reproof, because "Ryndin is the commander. He has full responsibility
for everything." The narrator renews his attack, challenging
Zhmyshchin's passive stance. Just because Ryndin has all the
responsibility does not mean that Zhmyshchin has none. Zhmyshchin
counters that he is just a "junior commander. He only does what he is
told." (Konovalov, 1981, 14)

The narrator rejects this line of reasoning. Junior officers have to
prepare to take on larger commands: a company, a battalion, a
regiment, an army. To do that Zhmyshchin needs to display the
initiative to turn things around in the company now. He needs to help
Ryndin where he can. This is exactly the point that Bogatov is making
in his portrayal of what happens to Lt. Blinov. Konovalov closes the
story with a positive happy ending. Zhmyshchin gets up early the next
morning and leaves a note for his friend, the narrator, which he signs as
"the Army commander," indicating that he has taken the narrator's
advice to heart.

As the narrator leaves the unit area, he encounters Ryndin going in
to work and hears him say something to the duty target acquisition and
tracking crew that Konovalov had gone to great lengths to establish as
one of Ustimenko's unique mannerisms. By doing so, Konovalov is closing
the circle to show that Ryndin has the potential to be a good
commander. As Ryndin and the narrator part company, Ryndin says
that he hopes that Zhmyshchin will help him understand what it was

that made Ustimenko such a good commander. This is how Konovalov indicates that Zhmyshchin's initiative will be welcomed by Ryndin.

Lt. Col. Viktor Mamontov takes a detailed look at the issue of initiative in his short story *The Zampolit*. The story presents an FTX scenario in which the battalion political officer, Sr. Lt. Glazov, is temporarily left in charge of the battalion while the commander, Capt. Surkov, is at regimental HQs. Glazov's orders are to take up a position in a grove in preparation for a river crossing. Before he can get the battalion under cover in the grove, they are overflown by an "enemy" photorecon mission. Recognizing the danger to his unit, Glazov moves them to another area three kilometers to the south.

When Capt. Surkov gets back from regiment, he reads Glazov the riot act for not following orders and refuses to listen to Glazov's explanation. "You acted of your own will, Petr Efimovich! And now who's going to get us out of this mess? This exercise is being graded. I suppose you know about that. ... We're not playing cowboys and Indians here." (Mamontov, 1983, 203) Before Surkov can finish his tirade, Mamontov brings the division commander on stage to further compound the negative reaction to Glazov's initiative.

Gen. Ivanov, recognizing Surkov as the commander and thus the culprit, immediately begins to read Surkov the riot act. "Why did you act of your own will? ... Back into the grove immediately. They will spot you here. At the front, these kinds of tricks cost you dearly." (Mamontov, 1983, 205) The general then turns on his heel and walks off without even bothering to ask why the battalion had been moved.

The general's appearance on the scene lets Mamontov make two important points. First it shows that the negative attitude to initiative is present throughout the command structure from battalion to division. Both Surkov's and Ivanov's reaction to finding the unit at a different location was the same. It also shows that the commander is immediately to blame for everything that happens in his unit, regardless of where he was when it happened or what he could have done to prevent it. This is apparent from Surkov's reaction to the general's tirade. Not only was the tirade directed at Surkov rather than at Glazov, but Surkov obviously understands why he is the one it is directed at. He recognizes the futility of trying to explain to the general and "takes his undeserved criticism silently," as befits a "good" Soviet commander. Surkov is ready to move the battalion back to the grove without delay. After the general's departure, he lays down the law. "Some people are supposed to give orders and other people are supposed to carry them out. To carry them out without deviation." (Mamontov, 1983, 205)

Glazov, however, manages to hold up the move through a small subterfuge until the inevitable airstrike on the grove takes place. Once that happens, Glazov is proven right and Surkov and Ivanov are put

firmly in their places. Mamontov gives an excellent description of the
general's discomfort, when he realizes that if this had been the front,
then he would have paid dearly indeed for his failure to listen to his
junior officers.

> Now Ivanov comprehended clearly, to the point of a
> pulsating pain in his temple, that he personally was the one
> responsible for the battalion being hit. ... And he, Ivanov, an
> experienced, seasoned, commander, did not think it necessary to
> look into the reason for [Glazov's] action and this is the result.
> To add insult to injury, he was the one who always said that
> initiative looks good on any officer. (Mamontov, 1983, 209)

In showing the gap between what Gen. Ivanov does and what he
says, Mamontov is, in fact, showing the gap between the official policy
and the reality of life in the Soviet military. Giving the character,
whose words are out of sync with his actions, the rank of general makes
a particularly strong statement in socialist-realist military fiction,
which has a tendency to confine this sort of mistake to much more junior
officers.

Glazov is not entirely without fault in this story, even though
Mamontov does not assign any of the blame to him or in any way paint
him as a negative figure. At the very least, Glazov should have
informed regiment where the battalion was and why it had been
moved. It is essential that the senior battlefield commander know
where his units are. Glazov's failure to do this is the one negative
aspect of his otherwise correct decision. Mamontov, however, does not
even hint at this aspect of the issue. His only concern is to show that
the two senior officers, Ivanov and Surkov, were wrong to immediately
assume that because their orders had not been followed to the letter,
something was amiss.

Mamontov is not satisfied just to show that Surkov and Ivanov were
wrong in their reactions to Glazov's initiative, but he also wants to
show that their people skills were lacking. In both cases, Ivanov and
Surkov yelled when they made their comments about the situation.
This is not an uncommon feature of similar episodes described by other
authors. To counter this poor people management technique, Mamontov
has Glazov, who is, after all, a political officer and, therefore, an
extremely people-oriented person, calmly point out to Surkov that a
little more tact in dealing with subordinates is in order.

> Every prediction, every general abstraction, the most
> insightful decisions will be brought to life by people. You can
> yell all you want, but if your tried-and-true idea does not get
> into their hearts, you won't achieve much. ... You have to

understand that harshness on the part of a senior officer can kill the initiative displayed by junior officers, dry up their desire to share their thoughts with you. (Mamontov, 1983, 204-205)

This is a very common problem in the Soviet military that is addressed by Sul'yanov, Kuleshov, Vozovikov and Polyanskij. In Polyanskij's short story *The Element of Surprise*, a battalion commander, Maj. Mel'nik, offers one of his company commanders some sage advice:

It's not what you say, but how you say it that's important! You can give a man a serious reprimand without offending him, if you have enough tact. It should not be the transitory burst of anger called forth by his action that controls what you say. It should be your respect for a subordinate, who does his duty well, but has made a mistake and is ready to correct it. (Polyanskij, 1984, 64)

Mamontov somewhat justifies Surkov's hot-tempered reaction to Glazov's initiative by showing that Surkov was not quite confident of his authority to command, because he is new in the job. Mamontov had set this up at the beginning of the story, when he showed Surkov speculating that "maybe they gave me a secondary role as the junior battalion commander, because they consider that the more experienced commanders will be the ones to win glory for the regiment." (Mamontov, 1983, 198) This is not, however, the primary reason for his poor tact in the story. After the general yelled at him, Surkov feels fully justified in having yelled at Glazov.

Because the battalion was not destroyed in the airstrike on the grove, it was able to take the "enemy" forces by surprise and save the bridgehead from their attack. After the battalion has saved the bridgehead, Mamontov redeems the general by having him apologize to Surkov for yelling at him in the field. This also removes the justification for Surkov's lack of tact. Mamontov, however, quickly redeems Surkov too by not letting him try to steal the credit for the insight to move the battalion out of the grove. He, unlike Capt. Dubrovskij in Bogatov's *Rise to Your Own Level*, gives full credit to Glazov.

Bogatov's Capt. Dubrovskij fought Lt. Blinov's ideas at every turn, yet he immediately tried to take credit for them once they were shown to be successful. He tries to justify his action by saying: "I was the company commander and any ideas that come out of the company belong to me. When they talk about the victories of a military commander, they are talking about him and not about the soldiers who achieved his victory with their blood." (Bogatov, 223) Bogatov rejects this notion as soon as Dubrovskij utters it. He has Dubrovskij's accuser counter that it is a military commander's tactics and operational plans that win him the glory, not the ideas of his subordinates.

Il'ya Mikson's novella *Officers* shows what might have happened to Glazov, if he had asked for permission to move the battalion instead of just doing it. The novella opens with an FTX scenario in which Lt. Krasnov is ordered to set up the firing positions for his tube artillery platoon in an area of the range where they have exercised many times before. Krasnov objects to the location of the firing positions, because they do not offer an opportunity to maneuver or to bring the guns directly to bear on the enemy in case of a direct assault on the emplacement. He views placing his guns in the position that has been used time and time again the same as placing them in a mousetrap. He tries to get permission to relocate to another, more suitable, position, but is rejected at every turn. "The area for the firing positions was chosen by regimental staff and we cannot change it of our own will." (Mikson, 9) "HQs knows better. It's not our job to pick firing positions." (Mikson, 8) Krasnov recites the formula that he learned in the academy: "without initiative, orders cannot be carried out the way they should be" (Mikson, 8), but this idea is dismissed with a subtle rebuff.

The battery commander, Capt. Strel'tsov, a war veteran, wonders to himself where does this green-behind-the-ears kid get off thinking that he can teach others. Where did he learn all that stuff about tanks, maneuver and direct assaults? He has never seen a live Nazi in his life. "They get all these babies together in the academy, tell 'em they are lieutenants and you have to suffer with 'em and be responsible for 'em." (Mikson, 9)

Mikson is showing, just as Mamontov did, that there is a gap between the official position on initiative (i.e., what they teach in the academy), and the reality of Soviet military life (i.e., what Strel'tsov says). In contrast to Mamontov, Mikson's criticism is directed at a hierarchical level that is more in line with the one normally found in socialist-realist military fiction.

Strel'tsov shows that he is not entirely a lost cause, because he finally gives in to Krasnov's initiative. He ponders why it is that, even though "this is not the first time that they have occupied this area, neither Krasnov's predecessor, nor he himself had ever thought about something so simple" as to dig foxholes along the ridge in case they needed to take up a 360-degree defense. (Mikson, 11)

Vladimir Vozovikov's novella *His Father's Son* is built around the same scenario. Lt. Ermakov, a tank platoon leader, has been called to the observation tower to talk with the military district commander, Col. Gen. Tulupov. Ermakov had misaligned the sights on the tank that was supposed to be used by his platoon in a live-fire training exercise, but one of the other platoons was assigned to this tank at the last minute. As a result of his "stunt," none of the other platoon's gunners hit a single target.

Ermakov had done this to make the exercise more realistic and keep his platoon on its toes.

> We only have one firing range and the range to all the targets has been measured to the meter. All the hills and gullies are numbered. And it's not surprising that, after one or two runs, the gunners can hit the targets with the first round right off the starting line. ... But what happens when they are in an unfamiliar situation? The sight gets knocked out of alignment during the attack? Will they be sharp enough to adjust their aim in that one second that they have to do so? (Vozovikov, 1977, 22)

Tulupov, unlike Mamontov's general, takes Ermakov to task for not informing his company commander and the range officer. In this part of the episode, Vozovikov skillfully shows what is going on in the minds of those listening to the conversation between Tulupov and Ermakov in one short sentence: "Ermakov is a your-own-will-nik." He immediately counters that impression by showing what Tulupov is thinking: "If this had been reported to Lt. Ordyntsev [the company commander], he would have probably rejected Ermakov's idea and given him a good dressing down to boot." (Vozovikov, 1977, 23)

Tulupov, in fact, liked Ermakov's idea, because he had been fighting against this problem himself. Ermakov's action showed him that his fight had not been successful. He let Ermakov's platoon fire from the tank with the misaligned sights. The first round is a miss, but the second lands dead center in the target. Tulupov is impressed and gives the regimental commander two weeks to teach the rest of his gunners how to do what Ermakov's people could already do.

In his parting words, Tulupov attacks the system's resistance to change. "It turns out that you can learn something from today's lieutenants. And by the way, it would be dangerous to assign someone to a command position, who had stopped learning from his subordinates, even to the position of squad leader." (Vozovikov, 1977, 25)

Col. Mikhail Sviridov further explores personal initiative and stale exercise scenarios in his short story *At Dawn*. While on FTX, Sr. Lt. Utkin[7] is defending a position against attack by his friend Sr. Lt. Volkov.[8] They have been at this training area before and the terrain is familiar.

Returning to the same range again and again tends, however, to draw the participants into a fixed repertoire of tactical scenarios.

Today Utkin and his troops are sitting in the trenches defending the position. The next time, someone else will be in the trenches and Utkin will be attacking. This is one of the major problems of providing realistic training for the troops. Familiarity with the terrain breeds contempt for the tactical situation to be played out there and gives way to a "we've-always-done-it-this-way-here" mentality.

Sviridov sets the stage for Utkin to display some initiative in a flashback to a conversation between Utkin and Volkov. Though they are essentially equals, Volkov has been promoted to battalion commander, while Utkin is still commanding a company. In a rather hostile monologue, Volkov tells his friend why he was promoted and Utkin was not. It is the memory of this conversation that prompts Utkin to want to try something different so that he can put one over on Volkov.

He is sure that Volkov will try a night attack to catch them off guard. Utkin would have too, if he had not remembered this conversation, and decided to do something different. He relocates two of his platoons to new defensive positions, leaving one platoon in the old position as bait. When the attack comes he will be on Volkov's flank and will take him by surprise.

Sviridov shows that this step is not entirely without risk for Utkin in a conversation between Utkin and one of his platoon leaders, Lt. Semin. Semin plays the voice of caution in approaching new ideas that is typical of the military in general, and the Soviet military in particular. He asks if they are going to catch it from the regimental commander, when he finds out that they are making a mess of the maps. Utkin assures him that he already got the regimental commander's approval for the change.

The conversation, however, makes Utkin have second thoughts about his initiative.

> Maybe all this fuss is for nothing. Maybe it wasn't worth it to undertake a flanking movement. Everything would have been fine, if the company had stayed at its old position. That's where the exercise plan called for it to be. Volkov would have attacked. He, Utkin, would have defended, firing blanks for all they are worth. At the exercise critique they would have said: "At a boy!" Now, just try and guess which way this initiative will turn out for you. (M. Sviridov, 1974, 15)

Utkin's initiative is only partially successful. Volkov is taken by surprise by the flanking action, but Volkov had kept a tank platoon and platoon of mechanized infantry in reserve and they were able to hit Utkin when he left his defensive position to attack Volkov. Volkov pats Utkin on the back with one hand for his initiative, while rubbing his nose in the mistake with the other. This goads Utkin on to plan to do better next time. "We'll catch up. It's not the last time we'll be in the field." (M. Sviridov, 1974, 15)

Sviridov provides another positive example of the display of initiative in his short story *Beyond the Blue Horizon*. Lt. Krasil'nikov is acting as the commander of a motor rifle company on an FTX. It is his chance to show what he can do. He ignores the order he has from battalion to attack across a natural depression that is notionally mined and covered by a gas cloud. Instead he uses maneuver to outflank the enemy and drive them into their own minefield and gas cloud.

At the end of the FTX Krasil'nikov is ordered to report to the regimental command post. He approaches the command post with trepidation, but finds that instead of a reprimand, he is invited to join the regimental and division commanders for breakfast. The division commander, Col. Shchukin, gives him a pat on the back. "You acted correctly. Initiative, daring and sensible risk are valuable qualities for a good commander." (M. Sviridov, 1982, 20)

Shchukin is so impressed with Krasil'nikov that he tells the regimental commander, Lt. Col. Kozyr', to put Krasil'nikov in to permanently fill the company commander's position rather than have Shchukin look for someone from outside. Kozyr' is hesitant, because Krasil'nikov has been out of the academy only for a year and a half, but Shchukin again supports Krasil'nikov by saying: "It's not how long you've been in grade, but how ready you are, that counts." (M. Sviridov, 1982, 20)

Kozyr's objection is the most common one about junior officers in military fiction, and Shchukin's support of Krasil'nikov in the face of it is quite surprising. Sviridov clearly supports the idea of giving young officers their lead so that they can rise to bigger and better things, but the number of stories, novellas and novels on this topic across the entire postwar period show that he is fighting an uphill battle.

Andrej Dyshev's novella *The Replacement*, explores the issue of initiative and command expectations in Afghanistan. The story centers around the conflict between two friends, one now a battalion commander, Maj. Petrovskij, and one still only a company commander, Capt. Oborin. Petrovskij is displeased with his one-time classmate, now his subordinate, because Oborin never has any combat operations and body counts or losses to report; no prisoners or captured weapons to turn in. This is due to Oborin's success in pacifying the local mujahedeen group leader. (A. Dyshev, 1989, 45 & 48) Petrovskij, however, views Oborin's dealings with the mujahedeen as mollycoddling the enemy rather than doing his duty. (A. Dyshev, 1989, 45) Oborin views it as doing exactly what he came to Afghanistan to do.

In a flashback to their garrison days together, Dyshev searches for the underlying reasons for the difference in their approaches to the same problem: winning the war. Oborin and Petrovskij started out together in the same class at the academy. They even served together as platoon leaders in the same regiment, and were both up for promotion. There was only one promotion and Petrovskij got it. The deciding moment for the promotion and the change in their relationship came at a demonstration during an FTX. Both platoons were advancing in line abreast toward an "enemy" position at the crest of a hill. Oborin had his platoon break ranks to flank the machine gun position, while Petrovskij had his platoon hold their line and charge the machine gun in a frontal attack. Petrovskij got the promotion, because he did what was expected of him.

As Petrovskij himself notes to his old friend, the audience at the demonstration wanted to see a dressed line and hear a throaty "Hurrah!", not the correct tactical action. (A. Dyshev, 1989, 47) Oborin's action was the right one for combat, but not the right one for a demonstration, when competing for a promotion.

In Afghanistan, Petrovskij is still doing what is expected of him by his superiors rather than what is called for by the tactical situation. Now, however, Oborin and Petrovskij are no longer equals. Petrovskij is Oborin's battalion commander and Oborin has to follow his orders. Petrovskij has always doubted Oborin's success in pacifying the local mujahedeen group and when there is hostile activity in the area, Petrovskij orders a search and destroy sweep against the group. He would feel much more comfortable with body counts and weapons to turn in to regiment than with words from some mujahedeen leader he has never seen or spoken to. Oborin sees no need to go on the sweep, because he is sure that it is not the local group that is the cause of the problem. He suspects that it is an outside group transiting the area.

Since Oborin's tour is up and his replacement has already arrived, Petrovskij settles the argument in his favor by relieving Oborin early and ordering the new company commander to take a platoon into the mountains on the sweep. While the platoon is assembling, Oborin argues with his replacement: "Sure we have to follow orders ... but who said that we have to be idiots? Who said that it is our duty to carry out stupid missions? Think about those who will have to pay for that highly idealistic stupidity with their lives." (A. Dyshev, 1989, 46)

As the story draws to a close, Dyshev makes it clear that Oborin is right again in Afghanistan like he was on the FTX. Oborin's faith in the mujahedeen group leader is justified when Dyshev reveals that the leader and his group went to the aid of the local defense force in a small vill and gave their lives to defend it against the outside hostile group that had been the one causing trouble in the area.

In his *Afghan Syndrome*, Anatolij Polyanskij looks at a very similar conflict about initiative from the other side of the war. The action of his novella takes place in a post-Afghan garrison inside the

USSR. The scenario is the same as in Dyshev's flashback: an FTX, where the tactical problem is to overcome the "blue" forces on a hill. Polyanskij's conflict is between a battalion commander, Capt. Kretov, an Afghan vet, and his regimental commander, Lt. Col. Voropaj, a brand new CGSC graduate, who has never seen combat.

Voropaj gives explicit instructions for a frontal attack, but Kretov uses his initiative, which was well-developed by his tour in Afghanistan, reasoning: "In Afghan[9], if there was even the slightest chance for maneuver, would we have made a frontal attack against the bad guys?"[10] (Polyanskij, 1990, no. 11, 83) His flanking movement is successful and he carries the day. He might have gotten away with not following orders to the letter, because his initiative was successful, if he had not suffered an exercise casualty. One of the BMPs threw a track on the mountain trail and gave the driver a concussion. He tries to shift the blame for the incident to the driver, but his arguments are rejected, showing again that the commander is responsible for whatever happens in his unit no matter what he had to do with it in reality.

Polyanskij adds a subplot to the standard conflict over initiative with a scene in which Kretov reports for duty and is dressed down by Voropaj for just being an Afghan vet: "Let's get this settled right from the beginning—None of your tricks! They let you get out of control there [in Afghanistan]. I won't tolerate that. My standards are the same for everybody." (Polyanskij, 1990, no. 11, 83) In the post-Afghanistan military, there was a new fault line in the command structure that had previously followed the generation gap. The new fault line divided those who had served in Afghanistan and those who had not.

Kretov is eventually forced to resign his commission, when the deputy military district commander, also a non-Afghan vet, comes to view a demonstration at an FTX in which Kretov is playing a leading role, and is displeased with another of Kretov's initiatives. Kretov should have taken the advice that Maj. Viktor Klyuev's battalion commander gave to Sr. Lt. Suponev in the short story *On a Winter's Day*. "There's a lot of high brass around. Everything's right out where they can see it. Don't think about trying to show off how smart you are." (Klyuev, 1970, 26)

Polyanskij comes down firmly on the side of giving young officers a chance to make mistakes as a part of their development in his short story *The Main Thing Is Your Duty*. Col. Bogdanchikov, Polyanskij's regimental commander in the story, is a strong proponent of this management theory. He realizes

> that the easiest thing would be to tell an officer to do this and this. But the easiest way of influencing their actions, does not help them, but only, in the final analysis, kills any confidence in their own abilities. The regimental commander, therefore,

from the very beginning made it a rule not to give subordinates ready-made recipes and to only become involved in exceptional circumstances, when the only thing left was to apply his authority. In all other instances, he considered it better to let an officer make his own decisions. You could guide him, suggest something, but you had to do it in such a way that he perceived your idea as his own. That is the essence of a commander's wisdom. (Polyanskij, 1984, 20)

Maj. Viktor Klyuev shows why this is the best policy for a commander in his short story *The Battalion Commander*. Capt. Yartsev is serving as a commander in a line unit for the first time. His previous assignments have been with a training unit and on staff. He has all the prerequisites to be a good troop commander: the knowledge, the desire and a love of people. His problem is that he tries to do everything for his subordinates. The battalion commander, Maj. Manin, tells him "you can't do everything in the company yourself. Don't you understand, Nikodim, that watching over them, baby talking them, taking over from junior commanders is not training them! You are in charge of a tank company and you have the fate of the troops in your hands." (Klyuev, 1971, 25)

Latitude for initiative is a key issue that the Soviet military needs to come to grips with. If it cannot, the troops, whose fate rests in the hands of commanders that are bound by the old system, will be the ones to pay.

NOTES

1. *Time*, 11 September 1978, p. 89.
2. The Inspector General's office is the one charged with oversight of military operations.
3. A play on the initialese for an incident such as a soldier going AWOL: Ch. P. = *chrezvychajnoe proisshestvie* [an extraordinary occurrence].
4. *Doveryaj, no proveryaj!*
5. Russian soldiers use the word "Afghan" to refer to the war in Afghanistan in the same way that American soldiers use the word "Nam" to refer to the war in Vietnam.
6. *Samovol'nichat'* : *samo* = auto (in the meaning of self; compare autokinesis); *vol'ya* = will; *nichat'* = infinitive suffix.
7. *Samovol'naya otluchka iz chasti*: *samo* = auto (in the meaning of self); *vol'ya* = will; *naya* = adjective suffix; *otluchka* = absence, *iz* = from, *chasti* = unit.
8. *Utkin* can be translated as Duck.
9. *Volkov* can be translated as Wolf.

10. *Dushman* is the Pushtu word for "bad guy" that was adopted by the Soviets in Afghanistan as the word for the enemy.

6

Wife: Unit of Issue, Each

If we had wanted you to have a wife, we would have issued you one.

Old Marine Corps saying

The relationship between a man and a woman as viewed in military fiction is more like a triangle than a one-on-one relationship. It is not how they relate to each other, but how they relate to the military that is important. Wives are an officer's "rear area," (Rezik, 384; Biryukov, 1975, 23; Kulakov, 116) and a strong rear means a strong front line.

"Long experience shows that married officers are more disciplined and serve better," says the Secretary of the Party Bureau, Capt. Baturin, in Anatolij Kuz'michev's *Nighttime Check*. (Kuz'michev, 1982, 147). Vasilij Rezik puts it a slightly different way in his *The Sky over Your Home*. Maj. Sedykh, the commander of a helicopter unit, is concerned with what the bachelors do in their time off, so he always gives them the Saturday missions. He knows where the married people will be: at home with their families, and that means fewer problems for him.

The political officer's interest in the family life of his subordinates is reflected time and time again in various episodes of assorted works of military fiction where a political officer is found:

- listening to a warrant officer's wife's complaint that her husband drinks, is playing around and isn't trying to get them an apartment (Polyanskij, 1978, 34);
- consulting with the chairwoman of the Ladies' Soviet, who is troubled by a mass of family problems (Polyanskij, 1978, 112);

- talking with the chairwoman of the Ladies' Soviet about day-care facilities for the children of the unit (Sul'yanov, 1982, 112-113);
- talking with the fiancee of one of the officers (Sul'yanov, 1982, 129);
- helping the distraught sweetheart of an officer, who has been transferred, to find a job so she can follow him to his new post (Gorbachev, 1977, 120);
- having a fatherly talk with the fiancee of one of the enlisted men (Strekhnin, 1977, 100);
- helping the family of a new battalion commander get settled while he is on exercise (Biryukov, 1975, 113);
- talking with the wife of one of the officers (Kuleshov, 1977a, 299);
- having a fatherly talk with the lightheaded wife of one of the division's officers (Kuleshov, 1981, 114 & 344);
- examining the divorce case of one of the division's officers (Strekhnin, 1977, 53-54);
- dealing with a letter accusing one of the young, single lieutenants of seeing another officer's wife (Bogatov, 115 & 154).

The political officer at a large unit is helped in dealing with the officers' wives by the Ladies' Soviet. Viktor Bogatov has an interesting example of how this works in his *Rise to Your Own Level*. The Ladies' Soviet called a meeting of all the commissioned and warrant officers' wives as the training year drew to a close. The keynote speaker was, of course, the unit political officer, Lt. Col. Rumyantsev. He called on the assembled ladies to help the unit in this time of heightened effort to close out the training year.

> Our success, in no small degree, depends on the welfare of and cordiality of relations within our families. Our commissioned and warrant officers work more effectively when they are in a good mood. ... Your husbands will be coming home tired. You have to, so to speak, create conditions for restful relaxation. Help them take care of their personal appearance. ... I hope that we can count on there not being any deviations from moral or ethical standards in our community on the part of our service families. (Bogatov, 109)

When a wife's actions begin to affect her husband's performance on duty, their relationship becomes a matter of military concern, and the unit political officer has to get involved. A political officer must be concerned with the lives of the families of the officers in his unit, because they are a part of the "morale factor" in combat readiness, reasons Lt. Col. Karelov, the political officer in Il'ya Davydov's *The Assignment.*

Karelov criticizes himself for not having paid enough attention to the families in his unit during an FTX. While they were in the field, one of the wives had almost gone home to her mother, because her husband could not get away from the exercise to come and pick her up from the hospital with their new baby. She was upset, because she had wanted to show off her husband, the lieutenant, to her hospital roommates, but instead she had been picked up by one of the other officers' wives like an unwed mother. If she had gone home, says Karelov, "a great part of the fault would have been mine!"

"What do you have to do with this? I didn't even ask you for help," replies her husband, a young senior lieutenant.

"I am supposed to know [that you need help] without your asking," answers Karelov, becoming quite agitated. (Davydov, 328)

This is the lead-in for Karelov to criticize the tendency of officers to be afraid to look like "drivelling humanists" (Davydov, 328) or, as Pishchulin put it, "crybabies" (Pishchulin, 1978, 10), by being too attentive to their families. Davydov adds weight to Karelov's view by having a general officer support it. Gen. Omel'yanov shows that families are important by taking the time, after his busy and tiring day observing the FTX, to go by the housing area and check on how they are doing.

Mikhail Sviridov presents a similar scenario in his short story *Beyond the Blue Horizon.* Lt. Krasil'nikov has been out in the field on an FTX. When he comes home his wife Lena is gone and there is an unfinished letter to her parents on the table. Before he even thinks of where his wife can be, Krasil'nikov gets a call from the duty officer. To show that he is mentally still in the field, Sviridov has him answer the phone using his field radio covername. It is the duty officer to tell him that his wife is in the maternity hospital and that they have a car waiting to take him to see her.

While offering Krasil'nikov a car to take him to the hospital is quite considerate for Soviet military standards, it is most probable that if the FTX had lasted longer, his wife would have come home from the hospital with one of the other wives too.

Lt Krasil'nikov's reaction to the news only serves to reinforce the point that officers' families come second to duty: "How can that be? Isn't it a bit early?" (M. Sviridov, 1982, 21) Sviridov quickly shows the reader that it was not early at all. Krasil'nikov has just lost track of the time in the rush of his duties.

In Maj. Viktor Klyuev's short story *The Battalion Commander*, Capt. Yartsev, the Chief of Staff, asks the battalion commander if one of the drivers can be released from an FTX, because his daughter is in the hospital. The commander refuses gruffly: "What kind of instructions do you expect from me? ... There's an alert and that's that." (Klyuev, 1971, 24) Throughout the course of the story and the exercise, the commander feels strangely uncomfortable. Finally, as the general is praising the battalion for a well-executed operation, the commander breaks down, and asks the general for permission to let the driver leave the exercise area to go to the hospital. The general, of course, immediately agrees, and tells the commander to send the driver to him. By having to resort to a character in the rank of general to show approval for paying more attention to families, both Davydov and Klyuev show how serious and well-entrenched the problem is. If it was only a minor problem, a major could have done the job.

I been in the field so long, my wife and kid call me mister.
U.S. Air Force Staff Sergeant, Rhein/Main Air Base, ca. 1969

Because of her husband's job, a military wife can expect him to be away from home a lot: in the field, on duty, at an unaccompanied post. This is a major cause of family problems. In Anatolij Polyanskij's novella, *Just My Duty*, Capt. Snegur is in the field so much that his wife, Tamara, who is an army brat, and used to garrison living, despite her usual patience, complained to him:

"I don't have a life, but rather just one long wait. Winter and summer, it's all the same color ..."
"What color?"
"They say it's blue."
"Why?"
"Don't you know what color lonely is?" asks Tamara.
(Polyanskij, 1984, 181)

Despite this, Capt. Snegur is sure that his wife understands, that this is all part of the job, and that he would not be happy in another one.

In Aleksandr Kuleshov's *The Nighttime Sun*, Sr. Lt. Chajkovskij's wife, Zoya, complains to him: "Listen! What kind of family are we? ... I counted up. Last month we saw each other for four days, this month for five. Do you think that's normal? ... you're like in that old song: 'Our wives are loaded cannon, our sisters—sabres sharp.' Your family is your company." (Kuleshov, 1981, 33-34) Considering Kuleshov's description of what Chajkovskij's schedule was like, it is surprising that they saw each other that much. "He's always in the barracks, doesn't sleep at home, leaves before it's light, comes home after dark. ... Then there's an exercise, a foray, a camp." (Kuleshov, 1981, 238)

In Vladimir Pishchulin's *Our Rocket Battalion*, Lt. Col. Kuz'michev's wife complains: "I don't remember the last time I saw my husband: he runs home, eats and then back to the barracks. All I hear is: I'm late, I'm late, no time." She says that she should have never married a military man. She can put up with the inconveniences of living at a remote post, but it's only seeing her husband once a week that she does not like. (Pishchulin, 1978, 73)

Lyuda in Vladimir Pishchulin's *Our Rocket Battalion* rejects Lt. Boris Zvonarev because she is a realist and does not want to live with a man who "is a guest in the house." She asked Boris to leave the Army for her, but he would not do it. She is sure that if he had loved her, he "would have done anything for her." (Pishchulin, 1978, 191) Sr. Lt. Rudnev, the Party Group Leader, sees her as being selfish, not caring what happens to others as long as she gets what she wants. Rudnev is sure that she would never have fit in with the Army community, which by implication has the exact opposite characteristics.

In his short vignette *The Sonnet* Ivan Ivanyuk takes a look at the same phenomenon from a slightly different angle, that of an officer discovering that he does not really have any family life. Capt. Krupaev has found the budget that his wife uses to keep track of family expenses and is leafing through it, when he comes across the empty heading of "Entertainment." This leads to the realization that they have not been to a movie in almost a year. As he continues to delve further into the budget, Ivanyuk shows how little Capt. Krupaev really knows about what it takes to run his home. He is amazed at "how many kilograms of flour, potatoes and meat" (Ivanyuk, 1986, 326) his wife has carried home from the store, despite her petite build. When he finds an entry for aerobics class, he is astounded that she did not even tell him anything about it, but comes to the realization that maybe she did tell him, but he just was not listening.

This is the kind of thing that can lead to the complaint from Sr. Lt. Rykov's wife in Babaev's *Conflict*. She is tired of being just "a cook" for him and she wants to separate for a while. This takes Rykov by surprise. He does not understand what the problem is. "She knew who she was marrying. ... What's happening to her? Maybe it didn't start yesterday, but before that? Maybe he just hadn't noticed? That must be it. When did he have time? He's busy from morning till night." (Babaev, 1986, 161)

In his short story *Urgent Mission*, Pronyakin tries to show that the constant call of duty affects the officers as well as their wives. It is Sunday. A winter storm just passed through the area. The commander of a wire communications company is called into the unit, because the storm took out one of their lines. With a gloomy look on his face, he picks two soldiers to go out and repair the break. The soldiers are not any more pleased by being chosen to go out in the cold to look for the line problem than the commander was to come in, and that is Pronyakin's setup for the moral of the story.

He uses the soldiers' interaction while they follow the line to rediscover Engels' dictum that freedom is the recognition of necessity. "Sometimes circumstances dictate your actions and you are forced to give in to those circumstances, whether you want to or not." (Pronyakin, 1974, 240)

Once the senior member of the party, Viktor, makes this realization, he immediately feels better. He comes to realize that perhaps the commander looked gloomy because he would have preferred to be home with his family on a Sunday instead of in the unit, worrying about a broken phone line. While this indirect approach to the problem does not have the same impact as a complaint from the commander, it is typical of the view of the problem in military fiction. It only serves to reinforce the fear of being called a "crybaby" described by Pishchulin and Davydov.

In military fiction, all these problems usually serve as a lead-in to the moral that it takes a strong woman with a strong kind of love to be the wife of a military man. "Don't be in a hurry to get married, Arkadij," says a post commander's wife in Davydov's *The Assignment* to young Lt. Tropilov. "Not every girl understands that becoming the wife of an officer is the same as entering military service yourself." (Davydov, 183)

Lt. Yurij Levashov's wife, in Kuleshov's *The White Wind*, does understand. Levashov gets called into the unit on a Sunday and as he gets ready to go, he apologizes to his wife. She muses his hair, telling him "don't do that, Yura. They are going to be calling you all your life, that's a fact of military life. And never apologize for it. I knew what I was getting into." (Kuleshov, 1977a, 211)

In Nikolaj Kambulov's *The Rocket's Thunder*, after the death of her husband, Lt. Col. Krabov, Elena Krabova gets a proposal of marriage from another officer. She recalls her life with Lev Krabov and decides that she has had enough of wandering "around remote garrisons." No, she would never marry a military man again, "it's incredibly hard and terrifying." (Kambulov, 1970b, 264)

Kambulov presents a more positive heroine in the person of Anneta Malko. Sr. Lt. Malko compliments his wife because

> she knows how to keep herself busy, when he is late because he was held up in the unit, and doesn't grumble when an alert tears him away from the family. He's also pleased with the fact that she turned out to be a good "pack rat": new things appear in their apartment—a mirror shining prettily in the corner, a couch along the wall that was comfortable to sleep on. (Kambulov, 1970b, 76)

Col. Korsunov, the chief of the Political Department of Polyanskij's airborne division, compliments his wife for having what he terms an essential quality for a military wife: never asking anything more than "Should I get you something to take with you?" when her husband is called away from home at night. (Polyanskij, 1978, 33)

Polyanskij presents a very similar portrait of warrant officer Zydin's wife in his short story *His Calling*, Zydin decides to take a cut in pay to accept a job as the motor officer in an airborne unit. They have two children, but he reasoned

> a man does not live by bread alone. The pay cut wasn't that big and, besides, the new job was more interesting. As far as his wife was concerned, she was understanding and would not stand in his way. Sure, she would grumble, that couldn't be avoided, but she would agree, because she realized that a person shouldn't be left in place to sour his disposition, if his heart was set on something else. (Polyanskij, 1984, 76-77)

In general, Polyanskij's wives are flat characters, only included to add a little local color. They are very much less individual personalities than the wives of other authors, but still, undoubtedly, have a basis in the reality of the service as Polyanskij lived it.

Pronyakin paints a picture of a military wife very much like one of Polyanskij's in *The Cloud*. Lt. Toropov[1] has only been married for a month and a half. His wife, Valyusha, would not let him go to post alone, set everything up and then call for her. She insisted on going with him, "even, if it's going to be tough . . . Besides, I want to be your mainstay". She is helping him get ready to go to the field on an FTX, but she gives Toropov a little more to take with him than Col. Korsunov's wife probably ever did. She gives Toropov the setup for the guilt trip that plays prominently in Pronyakin's story. She kisses him good-bye with the words: "Come back a hero!" (Pronyakin, 1974, 277)

Pronyakin gives Toropov a scenario in which he can come back a hero. He is the acting battery commander and a good showing on the FTX will most likely lead to making the temporary promotion permanent. Toropov, as is inevitable in any tragedy, fails to properly analyze the tactical situation on the aerial-recon photo that the umpire gives him, because of a cloud covering the target area, and thus misses the chance to shine in his new position. He knows that the news will get back to his wife through the other wives in the unit almost as soon as the FTX critique is over. He thinks about her and sighs heavily.

In military fiction, if a wife does not have a job, or at least an avocation, she is a negative heroine, who degenerates rapidly into a slovenly, unattractive housewife. (Gorbachev, 1977, 125) Military fiction shows its positive heroines as active, socially involved and usually professionally employed women, who also happen to be wives and mothers. (Rezik, 385)

Lev Snegirev offers a perspective on a military wife's lot that is exceptionally perceptive for the late fifties in his novella *Thaw at Midwinter*. Lt. Levchuk's mother-in-law helps her daughter, Lilya, keep house. When Lilya's aunt becomes ill, Lilya's mother goes to help her sister and the full burden of keeping house and taking care of their baby daughter falls onto Lilya's shoulders. "Even before this Levchuk had not been especially helpful around the house, and recently he had been coming home late, had had the duty a lot and kept going to the field." (Snegirev, 18-19) Lilya tried to balance the double job of being both mother and homemaker, but "she could feel the fatigue building up on her layer after layer." Finally, when she could not take it anymore, she asked Levchuk to help her around the house, but he tried to hide behind "the service taking up almost all of his time." As the narrator points out, Levchuk really sympathized with her problems, but "deep down inside, he felt that her problems were the age-old lot of all mothers." (Snegirev, 19)

Twenty literary years later, in Valerij Biryukov's *Only Three Days*, find Maj. Antonenko's wife, Viki, confronting the same problem. She is a music teacher and musicologist, the daughter of a professor used to big city life, and now her husband has dragged her off to a remote garrison. "Do you want me to become a broad?" asks Viki, when her husband tells her about the assignment. "What am I supposed to do there? ... Don't I have a right to the work that I love? Or am I supposed to forget about myself and dedicate my life to the kitchen, the washing machine, the children and waiting for you to come back off duty? Even you would fall out of love with me, if I became a broad." (Biryukov, 1975, 115)

Aleksandr Prokhanov paints a poignant picture of what Viki might have looked like some years later in his *The Muslim Wedding*. Lt. Baturin recalls a brief moment in his mother's life as the wife of an Army officer. She too was a musicology student. Her instrument was the violin. She graduated cum laude. Her only ties to music during their married life together had been the sound of marching songs and the banging of military bands. Once, when she thought that no one was looking, he had seen her take her violin out of the dark closet, where it was kept. She opened the case and looked at her violin. She had not dared to touch it. She could only look at its silent strings. (Prokhanov, 1990, 114)

Because many posts are in remote locations like Biryukov's garrison, most wives will probably also have a hard time finding a job, unless they have one of the standard "feminine" professions. In Vladimir Pishchulin's *Parting*, Lt. Col. Vinogradov jokes with one of his lieutenants that the lieutenant let the unit down by becoming engaged to a schoolteacher. The unit already had "a hairdresser, a teacher and a choir director," Vinogradov tells him that what they needed now was a dentist. (Pishchulin, 1974, 180)

According to the literary Ministry of Defense as cited in Nikolaj Gorbachev's novel *The Battle*, "doctor and educator are the most appropriate professions for the wives of military men. You can find a way to put your skills to work everywhere, as they say." (Gorbachev, 1977, 28) Unfortunately, even the Ministry is not always that well-informed. Teachers cannot always find a job. In Vladimir Pishchulin's novella *Our Rocket Battalion*, Sr. Lt. Aleksej Rudnev's wife, Nila, has been looking for a job for over a year. Aleksej had thought that she could get a job as a teacher, but he had come to the conclusion that it was not that easy. There were not many schools in their area and all the positions were filled. To Aleksej it seemed that there were only two ways out:

- let Nila go live with her mother in the city, get a job there and wait till he finished his nonresident CGSC course, after which there was a chance that he would be transferred to somewhere where there was a school,
- go to his commanding officer or the chief of the Political Department and try to wangle a job on the HQs staff, which was located in the big city, where there was a school. (Pishchulin, 1978, 9-10)

The first way out was no good, because he could not stand the thought of being separated from Nila. The second was no good, because he was afraid that his contemporaries would say that he was a "crybaby." Fate stepped in and presented him with a none-of-the-above solution. Nila was offered a chance to substitute for a teacher going on maternity leave. This was, however, not the ideal solution. The school she had to teach in was forty kilometers away.

For an American teacher, forty kilometers each way to school might be a bore to drive, but it is doable. For Nila, it meant taking two different buses that did not run that often. (Pishchulin, 1978, 11) One night she stayed late at school and missed the last bus back. She hitchhiked back to the nearest town and then tried to walk back to post. It was thirty below zero centigrade and she almost froze to death. (Pishchulin, 1978, 95 & 97)

If an officer's wife has another professional specialty, the task of finding a job can be almost impossible. In Viktor Bogatov's novella about life in the motor rifle troops, the wife of a company grade officer accepts the first job offered to her, even though it is not in her specialty, because she knows that "finding a job for an officer's wife in any garrison relatively faraway from a big city is a difficult, and in most cases unsolvable problem." (Bogatov, 129) "I was thinking about our ladies," says Nila Rudneva, who has been looking for work for over a year, "almost all of them have a degree, but not all of them have a job. It's not like I am the only one." (Pishchulin, 1978, 11)

In Davydov's novel *The Assignment*, Stanislav Leonidovich Sokol'skij, the contractor for the construction of an experimental rocket base at a remote location, deep in the heart of the USSR, introduces his wife Aleksandra Leonidovna:

> She was a design engineer, with a good future. I say "was," because I dragged her out here to this veil of fog. And so she wouldn't go crazy from the boredom after Moscow, I had her recertified as an economic planner. That's how we men ruin the talents of the women we love! (Davydov, 71)

In Arkadij Pinchuk's novella *Once and for All*, Lt. Col. Batashov's wife Polina had a degree in physical education and her specialty was that of a swimming coach. She too was not able to find work in her specialty and the first part of their marriage was spent first nursemaiding their daughter and then Batashov;

> Knocking around from post to post, and not a swimming pool anywhere in sight. Or Batashov either for that matter. He comes home at midnight and leaves at dawn. Disappears to the range for months at a time, and I'm left alone with the four walls. Me with my phys ed degree and no place to put it to use. (Pinchuk, 1985, 66)

When Batashov was at CGSC, she had started working as a trainer again, and even had two swimmers who looked like they could make it to the national team. She had thought she would be able to see her two swimmers through, because Batashov had been offered a chance to stay on at CGSC as a graduate student. Batashov, however, "stole her dream that time too." (Pinchuk, 1985, 15) He asked for a command position in the troops that took him to a small county seat. It was here in this remote location that she found a chance to work with swimmers again.

Polina had been offered a job as a swim coach and was now spending more time at the pool and with the man who gave her the job than with Batashov. Pinchuk shows his disapproval for her actions through her grown daughter, Valya, who comes to accuse her of letting Batashov down when he needs her the most. He thickens the plot by showing that Polina had not been all that thrilled to have a child in the first place. She felt that the birth of her daughter had made her "lose her favorite activity [competitive swimming] for the second time." (Pinchuk, 1985, 15) She had wanted to have an abortion, but Batashov had insisted that she have the baby. The baby, now grown up, has come back to take her away from swimming again and back to the man who dragged her away from it in the first place.

Pinchuk, however, does defend Polina to some extent by explaining her drive to continue working. "She did not want to be a dependent. She was convinced that being a dependent after you come of age was the fate of the disabled." (Pinchuk, 1985, 30) Batashov could understand this despite her unbending character and excessive pride. What he could not understand was how she could be "spiritually blind" to the pain she caused him with her words and actions. She did not even notice that she was being cruel.

Moving is a part of the way of life for those in the military. In works of military fiction, military families:

- "wander from one set of quarters to the next" (Davydov, 229);
- "migrate ... from one garrison to another" (Strekhnin, 1977, 189; Kulakov, 116);
- "move endlessly from one garrison to another" (A. Egorov, 1988, 57);
- "knock about from garrison to garrison" (Pinchuk,1985, 66);
- "roam from one God forsaken place to the next" (Rybin, 1984, 58); and
- feel like "civilization has passed them by" (Gorbachev, 1983, 83).

Viktor Stepanov draws a contrast between the attitude of a professional nomad in the service and a civilian in a sketch in his *At the Brandenburg Gate*. On a visit to his former commander, who is still a serving officer in GSFG, Semen Kashtanov remarks that Col. Prokhorov's apartment gives off the feeling that "nothing seems to have a place of its own, as if [Prokhorov was] living out of a suitcase." Prokhorov is not concerned by the comment and responds that "they say that things take on the characteristics of their owners. I've lived out of a suitcase all my life: here today, there tomorrow." (Stepanov, 1973, 91) This "disregard for things and for the stability of comfort" surprises Kashtanov, who had only been away from his village during the war, and had not gone anywhere since then.

In Yurij Strekhnin's *I Bequeath You*, Col. Surgin's wife Rina dreamed of going back to their hometown, Leningrad. She had often talked to her husband about how she was "tired of moving all the time, of government quarters, where nobody felt like a permanent resident," and how she wanted "to put down roots, like real people and calmly raise their son." (Strekhnin, 1977, 170)

Because of their nomadic way of life, some military couples do not
have any children. Lt. Col. Krabov of Nikolaj Kambulov's *The
Corporal of the Guard Has Not Come Yet* and his wife Elena had been
married for twelve years, but were still childless, because Krabov felt
that "the life of a military man is just one big move." (Kambulov, 1970,
41) This thought is echoed eloquently in Vladimir Pishchulin's *Our
Rocket Battalion*. The wife of a young lieutenant, who teaches in a
school with military dependents, complains to her husband:

> "We military people don't need children at all. Yesterday,
> I asked Sasha Mironov, the son of Capt. Mironov, where he was
> born. Sasha just stood there and didn't say anything. 'Why,' I
> said, 'don't you answer?' 'Well,' he said, 'I forgot the APO
> number.' Did you hear me? He forgot the APO number. He just
> doesn't know where he was born!"
>
> "What do you mean, where? In the Soviet Union," answers
> her husband.
>
> "You know what I'm talking about," flares his wife. "My
> home is my city, my town, and I don't want my children not to
> have a home! They have to have their own hearth, their own
> town, their own river. They are people after all!" (Pishchulin,
> 1978, 107)

For the lieutenant and the captain's son, home is something
different. Aleksandr Kuleshov describes it in this way in his *The
Nighttime Sun*. For the son of a military man

> used to travelling with his father from place to place, from one
> post to another, to changing cities and schools, he didn't see
> much difference between the hot southern areas and the harsh
> northern ones. It was interesting everywhere. That kind of
> newness is even attractive. It was more important to him what
> kind of homeroom teacher he got, what kind of physics teacher
> or judo instructor, than what the weather was like outside and
> how long summer and winter lasted. The main thing was that
> the duty was interesting. From conversations in the family, he
> knew, of course, that his father liked some places more, some
> less, and some not at all. But it was always because of the duty:
> what kind of superior officers, fellow officers, soldiers, what
> kind of unit, what kind of tasks. The cities, the quarters, the
> climate, they weren't the most important things. (Kuleshov,
> 1981, 136)

In A. Egorov's *Step onto the Line of Fire*, a political officer's twin
sons could not imagine another kind of life than the exciting and

dynamic one of a military garrison. For the twins, the people surrounding their father were "somehow special—energetic, purposeful, and full of life." Seeing them returning from an exercise, the twins imagined them "heroes from a fairy tale" astride tanks instead of horses. (A. Egorov, 1988, 57-58) The twins, of course, went on to become political officers themselves.

Other children are not as thrilled with the nomadic life of an Army officer. "I'm ashamed," says the daughter of Col. Leskov, "that we are homeless. Nobody in school believes me. ... I don't want to wander from one set of quarters to the next anymore." (Davydov, 229) The other extreme of this dilemma is that of the son of Gen. Grosulov in Nikolaj Kambulov's novel *Faithfulness*. Young Viktor Grosulov complains that he doesn't know his father at all. From the time he was eight—that is, when he started school—he had lived with his grandmother. Sometimes his parents would bring him out to their post for the summer, but his grandmother would not let them keep him with them. "I won't give him up. You'll ruin the child. You live like migratory birds. You don't have either house nor home. I won't give him up." (Kambulov, 1970b, 58)

Many women simply refuse to even consider putting up with the hardships of military life to be with a man in uniform. Others try and their marriages end in divorce or separation, but still others, the positive heroines of military fiction, succeed.

NOTE

1. His name is derived from the word for hurry and could be translated something like "Hasty."

7

Home Is Where the Army Sends You

What we value in Robinson is his belief in human labor, his
persistence in overcoming obstacles, his bravery and strong will.
Kornej Chukovskij
From his introduction to the 1951 edition of *Robinson Crusoe*

A great many of the problems that service wives encounter in military
fiction stem from the fact that posts are often located in the middle of
nowhere. The isolation of remote posts is frequently accompanied by
housing that will be substandard, with little inconveniences such as
communal apartments, no running water, wood-fired stoves for heating,
outdoor plumbing, and little or no social life.

Posts that combine these characteristics are sometimes referred to
as "holes" in the vernacular. While a requirement for developing a
positive attitude about serving at a remote post was not stated
explicitly by the MPD until 1981, it was a frequent theme in military
fiction before that. In a letter to his son, a brand new lieutenant, just
arrived at his first post, which is quite remote, Gen. Ignat'ev takes
those to task who think that a remote post is a "hole." "If we're to be
honest," writes the general, "those so-called 'holes' exist more in the
imaginations of some officers and their unfit-for-military-service
wives." (Kuz'michev, 1982, 68)

The general is right to some extent. An assignment is what you
make of it, but some posts are so remote that "you can't imagine that
such places exist" (Kuleshov, 1977a, 65), says the commandant of a
military academy to his cadets' dates at a New Year's Eve ball. Some
posts are:

- in "inaccessible places, where there may not be a house around for a 100 miles … not only no theaters, but no villages. Just bears" (Kuleshov, 1977a, 65);
- "at the world's end. Where there are no apartments, no water and no theaters" (Kambulov, 1970a, 47);
- in places where there is "not another soul around for miles. … no matter where you look, [all you can see is] wavy tundra with little islands of sparse trees touched with the yellow of fall" (Makhnev, 335);
- "in the steppe. Bare as bare can be all around. The hills were only just visible on the horizon. In the summer, the prairie dogs whistle. In the winter, the wind races with itself. There's not a hint of a living soul around for 50 leagues in any direction" (Khalturin, 1983, 194);
- where "the prairie dogs die from the heat in the summer and it's cold as the devil in the winter" (Kambulov, 1970b, 25);
- "in woods, faraway from big roads and settlements" (Kuz'michev, 1982, 5);
- "lost in the semidesert, where drought reigns in the summer and freezing blizzards in the winter" (Vozovikov, 1977, 91);
- "in remote desert lands" (Biryukov, 1975, 115);
- in places "forgotten by God …, where there are blizzards for eight months and rain the other four" (Vozovikov, 1972, 21);
- "where it snows 400 days a year," 400, because time at this remote post counts double for retirement (Pronyakin, 1974, 86);
- "where you have to stoke the heater, carry water in from the well, and the 'convenience' is outside" (Polyanskij, 1978, 147);
- "where, aside from the [garrison] gate, there are no tourist attractions" (Polyakov1988-14);
- "where Makar would never take the calves"[1] (Bogatov, 205).

As a nameless marshal in Leonid Konovalov's short story *The Silver Crane* says:

serving and living at these posts "on the other side of nowhere" is heroism and the people who do it, the soldiers, sergeants, officers and their wives and children, deserve a special feeling of respect. What's true is true. If you just look at the living conditions. The people at a small post are deprived of a number of conveniences: they do not have gas, they even have to stoke their heaters in the summer; there is no dairy store like there is in a city and so that the children can have milk every day, they have to send a special vehicle ten kilometers to the collective farm that has adopted them as a patron; they do not have their own library and there is an exchange of books

between battalions once every three months. The book exchange
is like a holiday. (Konovalov, 1981a, 20)

Mikhail Sviridov's heroine in his short story *Beyond the Blue
Horizon* is very unusual in military fiction. She is the daughter of a
general major, who uses her father's influence to affect her husband's
assignment, but not, as would be expected, to get him a good post in a big
city, but rather an assignment at a remote post in the Far East.

Sviridov presents this as a surprise ending to his story about the
relationship between Cadet Taras Krasil'nikov and Lada. Once their
relationship is firmly established, Krasil'nikov's buddy at the
academy, Yakov Nikonov, tells Taras that he should marry Lada, not
only because she is better than all the airheads he has been seeing, but
also because she is the commandant's only daughter and that will
undoubtedly mean a choice assignment when they graduate.
Krasil'nikov finds the suggestion revolting. He is amazed that
Nikonov could propose such a thing. Nikonov's idea, however, did
make him think about where he would be going after the academy and
wonder about what Lada would think about it. When he got his
assignment to the other side of nowhere, he was afraid to tell her for
fear that she would leave him.

Lada's reaction was a complete surprise for Krasil'nikov. She was
as happy as could be with their remote assignment, and her attitude
does not change once she gets there either. It was not until after they
had been at post for about a year and a half that Krasil'nikov found out
the truth. He came back from an FTX to find their apartment empty and
an unfinished letter to Lada's parents on the table. In the letter she was
asking for her father's advice on how to tell Taras the truth about his
assignment. She had wanted to make sure that Taras wanted to marry
her for herself and not for her connections. By having her father
arrange for a remote assignment for Taras before they got married, she
could be sure that he was not planning to do what Nikonov had
suggested.

More often, however, military fiction touches on those who do not
like living "in a land forgotten by God, at the end of the world", as Maj.
Antonenko's wife Viki puts it in Valerij Biryukov's *Only Three Days*.
(Biryukov, 1975, 23) She was a professor's daughter from the "big city,"
and had hoped that maybe her husband would stay on at CGSC for
graduate work or at the very least pick a decent city to go to. She was
mad at her husband, because, in spite of the fact that he had rated a
choice of assignment by being an honor graduate in his CGSC class, he
had chosen a garrison in the middle of the desert. Their quarrel over
the assignment lasted a whole month, from the time he told her about
it, right up until it was time to leave for the new post. He had not even
been sure that she would accompany him there. She had, but even after

they arrived at post, she kept threatening to go home to her mother. Without the intervention of the political officer and his wife, she probably would have.

Even the wife of a political officer is not immune to the call of the capital. Polina, the wife of Col. Korsunov, the political officer of Anatolij Polyanskij's airborne division in *The Right to Take Risks*, "had long wanted to go to the capital." She is, however, better disciplined than Viki Antonenko. Like Viki, she lost her chance to move to the big city when her husband turned down an offer for a staff job and probable promotion to stay with his unit at the working level. She never let her husband know if she agreed with his decision. All he knew for sure was that she had not objected to it. (Polyanskij, 1978, 8)

Yurij Pronyakin's battalion political officer, Maj. Yurenev, also had problems with his wife Nina due to their string of assignments at remote posts. "From time to time, Nina was homesick for the big city, but it never came to a family argument. The couple consoled themselves with the hope that they would some day be able to live 'like real people', but that 'some day' was always being postponed."(Pronyakin, 1974, 44-45) Yurenev had never made a goal of getting a staff job just to get them moved to the city, and for one operational reason or another he kept putting off taking the test for CGSC that would take them there as well.

In Anatolij Rybin's novel, *The Boundary Line*, Marina Avdeeva did object. She was mad at her husband, the lieutenant colonel, because he had turned down a chance to be the commandant of a School for Warrant Officers located in a big city in favor of a regimental command located in the middle of the steppe. She cried for a long time when she learned of his decision, and went to live with her parents. She felt that they had spent enough time "roaming from one Godforsaken place to the next", and that "it was time to join civilization." (Rybin, 1984, 58)

Rina, the wife of a political officer in Yurij Strekhnin's *I Bequeath You* wanted to join civilization too. She challenges her husband, Col. Surgin, about his choice of an assignment at a remote post over one in her hometown of Leningrad. "What do you want? To do all your service time in remote places?" she asks him, using the verb normally reserved for doing time in prison or in a labor camp. (Strekhnin, 1974, 177)

Maj. Chalov's fiancee, Valya, in Polyanksij's *The Right to Take Risks* was simply not ready to give up "the capital, where it was warm and comfortable, there was a subway, conveniences ... and mother." Polyanskij develops her as a negative character to show that she is not the right kind of wife for an officer. If Chalov had married her, thinks Col. Korsunov to himself, he would have gone "unaccompanied from post to post, cursing everything on the face of the earth. ... She would have visited him occasionally, traumatizing his soul. No, that's not the kind of wife you need!" (Polyanskij, 1978, 230)

Indeed, a wife, who is not prepared to move to a remote garrison is not what a career officer needs. In his short story *Commander of a Rocket Unit*, Col. A. Kulakov shows how such a wife can affect her husband's career. He relates the story of a nameless captain, who, on the face of things, has all the prerequisites for advancement, but who has been in grade in the same position for a long time. All his contemporaries have long since been promoted and have been given more important jobs. The captain goes to his commanding officer, Lt. Col. Anokhin, to find out just why his career is at a dead end.

Lt. Col. Anokhin reviews his file and sees that early in his career the captain had been offered a chance at advancement, but in a remote garrison. The captain, however, had turned down the assignment and with it his promotion. That was because his wife was finishing her degree and he needed to be with her. His superiors were understanding and had let him stay where he was. Two years later, they again offered him a chance at advancement, but again in a remote garrison. This time, his wife was finishing her dissertation, and how could she work on it "in the outback, in the woods?" (Kulakov, 116) At the point where the captain came to talk with Anokhin, it was already too late to do anything for his career. The captain was too old and Anokhin needed to give his most gifted lieutenants their lead.

If an officer can convince his family to come to post, then the next step is to find housing for them. A number of works of military fiction treat the problem of having to go to post unaccompanied and then having the family come later, once housing has been arranged. In Nikolaj Kambulov's two-volume novel *Faithfulness*, the new commander in chief of artillery troops for a military district even has to come unaccompanied to post at first. This was in the early sixties and the unit was just building married officers' housing. Even for the general, it was a year before he could bring his wife to post. What is good for the general is even more so for junior officers. One of Kambulov's lieutenants also has to delay his wife's arrival until he can find an apartment, and another has to delay his marriage for lack of an apartment. (Kambulov, 1970b, 23)

The commander of a PVO site at a desolate, uninhabited corner of the Soviet North asks a lieutenant newly arrived on a permanent change of station (PCS):

Did you leave your wife in Moscow or something? As you see, now everybody is doing that. When a young officer is assigned to a remote site, he lives alone for a year or so and then goes on leave and comes back with his wife. But there's no need for that kind of caution. We have an apartment ready for you here. It's not a palace, you understand, but it's not a hovel either I dare to assure you. (Makhnev, 334)

The apartment that the commander had to offer was located in the barracks area in the same building with the offices and work spaces, next to the commander's. There were no other apartments or other wives at the site. Hardly an enticement for the lieutenant's wife to join him.

This is much the same as the housing situation at Leonid Konovalov's remote PVO post in his short story *The Long Night*, where family housing is a single "standard, duplex house, with a tile roof and separate entrances." (Konovalov, 1981b, 13) One apartment was for the company commander, the other was for one of his three junior officers. While the number of apartments is undoubtedly appropriate for the size of the unit, there can hardly have been a lot of things for the two wives to do socially or professionally at a post two kilometer's walk from the nearest village, which itself had only about twenty houses in it.

Fedor Khalturin presents the parable of a political officer, who went to post without his family in the short story *And the Trains Are Still Running*. The nameless political officer works hard to improve living conditions for everyone at his new unit out in the middle of the steppe. He plants trees, sets up a library for the officers, and organizes a musical group. He even talks another officer's wife, who had had it with life in the bulrushes, out of leaving her husband. The irony of the story is that he cannot convince his own wife to join him at post. His wife torments him by alternating promises to come with outright refusals. "I'm not the kind of a fool," she wrote him once, "to swap L'vov for someplace out in the bulrushes." (Khalturin, 1983, 199) Khalturin undoubtedly intended the story as a positive character sketch of a political officer who, despite all his personal problems, continues to help others. The effect is seriously diminished, because Khalturin leaves the question of whether the wife will come to post open at the end. This leaves the officer in the same position Polyanskij's Maj. Chalov would have been in if he had married Valya. The critical reader cannot help but wonder how long he will remain effective.

When he gets the assignment to open a new PVO base on a nameless hill far in the North, where there were no facilities and everything had to be built from the ground up, Pronyakin's battalion commander, Maj. Ul'yantsev, is concerned for his family's welfare. He hints to his wife that she should take their daughter and return to her parents for a while, but she, in good socialist-realist style for a positive heroine, insists on coming along. Pronyakin thickens the plot around Ul'yantsev's decision to take his family to post or not with the major's consideration of: "what would his subordinates think," if he did not? (Pronyakin, 1974, 93) In the end, Ul'yantsev does bring his family to post and rents a private apartment in the nearest town, like those of his subordinates who had their families with them at post. The officers could not get into town every day, but it was better than serving an unaccompanied tour.

Despite the fact that renting a private apartment in town was a big financial drain on a lieutenant's or a captain's salary, when the married quarters were finished at the new PVO base, none of the junior officers wanted to move their families to quarters on post, because they were "in the backwoods, faraway from town." (Pronyakin, 1974, 93) Ul'yantsev and his political officer, Maj. Yurenev, set the example and were the first to move their families to the base. Soon afterward, the rest of the officers' families followed.

Because she had to give up a job that she had just started in town, to do so, the move to base housing weighed heavily on Galina Ul'yantseva. Despite this, she put on her smiley-face mask, moved to post and set about furnishing their new apartment like any good socialist-realist wife in military fiction.

Her life at the base gets but scant treatment from Pronyakin. He touches on it only briefly in a short episode in which Maj. Ul'yantsev returns home after a particularly bad day in the unit. He is going over his problems in his head, when his wife calls him for dinner. The call to dinner brings him back to the here and now of family life and he tells himself that "he will have to learn to leave all his problems connected with duty at the doorstep. Our wives don't have that much of a life here as it is." (Pronyakin, 1974, 96)

Leonid Konovalov presents a similar picture in his short story *The Long Night*. The PVO company commanded by Capt. Ustimenko was less fortunate than the one commanded by Maj. Ul'yantsev. Ustimenko had to wait through the winter before married officers' quarters were built and he could bring his family to post. During that winter, he had lived in the same hut with the other three officers in the company. The only concession to his rank was a thin partition to give him a living area separate from his three subordinates, who all shared a single room.

The amount of coverage that the topic of remote posts receives indicates that this is a problem of some scope, affecting not only the officers' wives, but the officers themselves. One of the 1972 prize winners from the literary contest run by the monthly magazine *Soviet Warrior* was on just this topic. In Vladimir Vozovikov's short story, *The Time of the Scarlet Snows*, Lt. Golovin has to overcome the feeling that his remote post is just a "hole" and that "real life" is in the big city "flowing in rivers of neon and human voices." (Vozovikov, 1972, 21) In the course of Vozovikov's story, Lt. Golovin comes to realize that the problem was not in the post, but in himself, and not even a transfer to Moscow itself would solve it. It is only after he makes this realization that he becomes a positive socialist-realist hero and worthy to be the winner of *Soviet Warrior*'s literary contest.

Nikolaj Gorbachev has a similar tale in his short story *Going Back*. In it he relates how Lt. Voronkov is assigned to a remote northern post and how he tried to trick his way into a transfer short of tour. Gorbachev sets the stage for Voronkov's antipathy toward the assignment well. Voronkov is stationed in his hometown. He has a wife and daughter and, as far as he is concerned, it is bad enough that he has to go to a "hole" up north, let alone take them along. When Voronkov arrives, his mood is worsened by the officer he is replacing, Lt. Skvortsov. Skvortsov tells him in confidence that "you've got my sympathy, lieutenant. I'm surprised that I was able to do the time. It was like some nightmare." (Gorbachev, 1983, 81)

Using a verb normally reserved for completing prison sentences, Voronkov thinks that Skvortsov is an idiot for having stayed out his tour. He decides that he is going to get out short of tour at any cost. He submits a false request for compassionate reassignment, basing it on his daughter's alleged illness. This is the weakest point in the story. It is hard to believe that Voronkov would have submitted a request based on something so easy to check as the state of his daughter's health, or that he would not expect the commanding officer to check on it.

When the commanding officer inevitably confronts him with the lie of his request, he offers to forget the whole incident if Voronkov brings his family to post. Voronkov rejects the offer and awaits his fate, reasoning that nothing can be worse than what they have already done to him by sending him to this post. Gorbachev then shows that the rest of the officers at post are also mad at Voronkov because of his chicanery. Just when it looks like Gorbachev is going to show the reader the power of being sent to Coventry, a blizzard breaks out.

Voronkov has the duty and has to go out to bring in the exposed guard posts. Since he is new to the unit, he gets lost in the storm. When he wakes up in the hospital, he finds out that the whole unit went out into the blizzard to look for him, despite the fact that he had deceived them. If they had not done so, he surely would be dead by now. Gorbachev's shift in focus from the negative power of the group to its positive power is very effective, and makes the story's point much stronger than if he had stuck to just one or the other.

While Voronkov recovers in the hospital, he has plenty of time to think about what he has done. His socialist-realist conclusion is that he has to go back to post to redeem his honor. He even plans to take his family with him this time.

In his *Court of Honor*, Pronyakin takes a slightly different approach to the topic of remote posts, by showing a reluctant volunteer, Sr. Lt. Savchenko. Savchenko was tricked into taking his present remote assignment by someone he had considered a close friend. When they were graduating from the academy, Savchenko had been given orders to Yuzhsk in the south and Valera, his "buddy," had gotten the assignment that Savchenko has now. As soon as the orders were published, Valera came running to Savchenko with a plea to swap assignments. He said that he had a fiancee in Yuzhsk and she did not want to go live up north. Savchenko had agreed to the swap out of friendship for Valera. On his first leave, Savchenko made a special point of dropping by Yuzhsk to wish Valera well in married life. It turned out, however, that Valera was not married and had never even said anything about a fiancee at his new unit. "It's a good thing," says Savchenko, "that he was at the range while I was there." (Pronyakin, 1974, 43)

Savchenko is contrasted to Lt. Nikolaj Danilin, who was an idealistic volunteer for his remote assignment when he graduated from the academy. Even though, as an honor graduate, he had a choice of assignments, he decided to volunteer for a remote, because he felt "that as an officer you should start your service where the going is tougher!" (Pronyakin, 1974, 9, 82 & 202) One night in the officers' mess, when Danilin lets it slip that he volunteered for the assignment, Savchenko, his roommate, pokes fun at him by asking what kind of grades he got in geography while he was in school. Savchenko gives him an "A" for "enthusiasm and idealism," because he volunteered, but gives him a "D" for his knowledge of geography.

Rather than make Savchenko the sole source of Danilin's further doubt about his decision to volunteer for a remote assignment, Pronyakin has Danilin recall what one of the officers said back in the academy. "It is better to serve on the northern shores of the Black Sea than on the southern shores of the White Sea." (Pronyakin, 1974, 9)

Pronyakin brings in yet a third character, Vasilij Korotkov, to deepen Danilin's doubts. Korotkov makes fun of Danilin very subtly by saying: "you military people, especially young officers, are real ascetics, volunteering to shut yourselves up in isolated, remote garrisons." (Pronyakin, 1974, 39)

Korotkov is presented, however, as an agent of anti-Communist forces spreading Samizdat literature, so as to discredit him and his opinions for the socialist-realist reader. It is Danilin's idealistic naivete, and by implication anyone else's, who reads Samizdat literature, that makes him fair game for Korotkov. Savchenko, the cynic, on the other hand, sees through Korotkov right from the start.

While discrediting Korotkov's arguments by disparaging his character, Pronyakin reasserts them with a memory of a conversation that Danilin had with his girlfriend Rimma. "You go off to a post," says Rimma, using a verb reserved for going to prison, "shut yourself off behind barbed wire and you're happy." (Pronyakin, 1974, 113) Even though she is a flat character, Rimma's comments about the military are uniformly negative. Pronyakin defends Danilin from Rimma's comments through his sister Lyusya, but her comments are nowhere near as completely rejected as those of Korotkov.

Not everyone at a remote post volunteered or was tricked into going. Viktor Bogatov shows that remote assignments were sometimes used as a punitive measure in his *Rise to Your Own Level*. In the course of resolving an ethical dilemma, Bogatov's main character, Lt. Nalimov, recalls an ethics lesson he had at the academy. The instructor used the example of

> an officer, who exposed a cover-up and blew the whistle on it. His whistle blowing did not appeal to those who did not need it. That was the beginning of hard times for the officer, but he did not give in. Even when they transferred him to some place from where his whistle could not be heard anymore, he did not give in. (Bogatov, 205)

The instructor was using this as a positive example of how to fight for ethical ideals. Nalimov, however, is not sure that it had the right effect. Certainly, he reasons, there were those who agreed with the instructor's conclusion, but there were equally as certain those who drew the opposite conclusion. "Don't rock the boat. Don't answer unless asked. Even if they ask you, try not to answer. Then you won't have to serve where Makar would never take the calves." (Bogatov, 205)

If they did not draw that conclusion then and there at the academy, then maybe they drew it later, after hearing other, similar stories. Even if it was not a conscious conclusion, it may have left its mark as a subconscious seed of "fear of the authorities, of cowardly yes-manism." (Bogatov, 206)

Nalimov struggles with himself, but in the end comes down firmly on the side of ethical idealism, but that takes a strong will or a socialist-realist pen. There were undoubtedly enough officers who listened to their subconscious voice of warning and did not make waves to avoid a remote tour.

Kuz'michev also takes a look at remote posts in his *Nighttime Check*. When the political officer, Maj. Kolodyazhnyj, asks Lt. Ignat'ev if he is pleased with his new assignment at their remote post, Ignat'ev answers frankly that he is not enthusiastic about the assignment, but "you've got to serve someplace." Kolodyazhnyj disagrees and agrees at the same time. He agrees that "you have to serve, and like they say: 'not out of fear, but out of conviction.'" (Kuz'michev, 1982, 10) He lets the comment about the location go without a reply. Kolodyazhnyj eventually does succeed in changing Ignat'ev's opinion about the assignment to give the novel its required socialist-realist happy ending.

One of the main issues in Pronyakin's *Court of Honor* is the system's lack of concern for the welfare of the officers and men serving in remote locations in its efforts to achieve combat readiness. This was undoubtedly in response to the resolution issued by the Central Committee of the CPSU entitled "Measures to Improve Party-Political Work in the Soviet Army and Navy" dated 21 January 1967, which raised the issue of improved living conditions for the troops. Pronyakin's political officer, Maj. Yurenev, maintains his commitment to improving living conditions for his officers and men throughout the novella, despite resistance from his superiors and the fact that his efforts have little apparent effect outside his own unit area.

He criticizes the misuse of the troops' enthusiasm and sense of romanticism as an excuse for not providing better living conditions for them at remote posts. In an episode in which he is taken to task for allowing the men to go into town for a concert, Maj. Yurenev responds to the reproach sharply. Rather than micromanage the unit, the people from HQs should be concerned with the broader issue of the living conditions of those on whom combat readiness depends. Here they are in the middle of the frozen North. The officers cannot have their families at post and do not get to see them for long periods of time. The construction of officers' quarters is only being pursued halfheartedly and the EM's barracks is only made out of clapboard. Should not the facilities for the officers and men be built at the same time as the launch positions for the rockets?

> Why is it that, when we are establishing something, setting it up and building it, that we often forget about those who are establishing it, setting it up and building it? We even praise them for living like troglodytes. We say enthusiasm and romanticism. Isn't that, sometimes, misusing these lofty ideals? (Pronyakin, 1974, 49)

Pronyakin underscores Yurenev's criticism with a comment from cynical Lt. Savchenko. "There it is, the thrill of military service: harsh climatic conditions plus an indifferent attitude on the part of the logistics people." (Pronyakin, 1974, 8)

The trip into town was the major's way of keeping up the unit's spirit. The trip was "to keep the backwoods, where the unit is located, from turning into a mental backwoods for the people stationed there." (Pronyakin, 1974, 49) If that were to happen, then the unit would cease to be truly combat ready. The senior officer visiting the unit, who called him on the carpet for allowing the trip, however, did not agree.

Pronyakin emphasizes the consequences of this lack of concern in his sketch of Yurenev's career. Yurenev, like most PVO officers, had served in one long string of remote posts. At first, life at a remote post appealed to the active, excitement-loving character of young Lt. Kostya Yurenev. When he got a chance to go into town, he would sometimes drop a quarter of his pay in a restaurant and then head straight for a dance hall.

> As the years went by, Konstantin Pavlovich's feeling of romanticism from serving as a PVO officer began to dim. He became reserved, a man of few words, as if the isolation of life at remote posts had left its mark on him. Looking at the present [late sixties] Maj. Yurenev, no one would have suspected that this was a man, who once managed to combine a love for his work with an enthusiasm for restaurants and dancing without any problem. (Pronyakin, 1974, 45)

Pronyakin stresses that even though that part of his nature did change, he kept the character trait that make a good political officer: the ability to quickly establish contact with people.

It is very likely that his ability to do this was also a result of his years of nomadic service at a series of remote posts. Constantly moving from post to post requires the ability to make friends quickly just to survive as a social animal.

The commander of Leonid Konovalov's PVO company in his short story *The Long Night*, Capt. Ustimenko, has also served all his career in "desolate places," but despite this, like Maj. Yurenev, "he had not lost his optimism or good spirits, and displayed an amount of zeal for his work that was amazing to [his] junior officers." (Konovalov, 1981b, 13) He too is a good people-person, who can "find a way to approach people" and can "find a common language with anyone." (Konovalov, 1981b, 14)

There is another side to small, remote posts that is most often overlooked, both in Soviet military fiction and in the West. There is a close sense of family at a small, remote post that does not exist at a big post near a big city. This results in the friendships that are made there being closer and more enduring than the ones made elsewhere. Part of this feeling of family is viewed by some as a lack of privacy. Everybody knows what everybody else is doing. This is not, however, a malicious invasion of your neighbor's privacy, as some see it, but part of being a family. The whole post knows, because it cares, not because it is nosy.

In his *Our Rocket Battalion*, Vladimir Pishchulin describes it like this: In a two- to three-year tour at a small, remote post, everybody gets to be friends, because everybody knows your "joys, ... sorrows, grief, grudges, quarrels, child's ills." (Pishchulin, 1978, 46) Nobody locks their doors. They just leave the key under the mat. If you need something—salt, bread, a school book, aspirin, TV tubes or just a needle—just stop by. If one neighbor doesn't have it, then the next one will. "This is because at a post at a remote 'site,' they have learned to appreciate human kindness. Woe be it to whoever ignores the unwritten laws of a small military post ... who thinks that what's mine is mine and what's yours is yours and don't bother me!" Those people will be quickly forgotten. The warm, open-hearted people, on the other hand, who were part of the family that is a small, remote post, with whom you celebrated, raised your children, went to the range and shoveled snow off the sidewalk, will remain special friends for the rest of your life. (Pishchulin, 1978, 46-47)

Il'ya Davydov presents the reader with the same story of remote garrison life in his novel *The Assignment*. At a "closed," remote post good news spreads like wildfire. (Davydov, 288) When the unit political officer, Lt. Col. Karelov comes to visit a new mother and baby, he just walks right in without bothering to ring the doorbell. This is because it had long been a tradition at this post to leave the key in the door on the outside so that folks could just walk in. (Davydov, 326) Mikhail Sviridov shows the same sort of openness in the remote community pictured in his *Beyond the Blue Horizon*. The people there just leave their keys under the doormat too.

Leonid Konovalov presents an especially good picture of the positive side of living at a remote post in his short story *The Silver Crane*. There he describes the housewarming given for a newlywed couple when they arrive at their remote, northern post by sled from the county seat. "The table had set itself somehow. God only knows where the marinated mushrooms, the cans of sardines, the pickled cabbage with onions, the steaming potatoes, the sliced kielbasa and other hors d'oeuvres came from." (Konovalov, 1981a, 22) All the officers and their wives turned out to welcome the bride and groom.

Stanislav Babaev echoes these sentiments in his novella *Conflict*. Sr. Lt. Rykov and his family have moved to a big garrison from a small remote one. They now have an Officers' Club, concerts, and it is not far to the county seat, but "they seemed to have been happier there [at the remote garrison]. Things were hard, but they were somehow happy, they made a holiday out of every insignificant event." (Babaev, 1986, 161)

NOTE

1. An expression sometimes translated as "the ends of the earth."

8

Dear Ivan

Forgive me, Ivan, but I filed for divorce. Our love, you know, was never famous for its real, no-holding-back feelings. Let's not deceive each other as long as there are no children. One last thing, please don't write me. All the more so, since I think that I have fallen in love with somebody else.

Letter to Sr. Lt. Ivan Trunin in Afghanistan

Nikolaj Ivanov

The Mountain Pass

An officer's or enlisted man's relationship with the woman he loves is most at risk when they are apart. When she is at post with him, if she packs her bags and gets ready to go home to mother, sometimes the political officer can help talk her out of it. If they are apart and she writes him a "Dear Ivan" letter, it is too late.

For the enlisted men, thanks to the mail, life is two-dimensional, reasons Pvt. Kupryashin in Yurij Polyakov's *One Hundred Days till the Order*. One dimension is here and now in his unit, the other is back home, when someone writes him a letter. It is when things go wrong in both these dimensions at once that things are worst for a soldier. (Polyakov, 1988, 64) Pvt. Kupryashin and his girlfriend Lena had it all figured out. They would not count the days until he got out of the Army and they would be together again, but the letters. They agreed to write each other only twice a week—they considered writing every day unrealistic. That meant that they only had to wait for 208 letters. He only got 38. (Polyakov, 1988, 12)

The effect of a broken relationship is the same, whether officer or enlisted man. It is what Lt. Levashov in Aleksandr Kuleshov's *The White Wind* calls "the influence of the morale factor on combat readiness." (Kuleshov, 1977a, 193) A Dear Ivan letter can ruin your whole day, not to mention a training exercise, a driver's test, an academy final exam or tracking a hostile aircraft.

Polyakov describes the Dear Ivan letter as "a common disease fraught with serious complications, affecting those in their first year of service." (Polyakov, 1988, 41) In his novella, Pvt. Kupryashin is not the only one with girl troubles by mail. Pvt. Elin left his girlfriend in the care of a "friend" back home, when he went off to do his compulsory service. She fell in love with the "friend" and they decided to get married. She could not get up the courage to write him herself, but had her new beau do it instead.

Elin's comrade in arms, Pvt. Kupryashin, tries to console him. Kupryashin gives Elin the advice that is standard in military fiction. He should break off the relationship cleanly. The letter shows that she did not really love him. It's better this way than, as is sometimes the case, when a girl is faithful to her GI "in her soul," but sleeps around all over the neighborhood. (Polyakov, 1988, 42)

Viktor Filatov provides the same advice for Pvt. Filipp Sokol in his novella *Recruits*, when Sokol gets an airmail letter from his Lena while he is in the field on an FTX. She has decided not to wait for him and has gotten married. His friend Stepan tries to console him with the typical philosophical answer of most authors to the Dear Ivan letter: "if I were you, I wouldn't be upset. ... If she didn't wait for you and married someone else, that means that she wasn't yours." (Filatov, 1978, 248) Kupryashin then philosophizes that you have to understand things from the girl's point of view. What if she waits faithfully for "Ivan" to come home and then when he gets there, he's not interested in her anymore? What about those two years of house arrest that she suffered through? (Polyakov, 1988, 42) This is a theme that is also echoed in Al'bert Usol'tsev's novel, *A Land of Soldiers*. There Usol'tsev's Klava waited for her soldier, but he did not wait for her. When he came back from the Army he had a wife and two sons. (Usol'tsev, 1981, 14)

This is hardly a satisfactory consolation for Filipp, who retorts that he'll see how philosophical Stepan is after Stepan's girlfriend writes him that she's gotten married to someone else. Polyakov does not resolve the matter. Both Elin and Filipp agree that they don't know what to do to make sure that their girlfriends wait patiently for them to finish their tour of duty.

Filatov's description of Filipp's reaction to his Dear Ivan letter is more like the description of a bad mood rather than the description of a major psychological shock. It is short and merely serves as a background event leading to a discussion of whether to enter a service academy after compulsory service.

For Elin, Kupryashin's advice does not help. Both dimensions of

Elin's life have gone sour at once. Not only did he get a Dear Ivan letter, but he is also suffering under the hazing that first-year draftees undergo at the hands of the Short-timers. For him the letter is the last straw. He goes AWOL and is run over by a train.

In Anatolij Kuz'michev's *Nighttime Check*, Lt. Nagornyj relates the tale of how he lost his love while a cadet in the academy. He and Lyudka had agreed to wait until he graduated and got his commission. Two months before final exams, she ups and marries some engineer and runs off with him to an overseas assignment. Nagornyj can imagine the Zhiguli[1] they bought at a special price and the cooperative apartment that they have undoubtedly already saved up for by being overseas.

Kuz'michev adds insult to Nagornyj's injury by throwing in a bit of Nagornyj's family history. It seems that Nagornyj's father was a corrupt member of the Party, who was on the take, and Nagornyj had always hated him for this. Lyudka's treachery is, therefore, all the more painful because he sees her motivation to marry the engineer and go overseas with him as the same kind of greed that he had always detested in his father.

Lt. Maslov in Vladimir Petrov's short story *The Philosophy of Battle* did not believe that "a letter, no matter what kind, could put someone out of mental balance," until he got one addressed to himself. Whenever one of the enlisted radar operators would lose a target because of a letter he had gotten from home, Maslov would call it "foolishness." After Maslov got his letter, he was present for duty in body, but absent in spirit.

The battalion commander, Maj. Likharev,[2] quickly notices Maslov's problem but does not know exactly what the cause of it is. Petrov keeps the story alive by avoiding the obvious, most desirable resolution of the problem: that of simply having Maslov tell Likharev what his problem is. Because Likharev has only been in the unit for three days, Maslov feels uncomfortable talking about a personal problem with him and dances around the subject, when Likharev calls him into his office to talk about another matter. This gives Petrov a chance to tie Maslov's personal problem with Liya together with his philosophical approach to the Army and life in general via a monologue that Likharev delivers to Maslov.

> There are rungs, just like those on a ladder, over which a person climbs gradually to achieve an end, the completion of some task. Philosophers maintain that the overall result is the sum of its small details. Am I belaboring the obvious? Maybe? But there are some people who do not take heed of this obvious fact. They ignore the details, *foolhardily* [emphasis added] jumping over some rungs so that they can get to the end sooner. And they get to the end, even though there are a lot of rungs

missing in their ladders. Sooner or later, however, you will have to step on those rungs and they will not be there. ... Some call this hastiness. Others superficiality or dilettantism. I call it a lack of thoroughness. Your problem is the result of a paradox. By trying to save time, you are wasting time. (Petrov, 1971, 16)

The monologue was directed at the way that Maslov had trained his crew. He has rehearsed a single scenario to perfection, but without giving his troops the depth and breadth of knowledge of what they are doing to be able to react to changes in the situation. By skimping on the details of their training, Maslov had achieved a good time for the completion of the exercise, but at the cost of only being able to do so with one fixed set of circumstances. When the situation was changed, they were unable to cope with it.

Petrov links Maslov's approach to training his crew with his approach to developing his relationship with Liya. They had been seeing each other for three years and Maslov had finally decided to pop the question. He wrote to her asking her to marry him and the letter with an answer from Liya, which opens the story, is the beginning of Maslov's problems. She turned him down. He had neglected one small detail. She wanted a bit more romance than would fit in a letter. Petrov makes this clear in her next letter, three days later, which has a handwritten P.S. that says: "there are things that you don't write about in letters, but say out loud in person, face to face. Do you really not understand that?" (Petrov, 1971, 16)

This turn of events drives home Maj. Likharev's lesson to Maslov as he realizes that maybe all is not lost. Maybe he was too hasty with his proposal to Liya. Petrov rounds the whole episode out nicely by bringing Maj. Likharev back into the conclusion, as Maslov retrieves Liya's picture from the trash can and pastes it back together. "What could be a better example of 'the summation of the parts into the whole'? Too bad that Maj. Likharev didn't see this. He would have appreciated it." (Petrov, 1971, 16)

Col. Mikhail Sviridov presents the reader with two very different views of romance by correspondence. One as positive as Cinderella. One as gloomy as a soap opera. His short story *Believe Rusakov!* centers around three letters that Pvt. Rusakov wrote to a girl that he had only known by sight. He saw her as she rode her bicycle past the area where his unit was working, but never talked with her. Rusakov never intended to mail the letters to her. Writing them had just made him feel better. It was Rusakov's friend, Pfc. Shumkov, who eventually sent the letters to the girl in question, because he knew that Rusakov was "an unhappy, shy weaver of rhymes, who would not do it for anything." (M. Sviridov, 1980, 21)

The girl wanted to find him, because the tone of the letters made him seem very sympathetic. The fact that he never intended to mail them gave the content of the letters a great deal of credibility. If Sviridov had let Rusakov send them, they would have seemed more like a standard soldier's come-on.

Her friends had advised her to go to the Political Department of the unit for help, where she is aided by Lt. Col. Samokhin, the chief of the department. Samokhin recognizes Rusakov from her description, but has to disappoint her, because Rusakov is no longer stationed in that garrison. He has been sent to Afghanistan. Samokhin gives her the address to write to Rusakov and, as the story ends, concludes that "she will wait" (M. Sviridov, 1980, 21) for Rusakov, even though she never met him in person.

Sviridov's other story about a romance by mail, *The Railroad*, has a socialist-realist happy ending, but with a strange twist. Pvt. Petr Lunev falls in love with Tanya while on leave from his railroad construction unit, which is working on the Trans-Siberian railway. He would never have thought about courting her before he went in the Army, but the Army had changed him enough so that he was willing to give it a try now. They danced and talked. He had told her about the work that he was doing. She had liked listening to his stories about life faraway in Siberia. His leave flew by.

When he went back to his unit, she wrote to him, but after about three months the letters became fewer and fewer. Then like "thunder on a clear day" his mother wrote to him with the news that Tanya had gotten married to Lesha Kurapov. Sviridov makes it a gloomy rainy day to match Lunev's mood. After a good night's sleep, however, he is over his depression and back to work building the railway.

The twist in the plot comes when Lunev gets the news that Tanya and Lesha have gone to Siberia to work on the Trans-Sib. Lunev is sure that his stories about what he is doing there were what prompted Tanya to take this step. The plot folds back on itself once more as Lunev picks up a hitchhiker, who turns out to be Lesha. Lesha does not recognize Lunev and in the course of their conversation, it becomes clear that Lesha does not have what it takes and that he is going back to civilization.

About a month later Lunev decides to go and look Tanya up at the construction camp. He finds her and they take a walk together, just like when he was on leave. In building to a socialist-realist ending more reminiscent of the boy-meets-girl-with-tractor novels of the fifties than of military fiction, Sviridov has Petr announce that he has decided to sign on for another hitch. He wants to go to the NCO[3] academy and come back to the railway. "I can't get along without it. I'm afraid that I'll turn sour." (M. Sviridov, 1982c, 259)

Even though Tanya wants to hear other things from Petr, she

realizes that she will not hear them this time. "The service and the railway have made him a man, who can control his emotions and subordinate them to the greater goal." (M. Sviridov, 1982c, 259) She tells him to stop by when he gets back from the NCO academy. She is not planning on going anywhere, especially since she knows where he is now.

It is not only a Dear Ivan letter that can ruin a soldier's whole day, but also letters from "friends" back home with reports of what the soldier's girlfriend has been doing with "Jody." Maj. V. Volkov develops two possible outcomes for this scenario in his short story *I'm Waiting for You, Soldier*. Pvt. Pochivalov hears from his "friend" back home that "I've seen your Svetka every evening with some guy, an irrigation technician. They're going to the movies and to dances together. I'd advise you to forget about Svetka." (Volkov, 13)

Needless to say, this news upsets Pochivalov, but his first sergeant notices it right away. The first sergeant in this story is a father figure, who advises Pochivalov that this seems a little out of character for the Svetlana that he has come to know from the letters that Pochivalov has let him see. Volkov then proceeds to relate the story of how the first sergeant had almost lost his Vera Alekseevna, now Mrs. First Sergeant, because of a "friend" back home. As it turned out, the first sergeant's "friend" was trying to get the first sergeant out of the picture so that the "friend" could have a shot at Vera.

Pochivalov follows the first sergeant's advice and writes to Svetlana to find out what is going on. Svetlana replies that the irrigation technician is really her cousin, who has returned to their village after finishing his studies and that, while Pochivalov is in the Army, "she has a reliable guard." (Volkov, 13)

This scenario is repeated in Maj. N. Kalmykov's short story *The Smell of Lilac*. In this case the Dear Ivan is Sergej Pavlov, a cadet at a PVO academy. He does not have a wise old first sergeant to turn to for sage advice, when he hears from another cadet that his girlfriend from town, Nina, "has been making time ... walking hand in hand with a sailor at the train station. ... so, my dear fellow, your ideal is nothing more than a soap bubble." (Kalmykov, 16) Practically on the eve of final exams, Sergej goes AWOL to check on this rumor, sees her with a sailor, but does not have the nerve to ask her about it face to face.

Kalmykov thickens the plot by throwing in an alert while Petrov is AWOL. Missing an alert due to AWOL is a serious offense. Petrov is expelled from the academy and sent to a line unit as an EM. This is normally a high enough price for anyone to pay for a mistake, but Kalmykov shows that for Petrov it is even higher. Becoming an officer had been his dream since his youth. He was the son of a career army officer, who had died on active duty, and he wanted to follow in his father's footsteps. Still, Kalmykov justifies the expulsion, because "an officer has to be an example of behavior for others to emulate. Sergej showed a weakness by placing his personal interests above his duty." (Kalmykov, 15)

Sergej leaves the academy without even talking to Nina. She only finds out about the expulsion from another cadet somewhat later. She is hurt that Pavlov believed another cadet and not her. She wavers, but finally writes Pavlov and the story ends happily: they get married, Sergej takes his academy finals as a nonresident, is commissioned and they live happily ever after.

In his novel *The Right to Take Risks*, Anatolij Polyanskij shows that you cannot believe everything that you read in a letter, even if it comes from your sweetheart herself. Polyanskij's Dear Ivan episode takes place in the immediate postwar period. Lt. Korsunov and Polina had fallen in love while serving together in the war. She had been wounded as the war drew to a close and was shipped back from the front to the Soviet Union to recover. At first their letters were warm and full of hope for the future, but then after she had been released from the hospital, the character of her letters changed.

He sent her long missives. She answered with short unintelligible notes. Finally, one "not so fine day" the Dear Ivan letter arrived. "I've met someone with whom I intend to tie my life." (Polyanskij, 1978, 216) Lt. Korsunov cannot believe his eyes. He is sure that there is "not one word of truth in the letter." He runs to his commanding officer (CO) and shows him the letter. The colonel only shrugs his shoulders and says: "I'm sorry. That's life, lieutenant. Be a man." (Polyanskij, 1978, 216) Korsunov insists that he does not believe what is in the letter and convinces the colonel to grant him a leave to go and confront Polina.

When Korsunov arrives in the town where Polina is studying and talks with her face to face, it all becomes clear. Because of her war wound and all the operations that she had to undergo afterward, she can no longer have children. She still loves him, but does not wish to saddle him with a barren wife. He yells at her and calls her an idiot, shoves her into her coat and drags her right off to get married that very day.

Lt. Col. Mamontov sides with Sviridov and Kalmykov in his conservative view of love and duty. In Mamontov's short story *Flowers on the Edge of a Foxhole*, Pvt. Andrusin is worried about his relation with Marijka. He has some serious competition from Grisha Petrov, a tractor driver back home on their collective farm.

As the story begins, Mamontov sets the stage for the moral to come by, relating how Andrusin was almost late back from pass when he tried to call Marijka one Sunday. He had placed the call early in the morning, but they had only completed it in the evening. This is the first small step to what almost becomes dereliction of duty.

There is a night alert and the next thing Andrusin knows he is on a chopper flying through the darkness. The choppers land just before first light and Andrusin and Pvt. Gorbunov, the Communist Party organizer in the company, are sent out to set up an observation post (OP) on a nearby hill. They dig in and Gorbunov goes off to report to the company commander, leaving Andrusin alone.

As the sun comes up Andrusin discovers that he is on the hill overlooking his home where he used to play when he was a kid. He can even see Marijka through his binoculars. Not only can he see Marijka, but he can see Grisha Petrov stop by on his motorcycle to try to pick her up. Andrusin picks some flowers to take to her. He figures that he can just run down there and back before the next scheduled radio check.

Because he was watching Marijka and Grisha, he missed the arrival of the tank unit that the OP was set up to watch for. If Gorbunov had not come back, he would not have seen them at all. Once the situation is corrected, Gorbunov reads him the riot act for neglect of duty. Andrusin tries to blame it all on his love for Marijka, but Gorbunov rejects his arguments.

> You use that word too easily, Roman. And that's too bad. Yeah, sometimes a guy will meet a girl, get acquainted with her and take off AWOL, forgetting about his duty, about his manly honor. And then he tries to excuse his actions with "it was Love." What kind of love is that, if, because of it, you let down the people that you sleep next to, eat with and who hold your fate in their hands? Is that Love? (Mamontov, 1979, 30)

Gorbunov thinks that Marijka would not even take the flowers that Andrusin picked for her, because he did it at the cost of his duty and his honor.

Gorbunov then relates a parable on love and duty from the war that his mother told to him just before he went off to join the Army. In 1941, Gorbunov's father had to withdraw in front of the advancing Germans and found himself on the outskirts of his own village. He could see his house from his foxhole. His father loved his mother ever so much and wanted to go to tell her he was there, but his sense of duty was stronger. He kept digging and held his position as the enemy tanks approached. He only left his position to attack one of the tanks, which he blew up right on his own doorstep. It was not until he came home in 1944 that his mother knew that he had been there and that he had won a medal for his action that day. The moral that Mamontov draws from this is that "the really big love is born out of a sense of duty. Everything we do is connected with the Motherland and its happiness." (Mamontov, 1979, 30)

The appraisal of the problem of Dear Ivan letters in an overwhelmingly male genre is, not surprisingly, primarily from the point of view of the soldier who has been Dear-Ivanned. Authors generally describe the soldier's depression; how it effects his training and combat readiness; how his friends or superiors try to help him overcome the trauma of a broken relationship. Female authors, who are very rare in the genre of military fiction, present a much different view of the issue.

Rimma Kovalenko turns the tables on Dear Ivan in somewhat the same way as Polyakov and Filatov do. In her short story *Pvt. Yakovlev*, Yakovlev did not write a single letter to his high school sweetheart the whole two years he was in the Army. Now that he is back home after his compulsory service, he wants to pick up things right where they left off. His sweetheart, however, has more sense than that.

Kovalenko's character sketch of Pvt. Yakovlev is one of an egocentric negative personality. Even when he tries to apologize to Zina at the end of the story, Kovalenko puts him firmly in his place. "You don't know what to do? Sit down and count how many times you said the word 'I' in the last three sentences! I, I, I, I ..." (Kovalenko, 40)

The girl Ivan left behind is more than just a flat character in Galina Sul'zhenko's short story, *A Letter for You*. At first glance the story is about a soldier and his correspondence with a girl back home. As the story develops, however, it becomes clear that it is the girlfriend and not the soldier who is the main character of the story. She is smarter than he is (he copied from her homework in school). She was accepted into an institute (he was not). She is the dominant one in their relationship. She was the one who suggested that they write to each other. When it is time to display an act of bravery in the story, she is the hero of our times, not he.

The action of the story takes place on the background of a generic military unit, where Masha's soldier is assigned. She is attending college in Moscow and writes often, which makes her soldier happy, but infuriates the cynical unit mailman, who has obviously already gotten a Dear Ivan letter from his sweetheart. He cautions:

"There's no point in your being happy, Beloshchekov,"[4] said the mailman with an evil scowl, "Your student-girl will only last another month and then ... She's studying in the capital in stylish surroundings. She doesn't need you. ... We've seen your type of happiness before. At first they write, but they don't wait till your tour is up. ... I don't deny that there is real love, friendship and faithfulness in the world ... but it's such a rarity. You never meet anyone who has found it. There's no point in your waiting [for a letter]." (Sul'zhenko, 330-331)

Beloshchekov is sure of Masha and makes a bet with the mailman.

If Masha stops writing to him, he will treat the whole platoon in the local snackbar. If she doesn't, the mailman will treat. Masha wrote through the fall and winter, but in the spring the letters stopped coming. Finally, the mailman said that it was time to pay up. True to his word, Beloshchekov treats the whole platoon to pastries and Pepsi at the local snackbar, which for a Soviet enlisted man, even at post-exchange (PX) prices, means a lot of money.

To put the amount of the bet into perspective, relative to an EM's disposable income, in Pronyakin's *Court of Honor*, when Pvt. Timoshin goes into town on a pass to visit his girlfriend, he buys two packs of cigarettes and 300 grams of chocolate and that is his entire "fortune." (Pronyakin, 1974, 129) For Beloshchekov, this was a very large sum of money indeed.

Three days later Beloshchekov gets a letter written with an unsteady hand. It seems that Masha had saved a child from being run over, but in doing so had been run over herself. Now after "months of immobility in plaster of paris armor" she was learning to write again. (Sul'zhenko, 331)

A tour in Afghanistan puts a different slant on romance by correspondence. There is a chance that Ivan might not be coming back, because he could be killed. Under those conditions it is not just something minor like a training exercise, a driver's test, an academy final exam that might go wrong, but a Dear Ivan letter could have a fatal outcome.

In Anatolij Polyanskij's *Afghan Syndrome* the relationship unravels from the other end. Capt. Kretov divorces his wife right before he goes to Afghanistan. They had been having problems before he got his orders. As Polyanksij puts it, they were too different to be married to one another. She was "too egoistic, too much in love with herself ... quarrelsome and unbalanced." (Polyanskij, 1990, No. 11, 82) Kretov had thought that this would all change, but it did not.

When he had done all his processing for Afghanistan, packed his bags and was getting ready to leave, he decided to make the break. He told her: "Come on, sweetheart, let's just go our separate ways with no heartache. You don't care if I get killed or not, so you can have all our property. Try to start a new life and let me go." (Polyanskij, 1990, No. 11, 82)

Nikolaj Ivanov presents a sweet and sour romance by correspondence from Afghanistan in his novella *The Mountain Pass*. Trunin is going through his footlocker, getting ready to leave his platoon-sized outpost area in the mountains. He has three stacks of letters that he has saved. One from his parents, one from his friends and acquaintances and one from Galya.

He calls her letters his four seasons. She had written him four times in the first year he was in Afghanistan. One letter in each of the seasons. He was not sure that he could pick her out of a crowd, but he could recognize her handwriting anywhere. He had read her letters over and over again. This romance is somewhat on the level with Pvt. Rusakov's relationship with the girl he had never spoken to. Trunin had only spoken with Galya for ten minutes before he left for Afghanistan.

Galya, however, is not the only woman in Trunin's life. He is married to Natasha. Ivanov sets the reader up for Trunin's and Natasha's cool relationship with the scene where Trunin is sorting his letters. There are none from Natasha. Sr. Lt. Trunin had been in Afghanistan for about nine months when she wrote him that she was divorcing him. This does not seem to disturb Trunin too much at all. He is not sure what happened to his love for Natasha. Perhaps it never really did exist. Her news only evokes a philosophical: "I don't know who Afghanistan puts more to the test. The officers here or their wives back in the Union.5" (Ivanov, 1987, 10)

Galya's letters are the high point of Trunin's existence in Afghanistan. He knows them almost by heart. In a scene reminiscent of an old western movie, Trunin burns the letters rather than risk the chance that they will fall into mujahedeen hands if the outpost is overrun and he is killed.

> If an enlisted man is always supposed to be confident of victory, then his commander has the right to postulate something worse. It was not the fear of his own death that bothered Trunin from the beginning of the battle. More than anything, he was afraid that the bad guys would get the letters and photos of his loved ones. He could trace this fear back to a magazine published in Pakistan that he had once seen. There was a photograph of a Soviet captain with two little boys sitting on his shoulders printed in the magazine. Their faces had been crossed out as a sign of scorn. It was hard to say how they got hold of the photograph, but Trunin could imagine how it happened right away just as soon as the attack started. (Ivanov, 1987, 44-45)

Trunin does survive the attack and Ivanov gives his relationship with Galya a happy ending. Just before he is ready to leave the outpost, he gets one last letter from Galya. "Some place to go on leave enroute to my next post," he thinks to himself as the story closes.

Andrej Dyshev's *The Replacement* is the story of the love of Sasha Stepanov and Olga. Sasha's approach to Olga is somewhat like Pvt. Rusakov's. Sasha is, however, more aggressive than Rusakov. He has seen Olga walking by in the mornings, but when he tries to talk with her in person, she ignores him. He eventually learns her name and address, and sends her a series of letters. When she still will not call him like he asked her to in the letters, he calls her. To his surprise, she agrees to see him.

Dyshev recounts their stormy relationship, relating its ups and downs as he builds to the moment of truth—Stepanov's announcement that he is on orders to Afghanistan. He had agreed to accept the assignment when their relationship was on one of its downs.

She represents a completely different type of woman than is most often found in military fiction. Even though she finds him attractive in uniform, and is prepared to accept him as an officer, she is not prepared to risk the uncertainty of him taking a tour in Afghanistan. "'Do you think that women need your medals?' she interrupted him, barely holding back her tears. 'Do you think we need your medals and your rank?'" (A. Dyshev, 1989, 59) She wants him to turn the assignment down.

He tells her that he could do that, but "they would hate him in the regiment for his cowardice. And even she would hate him too. Anyway, he already accepted the assignment." (A. Dyshev, 1989, 59) As he is about to fall back on the standard excuse of "I am a commander, and officer after all! I got my orders and I'm going!" (A. Dyshev, 1989, 59), he realizes that this is not the truth. He agreed to accept the assignment. She throws him out and he leaves with a feeling of guilt for having let her down somehow.

As the novella closes at the end of his first day in the war, he is lying on his back looking at the stars, trying to absorb all the events that have taken place that day. The horror of combat and the near presence of death are overwhelming. He feels detached from himself, as if he has not existed for days. When he looks for the event that triggered this feeling of detachment, however, his troubled relationship with Olga is ranked on a par with the death and destruction he has seen on his first day in combat. "How fragile everything in the world is. How untouchable it all is!" (A. Dyshev, 1989, 64)

NOTES

1. The Soviet-produced version of the Fiat. The dream of every Soviet Yuppie.

2. The name Likharev is derived from the word *likhoj* in the meaning of foolhardy, which is exactly what Likharev accuses Maslov of being.

3. The noncommissioned officers' academy trains enlisted men for duties in enlisted leadership positions.

4. Beloshchekov can be translated as something like *peach fuzz*, someone who does not yet have to shave regularly.

5. The Russians use the word "Union" to mean the Union of Soviet

Socialist States the same way that Americans use the word "States" to mean the United States of America.

9

The School of Socialism

The military is a school of endurance and discipline.
                                    Leonid Brezhnev
                                    XXV Congress of the CPSU

In addition to their role as a defender of the Motherland, the Soviet Armed Forces are also supposed to play a major role in socializing young people so that they can take a constructive part in Soviet society. This aspect of the Armed Forces' mission receives a great deal of coverage in military fiction. Because military fiction is a socialist-realist genre, its treatment of the topic throughout the socialist-realist period was uniformly positive and the success achieved by the Armed Forces in socializing young men is undoubtedly exaggerated. The goals for this effort and the reasons for wanting to achieve them, as stated in military fiction, are, nonetheless, valid.

Vladimir Pishchulin shows the effect that the military school of socialism can have on a young man. When Andrej Kolosov's sister comes to visit him in Pishchulin's *Our Rocket Battalion*, she sees how much the Army has changed him. "I didn't recognize him. It's Andrej, but it's not Andrej. He's matured, become more manly, and I can see that he is happy. It's as if he had grown wings." Kolosov's first sergeant explains to her that "It's the Army! The Army trains a man mentally and physically." (Pishchulin, 1978, 163)

Col. Surgin, the chief of the Political Department in Yurij Strekhnin's *I Bequeath You*, thinks that it would be good for his son to serve in the Army. "It would help him develop a real manly character, help him decide what he wants to do, like it has already helped so many." (Strekhnin, 1977, 152) Surgin catches himself thinking that he, too, like many parents, is counting on the Army to do what he could not do himself; that is, to raise his son to be a good citizen. He wonders why it is that he cannot find a way to reach his son, when he can easily reach the officers and men under him, who are the same age as his son, but Strekhnin leaves the question unanswered.

Surgin breaks parents down into two categories:

- those who cannot wait until their son is drafted so the service "can make a real human being out of him" and "finish the education that his parents and the regular schools started" (Strekhnin, 1977, 152 & 249), and
- those who "think that their child is already smart enough and there is no reason for him to lose those years to service in the military." (Strekhnin, 1977, 152)

Surgin thinks that

the years spent in compulsory service are good for everybody. The military not only gives you a sense of order and diligence, but also something more important. It develops a sense of responsibility. A school of responsibility. That is what the military is for a young man. ... Nothing makes you more grown up than a feeling of responsibility. The military is a school of fortitude, even if there is no war. And it's a good thing for everyone to go through it." (Strekhnin, 1977, 152 & 249)

Vladimir Komissarov shares Strekhnin's view of the military as the place for the distressed parents of problem sons to send them to be straightened out. In a conversation between Lt. Gorin, a platoon leader, and his girlfriend, Komissarov has her relate the tale of a man whose son is just finishing high school. The son is a poor student, a hooligan and has already started drinking. He has even been excommunicated from the Comsomol. His father has given up on him and places all his hopes on the military to bring the boy around: "If he only makes it to the Army, they can make a human being out of him there." (Komissarov, 60) Gorin, speaking as a representative for the system, is confident that they can do so.

Another common approach to the socialization mission of the Armed Forces in military fiction is to compare the Army to a regular school. Col. Korsunov in Anatolij Polyanskij's *The Right to Take Risks* compares his profession to that of his wife, who is a grade school teacher. "We both teach how to be human beings. ... And we have to make sure that our standards become theirs." (Polyanskij, 1978, 163) Korsunov's own son tried to get into one of the service academies, but did not make the cutoff on the entrance exam. The colonel is, of course, disappointed that his son will not follow in his footsteps as an officer, but he is pleased that his son will at least get to go through the school of enlisted service.

Just like Col. Korsunov, Maj. Morozov, the battery commander in Vladimir Komissarov's *Guards Lieutenant*, feels that his mission is the same as that of a school: the production of a human being. "Only in school, they shape them out of wax, here [in the Army] we chisel them out of marble." (Komissarov, 60 & 77)

Col. Loginov, the chief of the Political Department in Aleksandr Kuleshov's *The Nighttime Sun*, gets a great deal of pleasure out of his work, because he feels that "there is nothing more interesting than working with people." (Kuleshov, 1981, 221) He is proud of what the Army has done for all the young men he has worked with. "That is a political officer's mission: to produce citizens, not to produce them, obviously, but to put the finishing touches on them or something like that. The production of a citizen begins while they are still children—in kindergarten, in school ... and with their parents." (Kuleshov, 1981, 221)

Loginov does not give all parents equal credit for their success in raising good citizens. He relates the story of a young soldier he once had in his unit, whose parents only thought was to accumulate money. It was only after the boy came in the Army that, thanks to Loginov, he saw the truth of what they were and became a real *homo sovieticus*.

Loginov directs all his efforts to producing citizens who will be ready, if they are called on, to sacrifice their lives in the name of victory over the enemy. (Kuleshov, 1981, 256) This "moral steadfastness" is especially important on the modern, nuclear battlefield, because "the morale of the troops, their enthusiasm, their fighting spirit is particularly important. Only people with high moral qualities, people who disdain death in the name of a great and honorable goal, will prove themselves able to successfully carry out missions under these conditions." (Kuleshov, 1981, 306-307)

Vladimir Pishchulin echoes this idea in another variation of the common scenario of parents seeking the military's help to socialize their son. In his short story *A Sunday*, Pvt. Vasilij Artyukhin's mother writes to his commander, Sr. Lt. Khmel'nitskij, asking him "to smarten Vasya up. Make a human being out of him." (Pishchulin, 1976, 14) Pishchulin establishes Vasilij Artyukhin's character as that of an overconfident young man chafing under the discipline of Army life. He wants to do something important, skipping over the trivial detail of daily Army life, like shining shoes, making up beds, following rules and regulations. He wants to be where the action is and drive a rocket launch vehicle.

Khmel'nitskij sees that Artyukhin is not ready for this responsibility and sends him off to visit the retired company first sergeant who lives nearby. The first sergeant, Andrej Nikolaevich, teaches Artyukhin an important lesson on the value of the common good. "The main thing that you have to understand is where you are going and why you are going there. Some folks these days have been sort of blinded. They have the concepts of 'mine' and 'yours' down, but have forgotten about the concept of 'ours.'" (Pishchulin, 1976, 15) This is what socialization means to Pishchulin. This is what Andrej Nikolaevich fought for in the war.

To make his point, Andrej Nikolaevich takes Artyukhin to a nearby hill, where Andrej Nikolaevich stood firm against a German advance. Underneath the inevitable monument to mark the spot are the bodies of his friends, Mitaj, Semen and Vasilij Gromov, who fought with him on that day.

The last of the three names is Pishchulin's key to the change in Artyukhin's attitude. Not only does he have Artyukhin's first name, Vasilij, but his last name is reminiscent of the Norse god Thor (*grom* = thunder). The approach is rather transparent. He is the only one of the three whose last name is given. Pishchulin does not even give the first sergeant's last name and he is one of the main characters in the story.

Artyukhin is so impressed by the great deeds of his namesake on the day that he stood off the Germans to the death with Andrej Nikolaevich, that he changes his attitude to the service and becomes a good soldier, ready to take on the responsibility of driving a rocket launch vehicle. While this ending seems contrived to a Western reader, Pishchulin is only continuing the tradition of portraying the heroism of the war as a force that shapes destinies, just like Snegirev, Pronyakin and Vsevolodov.

In his novella *Our Rocket Battalion*, Pishchulin takes an even stronger stance on the value to society of having young men serve in the military. Stepan Gavrilin, the Comsomol group leader, had all "A"s in high school, but decided to enter the Army first, before going to college.

> I think that everybody should go to a second school after they finish the first one. The school of the Army. Otherwise, you'll live your whole life. Maybe become a manager, or maybe even become famous and you'll never have known the joy of doing a soldier's job or known what that job is worth. Believe me, Slavka, it's worth something. Even you know that. Our job as soldiers is not some abstract idea. It's not, how should I put it, not a job that produces something. Its product is combat readiness. How can you measure it and what scale do you use? You have to understand it with your mind and feel it with your heart. (Pishchulin, 1978, 113)

Pishchulin draws Gavrilin's thought through to the conclusion that combat readiness is what preserves the ability of all those, who do have jobs that produce something tangible, to continue their work. This, in essence, means that the product of a soldier's job is the combined product of all those who can work, because the soldier is on guard.

Pronyakin continues this same train of thought in his short story *The Strict Commander* in a speech by Sgt. Ryabukhin to Pvt. Kurban Shurapov on why they are in uniform.

> Wouldn't it be great right now to wander in the woods picking mushrooms? After that, closer to supper, to lie down in the meadow, with the birch trees whispering above you and with the clear, peaceful sky shining down through them? That's beauty! But, when you recall that you are the one who is responsible to the Nation for that beauty, you try to chase dreams like that out of your head. Duty, Kurban. When you take off the uniform, then it's another story. Take that shepherd, for example. What kind of worries does he have? Find a good place to graze the sheep so that there will be more milk and more meat. He doesn't have to worry about anything else, because he knows that Pvt. Kurban Shurapov is here on this hill with a weapon in his hands watching what is happening all around. He can see what's going on, not only just beyond the woods, but also over the ocean. ... when you think about who you are and why they gave you a weapon, then you look at things in a different light. (Pronyakin, 1974, 269)

This speech is the key to the change in Shurapov's attitude to serving in the Army and to his sergeant. He comes to the socialist-realist conclusion that Ryabukhin's nit-picking attention to detail and discipline is for his own good, and a part of keeping the peace.

One of the most common scenarios to show the success of the school of socialism is a reunion between the once-troubled young man, now an upstanding sergeant or officer, and his mentor. Col. Gennadij Gubanov's *Ashberries Ripen in the Frost* is a good example. In this story Lt. Nikolaj Kol'tsov is returning from leave when he runs into Maj. Laskin at a riverboat ticket office. Six years ago, it was Pvt. Kol'tsov, flight mechanic, and Sr. Lt. Laskin, assistant to the chief of the Political Department for Comsomol affairs. When they first met, Kol'tsov was being tried by a meeting of the Comsomol for his "impertinence and willfulness" (Gubanov, 1981, 39) for which they were considering excommunicating him from the Comsomol. Laskin defended him and prevented that drastic measure of Party justice from being applied to Kol'tsov.

Kol'tsov is pleased to see Laskin again and they talk about old times. In the flashbacks to Kol'tsov's days as an EM and before, Gubanov paints a picture of a young man who was headed down the road to prison. All this was caused by his "self-confidence and internal freedom, which overflowed into real foolhardiness." Kol'tsov's service in the Armed Forces changed all that. Now Kol'tsov is trying to teach other people some sense. (Gubanov, 1981, 39 & 41)

In the intervening years, Kol'tsov has learned that "no one can change themselves for the better unless they want to, unless they are dissatisfied with the way they are." Deception about your self-image, however, is what gets in the way of becoming dissatisfied with yourself, "and you pay for it dearly" later on. (Gubanov, 1981, 41) Thus far, the story is a typical success story for the school of socialism on the model of many others.

Gubanov shows that Kol'tsov is still deceiving himself about who and what he is. Kol'tsov is disturbed by the rush of what he perceives as insignificant details. He wants a fuller, more creative role to play, where he can "dig deeply into things, thoughtfully, thoroughly, not just halfway." Laskin puts this into perspective. All those little things are a part of the overall big picture of being ready to defend the Motherland. He thinks that Kol'tsov still needs to mature a bit more, because he, like most young people, is "inclined to exaggeration and black-and-white opinions." (Gubanov, 1981, 41) As the story draws to a close, Gubanov reveals that Laskin is on his way to serve in Kol'tsov's unit as the chief of the Political Department. He will be able to continue what he began six years ago and help Kol'tsov continue to grow as a person.

Gubanov wrote two versions of the story. The first, the magazine version, shows Kol'tsov as happy to be resuming the relationship with Laskin. The second, book version, changes the ending, giving the story a completely different tone. The change is in Kol'tsov's reaction to meeting Laskin. In the magazine version Kol'tsov is unhappy about meeting Laskin until he realizes all at once that "no, telling Laskin about himself so excitedly and frankly was not in vain!" (Gubanov, 1981, 41) In the book version of the story, Kol'tsov is sorry that "he told Laskin about everything so excitedly and frankly. It was in vain. He did not even want to travel together. If some reason to stay in town until the next sailing were to come up now, he would use it for sure." (Gubanov, 1986, 99)

While the officers of military fiction worked diligently during the day to imbue the troops with the lessons of the school of socialism, another socializing process took over at night. It was the tyranny of the draftees in the second half of their tour of duty over the draftees in their first half. This process, known as *dedovshchina* [grandpa-autocracy], was based on an unofficial hierarchical structure among the enlisted men based on time in service.

The life cycle of a Soviet draftee was defined by the biannual draft call. Each spring and each fall, when the new draftees arrived to begin their two-year tours of duty and the soldiers, who had completed their tours, left, a new cycle began. Each of the stages had its own name, which varied from unit to unit. Yurij Polyakov presented the life cycle of a draftee in a chart in his novella *One Hundred Days till the Order* (p. 8). Oleg Ermakov presents a similar breakdown in the narrative of his story, *Winter in Afghanistan* (1991, p. 341).

Cycle (in months)	Name	
	Polyakov	Ermakov
1 - 6	*Salaga* [no translation] *Synok* [Sonny Boy] *Dukh* [Breath, Smell, Spirit]	*Syn* [Son]
6 -12	*Skvorets* [Starling] *Shnurok* [Boot lace]	*Chizh < chizhik* [Sparrow]
12 -18	*Limon* [Lemon] *Cherpak* [Ladle]	*Cherpak* [Ladle]
18 - Day the Order is issued	*Starik* [Old man] *Korol* [King] *Ded* [Grandfather]	*Ded* [Grandfather]
Day of the Order - Discharge	*Veteran* [Veteran] *Dembel* [Demobilized soldier]	*Dembel* [Demobilized soldier]

The order referred to in Polyakov's chart is the one issued by the Ministry of Defense every six months to announce the spring and the fall draft calls. It also announces the discharge of those who have completed their obligatory service. It is issued approximately one hundred days before the draftees, who have completed their tours, are released from active duty.

In the U.S. military, a *Salaga* would have been known variously as a *Newk* or a *Weed*. A *Newk*, because he was so new or a *Weed* because he was so green. A *Starik* would have been known as a *Short-timer* because he only had a short amount of time left to serve until discharge. A *Veteran* would have been known as a *Double-digit-midget*, because he had 99 days or less to serve.

Polyakov was not the first author to write about the tyranny of the Short-timers over the Newks. His novella of the early eighties was, however, the first to attack the phenomenon from the point of view of an enlisted man and to show the full effect of it on those who went through the after-hours school of socialism. The victim of Polyakov's novella is Pvt. Elin, who was driven into going AWOL and killed by a train.

Oleg Ermakov presents some other possible results of this tyranny on young draftees. In his short story *Winter in Afghanistan*, one young man drinks the urine of a jaundice patient so that he can escape from the clutches of the Short-timers to the hospital for two or three months. Another tries, unsuccessfully, to shoot himself. (Ermakov, 1991, 344) Although it received only this kind of cursory treatment in military fiction, suicide due to the tyranny of the Short-timers over the Newks was and is a serious problem in the Soviet military.

The life of a Newk was not very pleasant. They lived in open-bay barracks with rows of bunk beds. Sleeping in the upper bunk was the lot of a Newk. Sleeping in the bottom bunk was a privilege of the Short-timers. (Polyakov, 1988, 5; Pustynin, 106; Ermakov, 1991, 438) The Newk in the upper bunk was essentially the slave of the Short-timer in the lower one. He had to:

- wash and mend the Short-timer's uniform (Polyakov, 1988, 5; Pustynin, 112),
- give up his new cap to a Short-timer (Pustynin, 106),
- make up the Short-timer's bed (Pustynin, 107; Polyakov, 1988, 28),
- know the Short-timer's day count, or face a beating (Pustynin, 106; Polyakov, 1988, 28),
- give up his blanket on a cold night so the Short-timer would be warm (Pustynin, 107),
- clean the latrine and police the area (Polyakov, 1988, 78).

In addition to this, Newks could not take baths, the Short-timers hogged all the shower time. (Pustynin, 107) Newks were the only ones who went to peel potatoes for the mess hall. (Pustynin, 109) The Short-timers even took the Newks' pay (Pustynin, 108; Polyakov, 1988, 37; Ermakov, 1991, 349), and only allowed them to leave the unit area to go to the latrine. It was not until they became Sparrows that they could leave to visit the library or friends from home serving in other units. (Ermakov, 1991, 354)

Polyakov's platoon leader, Lt. Kosulich, offers one possible origin of the tyranny of the Short-timers over the Newks. His theory is that it began in 1967, when the length of the obligatory tour for draftees was changed from three to two years. The men who had been drafted for three years "began to vent their anger on the two-year draftees and after that it was just a chain reaction." (Polyakov, 1988, 35)

Polyakov crystallizes the anger that the three-year draftees must have felt in a comment from Pvt. Kupryashin: "Terrifying!" Kosulich tells Kupryashin not to be so dramatic, but Kupryashin rejects Kosulich's downplaying of the impact of serving an extra year in a comment made silently to himself: "An officer, who signed on for twenty-five years in the first place, will never understand what it means to an enlisted man to serve an extra year." (Polyakov, 1988, 35)

While Kosulich's theory of the 1967 origin of the tyranny of the Short-timers over the Newks is plausible enough, Polyakov rejects it at other points in his novella. Kosulich immediately brings his own theory into doubt by citing an example of a caste system, based on time in service from the Page Corps in prerevolutionary Russia, that sounds very much like "grandpa-autocracy." Later in the story, Pvt. Chernetskij cites the example of a unit that was formed with draftees all from the same draft cycle. There were no Short-timers or tradition of grandpa-autocracy, but the draftees established something similar. Their caste system was based on might makes right. The strongest among them were the "Grandfathers." (Polyakov, 1988, 79) Polyakov has thus shown that this is a phenomenon that existed before the Soviets took power, making it a Russian character trait instead of a Soviet one. He also shows that other characteristics beside age can distinguish a ruling caste in a closed society like the military. He then takes the reader outside the military to show what the phenomenon looks like in the civilian world.

At the party to celebrate the rite of passage to Double-digit-midget status, Kupryashin is taken to task for his attitude toward the system of grandpa-autocracy by Chernetskij.

> Do you think that people are divided into Old-timers and *Salagas* just in the Army? You're wrong. Open your eyes: these people tramp to work on foot, these ride in mountainous, black cars, these crowd together in lines, and these are issued their goods in special stores, these ... Or here's an example. They kicked me out of the university for cutting class ... while my classmate, the son of the chairman of a regional executive committee, cut the whole semester, but he graduated cum laude and went overseas on his practicum. It works out to: he's a "Double-digit-midget" and I'm a "Newk." (Polyakov, 1988, 79)

This is a very cynical attitude and a severe criticism of Soviet society that, until the mid-eighties, would not have been possible, except in samizdat.

With characteristic twenty-twenty hindsight, it is possible to find reflections of grandpa-autocracy in works published prior to Polyakov's *One Hundred Days till the Order*. In 1961, Maj. V. Matreshin touched on grandpa-autocracy in his short story *Just a Bit*. It is the story of two medics, the Short-timer Sgt. Ershov, and the Newk Pvt. Puzikov.

Puzikov's cap is "just a little big" and his boots are "just a little tight." When he first got to the unit, he had a cap and boots that fit, but someone swapped them for the ones he had now while he was in the bathhouse. Ershov could not understand why Puzikov did not make a fuss about it. Matreshin was an officer, and may well have been out of touch with the realities of barracks life, but Puzikov was clearly an intelligent person and had recognized the danger inherent in making a fuss over it.

Matreshin does not implicitly blame this on grandpa-autocracy, but it is clear to see it in the characteristic condescension of Ershov toward Puzikov as they interact in the story. This link is further reinforced by the episodes in both Polyakov's and Pustynin's works in which Short-timers take Newks' new uniform items. As they explained it, it was a part of the ritual of being discharged. The Short-timers wanted to go home in a brand-new uniform and look sharp for their friends and relatives. (Polyakov, 1988, 49 & 65)

Matreshin produces the required socialist-realist change in Ershov's attitude toward Puzikov by giving Puzikov an impressive bedside manner that convinces Ershov that Puzikov is worthy of his protection. As the story ends, Ershov is on his way to the quartermaster to exchange Puzikov's cap and boots for some that fit.

In his short story about repairing a break in an overhead telephone line on a wintery Sunday, *The Urgent Mission* (1974), Pronyakin looks at the interaction of two soldiers thrown together in the isolation of the snow-covered countryside. Viktor is in the second year of his service; Mokshin is in the first year of his. Mokshin is directing an endless stream of questions at Viktor about why they were picked for this detail, which annoys Viktor, "who thought that the commander had been unfair to them, and here was Mokshin with his whining. Viktor, who had crossed the threshold of his last year of service, considered it disgraceful for him to let a *Salaga* see that he felt offended too, so he gave a curt answer." (Pronyakin, 1974, 240)

Pronyakin underscores the difference between them by using the Short-timer's first name and the Newk's last name. Just calling the Short-timer Viktor puts him that much closer to civilian life. Just calling the Newk by his last name places him much more firmly in the formal sphere of military life. Pronyakin's view of what is going on is that the slang is cute, but there is nothing sinister in their relationship. It is just an old hand helping a new man learn the ropes. When Mokshin climbs up a pole to repair the break, Viktor watches him with a "condescending smile" and thinks to himself: "was I really like that," [i.e. so clumsy and unsure of myself] when I was a Newk? (Pronyakin, 1974, 241)

In his *Only Three Days* (1975), Valerij Biryukov shows the reader one of the practical jokes that were played on Newks all the time, even in the U.S. military. Pvt. Urengaliev has been sent to the neighboring gun crew for an ST-1 clearance adjustment tool. When he got there, they gave him a large ST-ONE in a box and told him to take it right back. This was a common joke and the bigger and heavier the stone, the more the troops laughed. Biryukov comes down firmly against this sort of thing in his story by having the sergeant in charge make Pvt. Lyapunov, who had sent Urengaliev to get the ST-1, carry it back where it came from. This is an effective enough remedy for the problem, when applied in this manner.

Vladimir Stepanenko has a very short commentary on grandpa-autocracy in his novella *Nine Days without an Alert* (1977). An investigation of what was nearly a flight accident is in progress in a fighter aviation regiment. One of the aircraft was not serviced properly and the control panel fell out in the pilot's lap as he was preparing for take off. The flight commander, Capt. Nosov, tells his zampolit that they have to keep an eye on all the "Veterans," the word for Short-timers in Stepanenko's unit. "They often dump all their work onto the young airmen and this is the result." (Stepanenko, 69)

Stepanenko's point of view is still that of an officer. The primary focus is the potential adverse effect on the pilot, who could have been killed, rather than on the adverse effect on the new, young airmen, who get all the Short-timers' work to do as well as their own. Stepanenko's solution to the problem is that the Short-timer, who should have serviced the aircraft, is sent to the guardhouse for five days as a punishment. The punishment is not for having dumped his work on a Newk, but for the poor quality of the job that the Short-timer was supposed to have done. It ignores the fact that the work was done by a Newk and not by the Short-timer. It is not addressing the problem, only one of its symptoms. The Short-timer would most likely have felt that the Newk had let him down by doing a poor job and would have taken it out on the Newk when he got out of the guardhouse.

Aleksandr Belyaev's mention of the problem in his novel *The Runway* (1979) is so short as to be enigmatic for the uninitiated. It appears as a single sentence in a list of problems being faced by a new company commander. "The young soldiers were not getting along with the Old-timers." (Belyaev, 1979, 48) It is just a part of the background color and Belyaev does not return to it.

Anatolij Polyanskij was really the first to attack the tradition of grandpa-autocracy, but his short (two-page) treatise on it was buried in his novella *The Right to Take Risks* (1978) and did not attract much attention. Col. Korsunov, the chief of the Political Department of Polyanskij's airborne division, had noticed some discipline problems in the first battery of the division's artillery regiment. Up until recently, the battery had been one of the best and used to win prizes at

competitions. Korsunov sent his instructor to check out the situation
firsthand.

The instructor's report finds no problem areas, but Korsunov found a
detail in the report that alerted him to the source of the trouble. "'The
tone in the battery is set by the second-year soldiers and everyone is
subordinated to them,' he said with the most inane enthusiasm and
added happily, as if this was some kind of good news: 'You know what
they call them, comrade colonel? "Pheasants" and the second-year
soldiers take this nickname as their due. Isn't that strange?'"
(Polyanskij, 1978, 53)

Korsunov recognizes the problem immediately. He also recognizes
why his instructor, who has only been with him for a short period, did
not see it. He does not understand enlisted slang. Korsunov does and
Polyanskij points out that there are those who would question why he
would need to. Korsunov's answer to that question is "to be able to
understand the people." (Polyanskij, 1978, 53)

Maj. Nikolaj Kalmykov makes the same point in his *The Smell of
Lilac*. "An officer has to know a lot of things," said the main character
of the story, Sergej, when he was accused of trying

> to fathom the unfathomable. School lays the foundations of
> knowledge. The Army should form the character, teach one to
> value life and all that is beautiful in it. That is the
> cornerstone, on which, in the final analysis, conscience and
> discipline rest. Do you remember what Gorkij said? You have to
> study long and hard to have the right to advise cautiously. And
> how much you have to know to have the right to educate!
> (Kalmykov, 15)

To test his hunch about the problem, Korsunov asks the instructor if
it is customary in the unit at taps to call out: "Pheasants, good night!
You're one day shorter, that's right!" (Polyanskij, 1978, 53) The
instructor had not taken the time to stay in the unit until taps, so he
had no idea. In any event, he sees no problem with this not-so-poetic
goodnight wish.

Korsunov sees that he will have to go to the artillery regiment
himself and gives his inexperienced and naive instructor a lesson in the
facts of barracks life.

> The relationship between the second-year and the first-year
> draftees is not always straightforward and correct. The first-
> year draftees can and should have guardians, but sometimes
> the Short-timers dump all the dirty jobs on the new recruits.
> They play practical jokes on them that are very insulting and
> humiliating for these young men. You only have to overlook

something and an unpleasant situation will take shape in the *kollektiv* that will not promote either improved discipline or the proper education of our people. (Polyanskij, 1978, 54)

Polyanskij's description and evaluation of the situation is quite good and to the point. It is, however, too abstract and short to get the attention that Polyakov attracted with his novella. The primary difference is that Polyanskij's description is from the point of view of an officer and offers no details as to what it is that happens in the barracks that produces the unpleasant relationship between the Short-timers and the Newks.

The same is true of all the other official authors of the sixties and seventies. They all approached the issue from an officer's point of view. None of them shows what grandpa-autocracy did to the troops who endured it. Pustynin accuses the officers of ignoring the problem. "But where are the officers, the zampolit? They know, they all know, but it's easier for them not to notice." (Pustynin, 107) Polyakov's condemnation of the officers is not so universal. In his novella it is only Sr. Lt. Uvarov who is trying to use grandpa-autocracy to his advantage as a commander. The battalion political officer and Kupryashin's platoon leader, Lt. Kosulich, are opposed to it.

Even Pustynin's Afghan vet spent the night he had charge of quarters trying to convince the duty officer of the necessity of grandpa-autocracy, when he had become a Grandfather himself. (Pustynin, 112)

Communist doctrine has always taught that the ultimate wisdom lies with the masses, therefore listening to an enlisted man's opinion of grandpa-autocracy makes perfectly good, Communist sense. This is the "natural creativity of the masses" as Polyakov disdainfully classifies it. (Polyakov, 1988, 54) Lt. Levashov in Aleksandr Kuleshov's *The White Wind*, recalls what the psychology instructor at the academy taught them about learning from the troops.

Your professional qualifications are probably higher than those of any one of your soldiers taken individually. But the collective experience of the troops, taken as a whole, is a great thing. The collective wit, the collective intuition. Listen to what they say, look at what they do, maybe not at Tom or Dick, but to the whole platoon. Believe me, you'll learn a lot. And it won't hurt your authority any either. The primary quality of a commander, and of a political officer all the more so, is to see each individual behind the platoon, behind the company, and behind each individual, to see the platoon and company, the collective that he is a part of. (Kuleshov, 1977a, 177)

The coastal battery commander in Vladimir Borodin's *The Shyest Lieutenant* tells his new platoon commander, Lt. Murav'ev, "that learning from your subordinates is, of course, not bad, and even necessary, but the main obligation of a commander, in the final analysis, is not to learn, but to teach." (Borodin, 1980, 18)

When the new authors of the eighties (Pustynin, Ermakov and Polyakov) appeared with an enlisted man's viewpoint, they were careful to point out that their main characters were not as bad as the other Short-timers. Pustynin's Afghan vet recalls that the Short-timers liked to tell them "you think that we're running you ragged, well, in our time we were." His cycle had good intentions when they were still Newks, they "seriously thought that they would not beat anyone or humiliate them either." (Pustynin, 106 & 107) When, however, they finally get to be Grandfathers, things changed. Pustynin's Afghan vet recalls that they were giving a "blanket party"[1] and he was forced to join in. "And I was glad that they were not beating me, but him and that for today, at least, they weren't bothering me. ... They also kept at me to beat him. I had to do something that at least looked like I hit him to get them to leave me alone." (Pustynin, 110)

When Pvt. Kupryashin buys into Lt. Kosulich's advice about stopping grandpa-autocracy that the troops have to put a stop to it themselves, he is demoted from Double-digit-midget to *Salaga* by a court of Grandfathers. Ermakov's Double-digit-midget, Oreshov, comes off the worst of the three in the stark realism of Ermakov's Hemingwayesque prose. Oreshov was not "such a snake. Sure he busted people in the mouth and made them do all kinds of work for him, but he wasn't greedy and didn't hold a grudge and never made up refined tricks to make fun of the young troops, the 'Sparrows' and 'Ladles.'" (Ermakov, 1991, 439)

Kupryashin recalls the joke that they used to tell when he was in school, based on the political slogan that has taken on the quality of a proverb: "The Army is the School of Life." They would add " but it's better to go through it by correspondence." (Polyakov, 1988, 61-62)

NOTE

1. A "blanket party" is a beating delivered by a group in the barracks, where the person they are beating up has his head covered by a blanket so that he cannot see who is doing the beating.

10

Playing at War

The soldiers like training, provided it is carried out sensibly
Field Marshal Prince Aleksandr V. Suvorov (1729-1800)

Training is an essential part of life for the peacetime military. It is the only way to keep the troops prepared for the job that they may be one day called upon to do. The Soviet military's goal is to live up to the proverb "rough on the training field, easy on the battlefield," which is repeated time and time again in military fiction. (Zen'kovich, 8; Petukhov, 103; Kuleshov, 1981, 247) As Yurij Petukhov expresses it in his novella ... *Two Springs from Now*, "no commander wants to sustain heavy losses in combat, and the knowledge of how to survive under enemy fire is developed in training." (Petukhov, 103)

Col. Bogdanchikov, the regimental commander in Anatolij Polyanskij's short story *The Main Thing in Your Service*, "understands the necessity of teaching people under conditions approximating to those in combat. Working under maximum load, the troops are tempered and gain the requisite skills." (Polyanskij, 1984, 18)

This is a long drawn-out process as Viktor Bogatov shows in his *Rise to Your Own Level*. Lt. Blinov is talking to one of his sergeants about the changes the sergeant feels have taken place in him since he has been on active duty. He has an increased sense of self-assurance and resoluteness that seems to have crept up on him little by little. Being the good Communist that he is, Blinov explains this as a part of the theory of dialectic materialism, the change of quantity into quality. He brings it down to the sergeant's level by using the analogy of a brickwall. "One brick in a wall would seem not to add anything to it. But still, it's not the same wall that it was." (Bogatov, 21)

Blinov, who is a mustang[1], goes on to recall a winter FTX during his enlisted service. They made a long march on cross-country skis and were out for two full days of field training. When it was all over and they were returning to garrison, Blinov was so tired that he was ready to collapse. He felt that way the whole forty kilometers they had to cover to get back. The only thing that the troops remembered after that FTX was the exhaustion and, to a lesser extent, the cold. As with his sergeant now, it was only later that Blinov came to realize that the FTX had given them more "courage, daring, initiative, resourcefulness. Just a bit more endurance and a capacity to overcome hardships. ... I was ready for them, not just physically, but most importantly mentally." (Bogatov, 21)

To get the troops ready, both physically and mentally, the Soviet military strives to create exercise conditions that are as close to those on a real battlefield as possible. They believe in all-weather training and the extensive use of pyrotechnic, light and sound effects. Some of the descriptions of these simulations in exercise episodes in military fiction are quite detailed and suggest that the Soviets are very successful at them.

In his novella *His Father's Son*, Vladimir Vozovikov shows Lt. Ermakov surveying a tank firing range. He sees the burned-out shell of a tank, a telephone pole lying on its side, the wrecks of a bomber and a helicopter, a crater in the side of a hill. "Barren land, a naturalistic portrait of war, with the traces of destruction and death that have been the same since time began. A soldier gets used to it day by day, so that, if he ever has to, he can stand in the enemy's way without flinching." (Vozovikov, 1977, 16)

Vozovikov has an extensive description of an opposing forces FTX in the same novella. Conditions in the exercise training area are more like those on a real battlefield.

> On the left flank, from where the wind was blowing, the report of a gun sounded dully and large fiery balls, orange, reddish-brown, pale green, yellowish-blue sprang in huge arcs along the company's front. [Ermakov could see] a muddled road march formation of somebody else's tanks beyond them. A small column of BTRs[2] out of which troops were hurriedly sprinkling. *Most of the vehicles were on fire.* Tanks moved about senselessly in the yellow dust and black soot. The figures of people rushed around in the white flashes of the explosions and in the crimson tongues of fire." (Vozovikov, 1977, 66 *emphasis* added)

Unless they were using live rounds or a vehicle strayed near a pyrotechnic effect, none of the vehicles should have been on fire. They are, after all, operational vehicles from motor pools in line units and setting an operational vehicle on fire just to add realism to an exercise is expensive, both in terms of money and in operational readiness.

The danger of pyrotechnic effects is demonstrated in an episode from Aleksandr Kuleshov's novel *The White Wind*. Kuleshov's zampolit, Lt. Levashov, is supervising the placement of the pyrotechnic simulation for an exercise. The exercise scenario calls for an air strike to soften up the landing zone (LZ) for the air drop to follow. To simulate the air strike, Levashov's unit has "to plant explosive charges at prearranged places and detonate them on cue, imitating the detonation of the bombs." (Kuleshov, 1977a, 12) This was to be followed by a firefight between the para drop and the defenders, culminating in the destruction of the defenders' rocket emplacements. The charges had to be well-marked and their detonation well-coordinated, because there would be people on the ground and they had to be kept away from the charges as they went off. Levashov was worried that perhaps the markers would be trampled in the heat of the attack and that someone would be in the danger zone when a charge went off.

He personally went out to check the arrangements before the exercise and found a charge not properly marked. Kuleshov uses this episode to show Levashov's conscientious attitude to his duties, but at the same time, he inadvertently shows the inherent danger to the troops participating in the FTX. Certainly not everyone would have been as gung-ho as Levashov, who was essentially a model officer. Any less conscientious effort to check the training area would ultimately translate into exercise casualties as a result of the effort to achieve "conditions maximally approximating those in combat."

Vozovikov returns to a somewhat more realistic description of the simulations in his episode in which there is a notional nuclear strike. "A blinding flash of flame and a deadly mushroom." (Vozovikov, 1977, 68) Ermakov's company was well past ground zero, but "the shockwave caught it well past the converging steep slopes and in the worst instance—if it had been real—would have only blown off their external fuel tanks. But when the giant mushroom cloud of dust and smoke rose up behind them, communications were lost with battalion," and regiment as well, "as if there were a dense zone of ionization all around." (Vozovikov, 1977, 69) While he emphasizes the simulation of the shockwave on the one hand, the element of lost radio communications across the ion cloud that was created by the blast is very realistic. It would have required a well-coordinated effort with an electronic warfare unit to produce the jamming required for the simulation.

In his novella *Recon*, Valerij Kuplevakhskij shows how hard it is to turn sounds into words. His description of the use of magnetic tape recordings to simulate battle noise on an indoor obstacle course used by his recon unit loses something in the translation from sound on tape to words on paper. "The hall shook with screams, wheezes, groans, the whine of shells, explosions, machine gun fire. ... Screams and screams, the kind that make the back of your head go numb." (Kuplevakhskij, 1983, 34)

In his *Nighttime Check*, Anatolij Kuz'michev also tries to describe the use of combat sound effects as Lt. Ignat'ev undergoes a simulated air strike. Ignat'ev had never heard anything like it before, except, maybe, in a war movie, but that was nothing compared to the exercise soundtrack. "The high-pitched roar of jet engines, the whine of bombs, the boom of heavy ordinance, followed by roar, whine, boom." (Kuz'michev, 1982, 158) It almost seemed as if his eardrums were going to break.

Regardless of the difficulty of conveying its effect in the print medium of military fiction, noise is a major component of a soldier's overall perception of the battlefield, and, like the visual effects, is something that the troops have to get used to.

Having replicated the battlefield environment with naturally occurring wind, rain, sleet or snow plus pyrotechnic, light and sound effects, the exercise control staff needs one more element to make their simulation complete: the gods of war. On an FTX, the umpires attached to a unit represent the interests of the notional enemy. (Vozovikov, 1977, 62) "On an exercise, an umpire cannot sympathize or empathize with his charge. He can only arbitrate and judge, give or deny permission, record victory of defeat. Therefore, an umpire on an exercise is the detached objectivity of real combat." (Vozovikov, 1977, 66)

The exercise staff cannot favor one side over another. Both sides are theirs. "Their wish is to place both of them in conditions as close to real combat as possible." (Vozovikov, 1977, 69)

M. Kolosov reiterates this point in his short story, *A Lieutenant's Diary*. He shows a regimental commander addressing the umpires prior to an exercise that they will be grading for his regiment. He enjoins them "not to cut corners. To turn the situation on the map into real life." (Kolosov, 158)

Be the simulation ever so good, if the exercise participants refuse to suspend their disbelief and act as if they really were in combat, the extra effort expended to implement the simulation has been wasted. The failure to suspend disbelief appears to be a widespread phenomenon. There are a large number of works of military fiction that direct their socialist-realist criticism at exactly this problem. Authors find it at all levels of the hierarchy from private soldier to general.

In Valerij Biryukov's *Only Three Days*, Lt. Col. Savel'ev is breaking in his replacement, Maj. Antonenko. For Savel'ev, "an exercise is the same as combat." Antonenko, a recent CGSC graduate, dismisses exercises as just games. "When the battle is real, there will be a combat attitude to go with it," he proclaims. Savel'ev does not accept this, saying:

> Let's say that it is a game. You can't avoid a certain amount of pretend on an exercise. There's nothing you can do about it. But I demand that they treat the game as if it were real. That way, when it's not a game, they won't be confused, they won't need any time to think about what to do. It'll be habit. I want them to react automatically to any unexpected thing that the enemy might throw at them. (Biryukov, 1975, 46)

In his novel *The White Wind*, Kuleshov addresses the topic on another hierarchical level in a brief episode from an FTX, in which one of the new troops is taken to task for his attitude that the FTX is only a game. The new soldier has been designated as "wounded" by the umpire and has to be carried on a stretcher. He complains that he is ashamed to look the stretcher bearers in the eye. He feels like a plantation owner being carried around by black slaves. He suggests that they swap places every kilometer so that nobody gets worn out and they can all get a chance to rest. Everybody gets a big laugh out of his proposal.

One of the Old-timers chimes in sarcastically with "too bad we didn't bring the 'dead' with us. They could have helped out too. What do you think? In combat are the wounded going to swap places with the stretcher bearers? Well?" (Kuleshov, 1977a, 177) The new soldier defends himself by saying that, if this were combat, then things would be different. The Old-timer immediately challenges that assertion. This is combat as for as he is concerned.

Vozovikov then takes the reader back up the chain of command. Cut off from the main body of his division by the notional nuclear strike, Lt. Ermakov continues to advance, taking his company deep behind the notional enemy's lines. At their original object, a river-crossing bridgehead, they encounter a SCUD battalion as it is crossing the bridge and "wipe it out" in a stunning surprise attack. The commander of the opposing side, to which the SCUD battalion belonged, appealed to the military district commander, Gen. Tulupov, to annul the umpires' decision that wiped out his SCUD battalion, because it was based on what he considered some "absurd chance happening. ... Is it worth it to take a rocket battalion out of 'the game,' because of some lost company or other?" (Vozovikov, 1977, 80)

Gen. Tulupov responds angrily that he has no intention of annulling the decision, unless, of course, the opposing division commander wants to admit that it was a joke. He believes in chance, but not in absurd chance happenings.

As for "game," you can tell him: I know the games of soccer, hockey, billiards, and even solitaire. But when thousands of people are deployed round the clock without sleep or a chance to rest, when hundreds of expensive vehicles are using up engine hours and burning fuel, I don't see any game at all. This is combat training and people are learning to fight on the modern battlefield and not to play. (Vozovikov, 1977, 80)

Rybin spends a lot of time in his novel *The Boundary Line* criticizing those who think of field training only as a game. In it he relates how Lt. Col. Avdeev, a new regimental commander, even though he is supported by the division commander, is confounded at every turn as he tries to conduct troop training under conditions as close to actual combat as possible without cutting any corners.

While observing an exercise, Avdeev notices two soldiers bringing up the rear of an assault on a hilltop emplacement. They are walking up the hill instead of running and one of them has his rocket launcher slung under his arm like a boom box instead of at the ready. When he confronts them, one of them replies: "There's not really any enemy. ... And they forget about us anyway. How do you simulate aircraft? You really need more than just the words 'Hostile aircraft.' And there aren't any targets anyway." (Rybin, 1984, 66) Rather than blame the troops, Avdeev blames the company commander for not issuing a combat order that insured that the rocket launcher team was assigned a part of the exercise.

Avdeev's deputy commander, Maj. Krajnov, is just as guilty as the company commander. When Avdeev asks for Krajnov's help in selecting a location for an upcoming exercise, Krajnov selects an area without hesitation. When asked why, he explains: "Our officers and men feel right at home there, comrade lieutenant-colonel. Therefore, there will be fewer mistakes there. I've personally crawled over every meter." (Rybin, 1984, 88) Avdeev disapproves of the suggestion, because using a known training area is one of the ways of cutting corners on the reality of the exercise situation.

Lt. Col. Savel'ev shows why an officer would want to do this, when he warns Maj. Antonenko in Biryukov's *Only Three Days* about Sr. Lt. Avakyan, the commander of the second battery, who likes to try

to look better than he really is, to create the impression of well-being in his battery. After all he's only twenty-five years old. I've outgrown that a long time ago. I don't need a superficial result, but a true grasp of the state of readiness in the battalion. And it's not important for me to conceal or brush over the problem areas in the training of my subordinates, but to find all of them, so that I'll know what I still have to work on.

I don't take people to task for shortcomings that were the result
of ignorance or of not knowing how to do something. Why
should I, if this is the result of my not doing my job? On the
other hand, I really make them answer for fakery. (Biryukov,
1975, 87)

This attitude is all well and good for Savel'ev, who is retiring, but
active duty officers were often concerned with the rating that their unit
would get on an exercise and the subsequent effect that it would have on
their careers. Capt. Ordyntsev, the company commander in Vladimir
Vozovikov's *His Father's Son*, expresses his concern on this issue curtly
and to the point: "This is a real exercise with real "D"s, which will not
be forgotten for years!" (Vozovikov, 1977, 64)

Viktor Filatov presents an episode describing Pvt. Kholomkin on
exercise, in which Kholomkin both rejects and then accepts the reality
of combat training. Kholomkin has dug in, but it cost him six blisters on
his hands. It is raining and his foxhole is filling up with water. They
have been making one assault after another. Running up the hill to the
notional enemy position there and then back down again. Each time the
assault has been rated unsuccessful. His blisters have broken and his
hands are sticking to the stock of his kalashnikov.

Kholomkin begins to think about what they are doing out in the
field in the rain.

This exercise—running up and down the hill—doesn't do a lot
for you in real combat. After all, when you come right down to
it, this is a game. And what's the lieutenant trying to do? Get
us all to run up the hill in step? OK, so we run up the hill for a
while. So what? Will that make us feel like we've been in real
combat? Of course not. It's a useless waste of time. We all know
that this "war" will be over in an hour and a half, tops. You can
always be ready for this kind of war. You win some, you lose
some. It doesn't matter. (Filatov, 1978, 162)

This is a strong setup for a rejection of the usefulness of an exercise,
made all the more so by being presented from the point of view of an
enlisted man, who is ultimately the one who has to carry the battle to
the enemy.

Filatov then shows a transformation taking place in Kholomkin.
"His pride wounded by the unsuccessful assaults, his pumped up
ambition, his anger directed, it seemed, at their senseless actions, at
the bad weather, at the slippery slope of the hill, at the pain he felt
all over his body, at his soggy boots, turned into hate and resolution."
(Filatov, 1978, 162) Together they gave form to the imaginary enemy at
the top of the hill and pushed him on to victory over that enemy.

Filatov's description of the transformation, which is the desired goal of the exercise, is too short. It compresses what Bogatov and Vozovikov present as a long, drawn-out process and rushes Kholomkin from his extreme rejection of the usefulness of the exercise to a change of attitude that culminates in his deciding to remain on active duty and become an officer.

Viktor Stepanov's narrator in his *At the Brandenburg Gate* repeats the pattern of Filatov's story of Pvt. Kholomkin. "No matter how loudly the machine guns thunder or the explosive charges boom, everybody understands that this battle is only an exercise. Nobody is going to get killed in this battle or even wounded. Even the word 'enemy' is so helpless that it has to be written in quotation marks and is not said out loud seriously, but as a joke." (Stepanov, 1973, 93)

Despite this, the troops taking the field that day were as enthusiastic as if there was a real enemy in front of them. Their zeal warmed the hearts of the grey-headed generals, who had come to see them in action. Stepanov's narrator attributes their enthusiasm to the fact that they were in Germany on the forward edge of the embattled Communist Commonwealth. They could feel the threat to their existence that smelled of napalm. That meant that the "enemy" was not so abstract after all. That you could write the word without quotes. You only had to look in the international column of the newspapers everyday to see who this concrete enemy was. (Stepanov, 1973, 95)

Both Filatov and Stepanov have clearly defined the problem: find a way to motivate people to suspend their disbelief. Filatov's string of objects for Kholomkin's anger stumbles on "their senseless actions." All the rest can be motivators on the field of battle, but senseless actions are things to be avoided. Kholomkin's real motivation was probably a realization of necessity as Friedrich Engels put it. If Kholomkin did not show some enthusiasm, the lieutenant would keep them at it all night. Stepanov's identification of a concrete enemy and his reiteration of the threat that this enemy poses is a much more effective approach.

In Aleksandr Kuleshov's *The Nighttime Sun*, Gen. Chajkovskij thinks about the importance of training in terms of his experience in the war. He had always been taught to act as if he were not on an exercise, but in actual combat, which "is like ABC in any exercise." He had seen people training with him, who were just doing the minimum, because "they considered training just training and not combat." While he never kept count, they always seemed to be the first to get killed. "They paid for the sweat they saved then in blood. Everybody knows the truth in 'rough on the training field, easy on the battlefield,' but, unfortunately, not everybody pays heed to it." (Kuleshov, 1981, 247)

Yurij Pronyakin echoes Kuleshov's dire warning in his novel of service academy cadets in the late forties, *Cadets*. Sr. Lt. Antonov is making the rounds of his student company on FTX to see how well each of the cadets had dug in. He finds one cadet who has dug in behind a boulder, which obstructs his field of fire. When pressed, the cadet admits that the location that he chose for his foxhole was not a good one. Antonov attacks him for his indifferent attitude to their current field exercise.

> You decided that it's night, nobody's going to notice anything and there's no real, live enemy anyhow, so what difference does it make where I dig my foxhole. ... And that's very sad. If you don't learn to skillfully pick a location for a firing position during the hours of darkness here, it'll be worse at the front. You'll have to pay for the lessons there in blood. (Pronyakin, 1954, 52)

Pronyakin's and Kuleshov's approach is to motivate people to serve their own self-interest of survival on the battlefield. The use of this approach, however, fell off sharply as the last of the World War II veterans disappeared from the scene.

The Soviets can produce the sights and sounds of the battlefield, but the gods of the exercise only have the power to remove people from the game. They do not have the power of real death. Death and the fear of death are the primary elements missing from any exercise, no matter how otherwise realistic. Like Stepanov's narrator said, "Nobody is going to get killed in this battle or even wounded." (Stepanov, 1973, 93) In real combat, people do get killed, and the realization of this fact is hard to achieve on exercise, even though the Soviets do try.

The failure of a commander to make the realization that "they are not firing blanks here, but live rounds that separate the quick from the dead" (Ivanov, 1987, 39) can easily lead to officers, who treat their troops like expendable "paper soldiers" (Kikeshev, 1992, 53) instead of like people: if one of the old ones gets torn up, then just get some new ones.

NOTES

1. A mustang is an officer, who served as an enlisted man before getting his commission.
2. BTR is the designator for a Soviet-produced armored personnel carrier.

11

They Shoot Intruders, Don't They?

And I would say that even [the] political leadership will not dare to punish the military. The military did what they have to do. They would be court-martialed, if they wouldn't fulfill the order from ground control. There is a law; there is a regulation. ... It was [the] Politburo and the political leadership, who approve these laws, which permit—not permit, but order the pilots to shoot any intruder in Soviet [air] space.

Arkady Shevchenko
on the KAL 007 shoot down[1]

On 24 March 1985, Maj. Arthur D. "Nick" Nicholson, Jr. of the United States Military Liaison Mission (USMLM) to the commander, Group of Soviet Forces, Germany, was shot and killed by a Soviet sentry near Ludwigslust in East Germany. This incident produced an outpouring of enraged indignation among the American military. There was a feeling that the Soviets had changed the rules under which USMLM and the Soviet Military Liaison Mission (SMLM) in Frankfurt had operated during the Cold War.

There are five works of postwar Soviet military fiction that touch on the issue of a sentry firing on an intruder. Four of them were written before 1985 and one after. These stories present firing on intruders as standard operating procedure (SOP) in the Soviet military. The inclusion of these episodes in the socialist-realist genre of military fiction was frequent enough to indicate that this was a real-life issue worthy of the attention of the authorities and official writers. The number of episodes is not, however, suggestive of something that was a daily occurrence.

The first work of postwar military fiction to approach the issue of the use of deadly force to protect military facilities in peacetime is Vladimir Komissarov's *Guards Lieutenant*, which plays in 1948. In Komissarov's story, Lt. Poplavskij and Nina are out walking on base together at night and lose their way. They wander into an area under guard and are challenged by a sentry:

> "Halt! Who goes there?"
>
> Nina shuddered and clung to Poplavskij in fear. He put his arm around her.
>
> "What's the matter, silly? They're not talking to us."
>
> He took a step forward and the hoarse voice, which now had taken on a threatening quality, said again:
>
> "Halt! Who goes there?"
>
> "Damn it," mumbled Poplavskij. "Where the devil have we gotten to, Ninka? Friend!" he yelled loudly. "What are you yelling for? Your post is way over there and we're going over there."
>
> "Halt! Who goes there? I'll fire!" yelled the voice in the dark, this time even more threateningly.
>
> "I'll fire you!" yelled Poplavskij, trying not to let his voice shake. "Don't you have anything to do? It's me, Lt. Poplavskij."
>
> There were several seconds of silence, then Poplavskij turned round decisively, took Nina by the arm and they left. (Komissarov, 85)

This scenario is repeated almost exactly in 1979 in Aleksandr Belyaev's novel *The Runway*. Belyaev, however, takes the scene a bit further than Komissarov. In Belyaev's story, Capt. Kol'tsov and Yulya are out walking on base together at night and lose their way. They wander into an area under guard and are challenged by a sentry:

> "Halt! Who goes there?" said a forceful shout, coming unexpectedly out of the dark.
>
> Kol'tsov and Yulya stopped, taken aback.
>
> "Damn it!" suddenly cursed Kol'tsov in a whisper. "I forgot that they put a guard post out here."
>
> "Halt! Who goes there? I'll fire!" said the voice again in the dark.
>
> "It's me, captain Kol'tsov!" said Kol'tsov identifying himself ...
>
> "On the ground!" commanded the sentry and an automatic weapon burst resounded in the dark of the night.
>
> Without hesitation Kol'tsov grabbed Yulya by the

shoulders and threw her on the ground. ...

"Don't get up for anything!" he warned her in a whisper.

"Why did he shoot?" asked Yulya, also in a whisper.

"Regulations."

"Nice regulation!"

"Sentry, it's me, captain Kol'tsov. Don't you recognize me?"

The sentry was silent.

"What? Won't he listen to you?" asked Yulya with a touch of irony this time.

"He's not permitted to talk with us at all."

"Are we going to lie here a long time?"

"Until the corporal of the guard comes."

"Is that also part of the regulations?" (Belyaev, 1979, 59-60)

Both these amazingly similar scenes present the use of deadly force by sentries as a relatively commonplace incident. There is no subsequent follow-up in either story. The incidents simply appear to be part of the background of life at a military base. Belyaev's episode is much more serious than Komissarov's. Once the sentry fired his warning shot, the incident could have easily escalated, if Capt. Kol'tsov had not gotten down and stayed down still until the corporal of the guard came.

Aleksej Kireev shows that it could have been much more serious indeed in his *The Pines Roar Ominously* (1983). Jr. Lt. Stepanenko wanted to check up on the sentry from his platoon standing guard at post number seven, the arsenal. He crawled up to the post in the dark so as to take the sentry by surprise and see if he was really awake or not. The sentry was awake and noticed Stepanenko approaching his post: "Halt! Don't move!"

Stepanenko froze, but did not say anything. Even though the sentry recognized Stepanenko, he commanded: "On the ground, or I'll fire!" Like Kol'tsov and Poplavskij, Stepanenko tried to talk his way out of the situation, but the sentry stuck to the regulations. Raising the stock of his weapon to his shoulder, he commanded: "I'm warning you! If you don't get on the ground ..." (Kireev, 90)

With Stepanenko on the ground, the sentry rang the alarm to call for the corporal of the guard. After the corporal of the guard had freed Stepanenko from his predicament, Stepanenko walked off without saying a thing. The corporal read the sentry the riot act. "He'll have us all thrown in the guardhouse now," and pulled the sentry from his post early.

The sentry calmly stood his ground and said that he had only been following the regulations. Kireev backs him up. When the commandant of the academy, where the action of the novella takes place, hears of the incident, he calls Stepanenko in and reads him the riot act: "How could you, an expert on the regs, do something like this? Were you

trying to catch yourself a bullet, my dear? ... Were you trying to get to
the next world early, or something? That boy could have just as easily
pulled the trigger, and then try and figure out what happened."
(Kireev, 91) To insure that the lesson sinks in to Stepanenko, the
commandant then proceeds to give the sentry a ten-day pass as a
reward for following regulations to the letter.

Vladislav Sosnovskij's novella *Cold and Hot* (1976) approaches
the issue from a slightly different angle. Sosnovskij explores the
psychological questions raised by a young draftee as he contemplates
the possibility of having to use deadly force while on guard duty in
peacetime. Sosnovskij is the first to show that there really is a reason
for the SOP. He presents a conversation between Pvt. Repkin and the
commander of the radio beacon detachment where he is assigned, Sgt.
Letov. Repkin asks what should he do if he saw something moving
towards his post in the dark. Sosnovskij has him answer his own
question.

> "According to the regulations, you are supposed to holler:
> 'Halt! Who goes there?' Let's say I holler and it still keeps
> coming. Then according to the regulations you are supposed to
> yell: 'Halt! or I'll fire!' But it still keeps coming. Now it comes
> down to firing into the air. You fire and it's still coming. What
> do you do then? There's only one thing left and that's to put one
> into the intruder. Right?"
>
> "Right, but there is still the alarm," said Tkach [one of the
> other EM at the detachment].
>
> "That's for sure, but the alarm could be a long way away
> and this person close by. So I bring my rifle to the ready,
> bang—and that's it. It turns out that he was deaf or something,
> or drunk, been out carousing with his buddies and is on his way
> home to his wife and kids, or maybe, he was just in love and
> was wandering around in a fog and did not hear anything. How
> am I supposed to live with myself after that? Our Spak [the
> deputy detachment commander] got all wound up yesterday.
> You have to do your duty, he yells, no matter what."

Sgt. Letov responds by recalling an incident that happened a while
back. A soldier named Vasilij from the neighboring company was on
guard duty in the motor pool in the middle of town. That is a real low
threat area.

> But, all of a sudden, in between the vehicles, there was this
> some guy he did not know. Vasilij noticed him and said: "Halt!
> This isn't a dance hall." The guy started to cry, he was
> apologizing: "I'm sorry," he says. "I didn't mean to. I got lost."

O.K. so Vasilij put his gun back on his shoulder and walks up to him. "If that's the way it is, I'll walk you out." He didn't even get the words out of his mouth before this guy sticks a knife into him right up to the hilt. Vasilij was a strong cuss and with the last of his strength he got off a shot and wounded the SOB. The guys caught the jerk, but Vasilij was gone. ... Therefore, a post is a post and we don't wear our uniforms for sentiment's sake. (Sosnovskij, 35)

Sosnovskij's story of an armed intruder suggests a higher level of violent crime in the Soviet Union than was commonly believed to exist. This is apparently the reason for the existence of the SOP for the use of deadly force on guard duty.

The next work of military fiction to explore this issue was the one written after Maj. Nicholson's death. Anatolij Polyanskij's *Afghan Syndrome* (1990) is a postsocialist-realist work, which is subtly different from the other socialist-realist works before it. It shows that the SOP for the use of deadly force to guard military installations still stands, and that crime by armed robbers is still the reason for it. Polyanskij clearly shows that his main character, Capt. Kretov, an Afghan vet, firmly believes in the use of deadly force to deal with intruders, but the ending of the story reopens the question and leaves it unanswered.

The scene is a garrison inside the Soviet Union. The players are Afghan vets. Capt. Kretov has resigned his commission because of the reception that the regular Army is giving Afghan vets. Vanya Pospekhin served as a private under Capt. Kretov in Afghanistan. He has been driven to a life of crime by the reception that society is giving Afghan vets. As the scene opens, Kretov has relinquished his command and is pulling other duties as assigned until his discharge paperwork is complete. He is checking the guard posts, when shots are fired at post number two.

The sentry at post number two had heard some noise at the next post and fired at something moving in the shadows. They run to the next post, where they find the sentry tied up with a gag in his mouth and the door to the arsenal open. It was a professional job. They had even taken out the alarm system so that it did not ring at the corporal of the guard's shack.

Kretov heard a sound in the bushes on the other side of the barbed wire and rushed to see what it was. The barbed wire had been cut. The sound got louder. Kretov yells: "Halt!" and takes out his pistol. The intruder begins to run and Kretov begins to run after him: "'Halt, or I'll fire!' and fires into the air."

Kretov thought that he saw something familiar in the large, ungainly figure of the man that he was following. But there was no time to figure out what it was. Besides, that was stupid, of course! Kretov raised his pistol. For a moment, he hesitated: that's not a bad guy, but it is a bandit! Am I going to let him get away? Not for anything! (Polyankskij, 1990, No. 13, p. 87)

Kretov did not let him get away. His second shot was on target. When he gets to the body, he sees that the intruder was armed with an automatic weapon. "'Why didn't he shoot?' thought Kretov with detachment and turned the man over on his back with a jerk. He took a look and froze. The hair stood up on his head. It was Vanya Pospekhin, his faithful war buddy, who had once saved his life, lying on the ground in front of him." (Polyankskij, 1990, No. 13, p. 87)

An ending like this would not have been possible under socialist-realism. In Sosnovskij's story, it was the sentry who got killed, but he was only a flat character. Pospekhin is someone the reader knows. He is a lost, but gallant soul. He has saved Kretov's life again, this time at the cost of his own.

As the story draws to a climax, Polyanskij plants the seeds of doubt in the justification for the use of deadly force. He has Kretov hesitate, when he thinks that he recognizes something familiar in the fleeing figure of the intruder. Taken to its logical conclusion, Kretov's hesitation would have become a decision not to fire, if he had recognized Pospekhin. This seed of doubt is the first step of calling the whole policy of the use of deadly force into doubt. Something that the death of Maj. Nicholson failed to do, but the sentry who shot him did not know him.

NOTE

1. The MacNeil/Lehrer News Hour, 6 September 1983.

12

Afghanistan

When you're wounded and left on Afghanistan's plains
And the women come out to cut up what remains
Just roll to your rifle and blow out your brains
An' go to your Gawd like a soldier.

Rudyard Kipling
The Young British Soldier (1892)

These lines from Kiplings's poem, even though written over a hundred years ago, are not at all out of place alongside the modern prose of Soviet authors writing about the war in Afghanistan. The reality of combat on the ground in Afghanistan was much the same for the Soviets as it was for the British. Valerij Povolyaev's hero, Sgt. Knyazev in *"H" Hour* even notes that the bad guys are still shooting at the Soviets with old flintlock rifles left over from the time of the English Expeditionary Corps. (Povolyaev, 147 & 196)

Kipling recommended that wounded British soldiers blow out their brains for the same reason that the Russians dreaded the thought of capture by the Afghans. The fate of the wounded and captives was not very pleasant. In his short story *Krez and Cleopatra*, Leonid Bogachuk shows that "cut up what remains" is quite literally one of the possibilities: "Working with knives, they cut off the dead men's hands, ears, sexual organs and mutilated their faces. That was what they had been ordered to do to the enemy to instill fear in the rest, who had sold themselves to the unfaithful." (Bogachuk, 397)

The tactic was certainly successful with the Soviet troops, as can be seen in Sergej Belikov's *A Foreign Sky*. Belikov describes Lt. Soloshchenko's dread of being taken prisoner after his chopper goes down in hostile territory, leaving him injured and unarmed. For Lt. Soloshchenko

> death is a lesser evil than capture. At best they send you to a POW [prisoner of war] camp in Pakistan to croak slowly from hunger and beatings and you don't even want to think about the worst case. They chop off your hands and feet, poke out your eyes, cut off your ears and nose and castrate you. (Belikov, 67)

Belikov follows the lieutenant's efforts to exfiltrate to friendly territory for three excruciating days until, finally, the lieutenant is seen by a young Afghan girl drawing water at a pond. Instead of killing her to prevent her from giving him away, he lets her live. The story then builds to its climax as the mujahedeen chase Soloshchenko into the mountains using dogs to track him. As they close in on him, he longs to be able to take some of them with him, but injured and unarmed, he can only continue to run. Finally, exhausted and at the edge of a cliff, he does the only thing he can do to humiliate his tormentors before he steps over the edge to escape them in eternity: he shoots them the finger.

Aleksandr Prokhanov's main character in *The Mountains*, Sgt. Vagapov shows the same resolve not to be captured. Prokhanov's description of the torture awaiting POWs is not as vivid as Belikov's, but it echoes his terrors well enough: "burn him with red hot pieces of metal, cut him to pieces." (Prokhanov, 1989, 240) Vagapov, however, unlike Soloshchenko, has two grenades and knows what to do. The political officer has talked about this kind of situation at meetings before. Vagapov has read about it in the Unit Newsletter.

He is going to take one grenade in each hand and as the mujahedeen get close enough, he is going to pull both pins out with his teeth and hide the grenades behind his back. Then he will wait until they come to get him and take them with him. (Prokhanov, 1989, 242) Vagapov is much luckier than Soloshchenko. The air cavalry arrives at the last minute to shoot up the bad guys and pick him up. He eventually even makes it back to the USSR to get married and start a family.

Nikolaj Ivanov covers the same ground in his novella *Storm over Gindukush Mountain*, but does it from the point of view of the bad guys. This is a very effective propaganda piece for showing how brave the Russians are and how much respect the bad guys have for them. This approach, however, lacks the impact that stories have when told from the point of view of the man making the decision to pull the pin.

As the bad guys close in on the wounded and unconscious Lt. Spirin and Sgt. Novikov, the band leader comments to himself on how brave they have been. If he had men like these he could really fight a good fight. Not only would the government troops be afraid of him, but the other bands as well. When he gets nearer, he sees the outlines of a grenade in the lieutenant's hands, and yells for his people to get back. (Ivanov, 1986, 46) The image is a very strong one, showing that the bad guys are even afraid of unconscious Russians. For Spirin, just like Vagapov, the air cavalry arrives in the nick of time and he returns to the USSR to get married.

The number of times that the scenario of a soldier alone, deciding to seek death rather than submit to the horrors of capture, is repeated by different authors, including Kipling, points to a phenomenon that is undoubtedly part of the common experience of Afghanistan, which is shared by every Soviet who served there. Even if they did not experience it themselves or know someone who did, the widespread propaganda effort, hinted at by Prokhanov in his episode with Vagapov, certainly would have made them aware of it.

Aleksandr Prokhanov takes the reader into captivity in his story *The Grey-headed Soldier*. Prokhanov's main character, Pvt. Nikolaj Morozov, actually does get captured by the mujahedeen. He is taken to a vill in the mountains, where he is approached by an Englishman, Mr. Edward Staf, ostensibly working for Reuters. Staf asks that Morozov give him a recorded interview, in which he tell the world why he defected to the Afghan freedom fighters. Staf says that if Morozov gives him the interview, then he will be protected from the mujahedeen by the notoriety that the interview gives him. If Morozov does not want to give Staf the interview he is asking for, then what happens to Morozov afterward is entirely out of Staf's hands.

Once Staf is gone, maybe the mujahedeen will cut off Morozov's hands and feet "for fun," or maybe they will tie him to a horse and drag him around the vill "for fun." Maybe, and this is the best of the alternatives, they will just put a bullet through his head, but then again they might pump him full of opium, so that he will not try to escape, and take him on the road with them through the mountains, where he will die of heat stroke after a week or two. (Prokhanov, 1987, 367)

Prokhanov lets us in on Morozov's thoughts as he faces off against Staf in a battle of wills. Morozov appears to have been even less prepared for capture than Prokhanov's other character, Sgt. Vagapov. Morozov knew that the training he had received in the garrison just across the border in Turkmenistan on how to shoot, throw grenades, hold a defensive position in the mountains would not help him in this battle. (Prokhanov, 1987, 362) Nevertheless, he finds the inner strength to make Soloshchenko's choice and not to give in to the blandishments of the Englishman.

In looking for a place to conduct the interview, Staf takes Morozov to the edge of the vill where the slope of the mountain drops steeply off through jagged rocks and a minefield to a river below. (Prokhanov,

1987, 363) Morozov follows Soloshchenko's lead and jumps over the edge rather than betray his country and friends. Unlike Soloshchenko, however, Morozov amazingly survives the fall and the mines and Prokhanov continues the story with a description of his agonizing trek through the mountains for two days before he is found by friendly Afghans and returned to his unit.

This short story is clearly a reaction to the reports in the Western press about Russian soldiers who had defected to the mujahedeen and later were exfiltrated to America and the United Kingdom. The statements that Staf is trying to get Morozov to make echo those that appeared in the Western press from the defectors.[1] Staf just wants Morozov to

> talk about the horrible situation that you got pushed into. How much misfortune you have seen. How much you have been tormented by thinking about this. Then finally you made your choice. You ran away to the Afghan freedom fighters from your garrison, from your cruel commanders, who keep sending you out to face death. (Prokhanov, 1987, 357)

Staf's pitch to Morozov to do an anti-Soviet article for the Western press is just a throwback to the Cold War propaganda of the late fifties. It is paralleled in Vadim Sobko's novel in a less pressurized scene, in which a German writer, Gerhart Boler, is approached by an American correspondent with a prewritten article "full of lies about the Soviet occupation Forces." (Sobko, 138) All Boler has to do is put his name at the bottom. Like Morozov, Boler shows the necessary willpower to reject the pitch of the agent of imperialism and goes on to write a positive novel of life in the Soviet zone of occupation.

Prokhanov presents a very strong picture of the psychological pressure that Morozov is under, so that the reader will find it easy to believe the standard Soviet response to statements from deserters: the statement was made under duress and cannot be true. He sets the stage for the pitch to the young soldier in gory detail. First Morozov sees the ritual slaughter of a calf right in front of his cell. The carcass is hung on the wall opposite the cell so that it can be butchered, but before the butchers are finished, the guards come for a nameless Afghan soldier in the cell with Morozov. (Prokhanov, 1987, 353) At that point, Prokhanov skillfully ties the fate of the soldier with that of the calf by having Morozov notice a facial resemblance between the two. They march the soldier up to the wall, where the carcass had hung minutes before, with the Englishman taking pictures the whole while. Just as Morozov expects to hear a rifle shot ending the soldier's life, the Englishman stops the execution and the soldier is marched back away from the wall toward the cell. Morozov breaths a sigh of relief. This was just a mock execution put on for his benefit. Morozov can see the soldier's face. It is pale and lifeless. The expression on it "is as if he [the soldier] had lived through his own death and was now walking around dead." (Prokhanov, 1987, 360)

Morozov was wrong. The only reason to march the soldier back to the cell was that the Englishman had to change cameras. The first march to the wall had been photographed in color and Staf wanted to do it again in black and white. When they get the soldier to the wall the second time, they really do put a bullet through his head.

While the mujahedeen are clearly the negative heroes in Afghanistan, the positive hero is the gallant Soviet knight in shining armor, who is morally superior to the capitalist enemy. In his novella *The Mountain Pass*, Ivanov describes an episode in which the Russians are in a vill to get water at the well there for their detachment. While they try to find a bucket to draw water from the well, a group of boys comes up to their BMPs and asks for food. One of the soldiers rips open a packet of K rations and starts handing out rusks. Before he can finish, the Soviets start taking fire from the mujahedeen. When the shooting starts, all the boys disappear, except one, who stays behind only just long enough to place a satchel charge under the water tank and blow it up. This is a very serious blow to the detachment guarding the pass, because the well in the vill and the water tank are the detachment's only source of water. With hostile activity increasing in the area, not having water in supply places them in a precarious tactical position in the parched mountains of Afghanistan. The soldier, who had been handing out the rusks, is lining up his sights on the boy, who placed the charge, when his squad leader stops him, admonishing: "It's only a kid, Kostya!" (Ivanov, 1987, 30) The squad leader cannot bring himself to permit a subordinate to shoot at children even if they are obviously hostiles.

Ivanov presents a slightly different version of big-brotherly concern in his novella *Storm over Gindukush Mountain*. He shows the reader how the Russians save a thirteen-year-old girl from a hostile mujahedeen band by interposing their BTR between the girl and the band. The BTR immediately takes a hit from a rocket launcher and one of the crew is seriously wounded. (Ivanov, 1986, 30) As they are loading the girl and the wounded man into a chopper, still another member of the crew is shot in the back. (Ivanov, 1986, 36) Specifying that he was "shot in the back" serves to make the bad guys seem even more dastardly than they were before.

The same type of gallantry, at an even higher personal cost, is displayed by Lt. Soloshchenko in Sergej Belikov's *A Foreign Sky*. Soloshchenko, alone and unarmed behind enemy lines, makes a conscious decision not to kill the Afghan girl, who sees him at a pond, even though he knows that she will give him away and "will become the cause of his death." As the mujahedeen close in for the kill, Soloshchenko reviews his decision and is not sorry for it. He wishes the girl well and hopes she has lots of kids. (Belikov, 73)

In Nikolaj Burbyga's *The Pacification Detachment* we see young Sgt. Sergej Lebedev give his life trying to rescue an Afghan boy who is being used as a hostage by the mujahedeen. (Burbyga, 279) Burbyga contrasts this gallant deed to the rumors being spread by the mujahedeen that the Soviets eat children. The Russians in the story are confronted by the reality of the rumor when they meet a little girl in a vill, who begs them not to eat her. They, however, quickly convince her that they are the good guys by giving her some food and candy. (Burbyga, 272) When they leave the vill, she comes out to wave good-bye to them.

The overall impression from scenes of this type is one of a black and white cowboy movie, where the good guys wear Aussie hats and the bad guys wear turbans. This is typical of the black and white contrasting picture of Afghanistan in socialist-realist Soviet military fiction. The mujahedeen are ruthless and cruel. The Soviets are gallant and kind.

While the Soviets are in Afghanistan giving their lives for the greater glory of the Internationalist movement (Selikhov, 95), the mujahedeen are only in it for the money as far as authors of military fiction are concerned. Nikolaj Ivanov's mujahedeen leaders both talk about the money they get for their efforts and how their troops' reliability increases with the amount that they are paid. (Ivanov, 1987, 53-54; Ivanov, 1986, 23 &25)

Kim Selikhov, whose heroes are Afghan rather than Russian officers and whose works are peppered with Pushtu words, shows the same thing in his novella *Echo of the Mountains of Afghanistan*. Money and presents are the reward promised by Selikhov's evil Lt. Col. Lewis of the CIA for every dead heathen. (Selikhov, 130) One of Lewis' mujahedeen minions, in showing off how much he has already earned from his bosses, brags that they are not miserly and "pay well for the blood of the unfaithful." (Selikhov, 133)

In Aleksandr Prokhanov's *The Muslim Wedding*, the cooperation of Sejfuddin, one of the local warlords, is bought by Kabul. (Prokhanov, 1990, 93) Prokhanov's intelligence officer, Lt. Col. Berezkin, is pleased with the success of his idea to buy Sejfuddin's loyalty.

I've become convinced, comrade colonel, that all this talk about Islam, a Holy War, the Green Flag of Allah, that those embassy eggheads put out, is just a screen. The East recognizes strength and submits to it! And takes money, no matter who is handing it out! And Allah favors those, who have the most knives and afghanies.[2] (Prokhanov, 1990, 102)

In his *Hit Parade on the "Anaconda"* Col. Nikolaj Kikeshev gives the reader a glimpse of the frustration of the troops in Afghanistan at not being able to persecute the war successfully, because of all the restrictions placed on them by the high command. This has a certain similarity to the way that American troops in Vietnam were hamstrung by their rules of engagement. Kikeshev shows the reader a skit put on in a spetsnaz unit that is worthy of a Gilbert and Sullivan operetta plot.

An actor comes on stage dressed as a general with theatrically oversized red stripes down the sides of his trouser legs and a comically long sabre. He puts on a pince-nez and then proceeds to discuss an upcoming operation with Lt. Ivanov:

> "Comrade general, I've decided to attack the rebels here!"
> "No, no, it's dangerous there."
> "Then would you approve here?" said Ivanov, looking at the general imploringly.
> "No, no and no! The mountains are high there."
> "What if we flank the bad guys' stronghold from the rear?"
> "Can't go there. That's the border. I for-bid it!"
> The general draws his sabre and starts to point with it.
> "Can't go here! Can't go there! Can't go anywhere! But tomorrow you have to report that you annihilated the enemy group or I'll cut off your head with this sabre."

The last line of the skit also hints at the pressure that Petrovskij was under from Oborin to get body counts and weapons to turn in. Having seen the skit, Kikeshev's Maj. Bokov finds it so true to life that he breaks out laughing. He had been in the same situation several times himself. (Kikeshev, 1992, 55)

Nikolaj Ivanov, a professional political officer and one-time editor of the magazine *Soviet Warrior*, provides a positive, socialist-realist description of what went on inside a good commander's head in Afghanistan. In his novella *The Mountain Pass*, Ivanov lets us look over the shoulder of Sr. Lt. Trunin, the commander of a platoon in a remote outpost guarding a mountain pass. As is to be expected from Ivanov's background as a political officer, concern for the lives of his men is the basis of Trunin's world view as a commander. It is Trunin's belief that, when you are responsible for the lives of others, you are more careful and weigh a course of action more carefully before implementing it. He opines that "the weight of responsibility for subordinates in combat often is a determining factor in the success of the mission," because it prevents you from taking rash, unpremeditated actions. (Ivanov, 1987, 24) He is loath to risk the lives of his men unnecessarily, and feels that "the only feat of valor that is required of a commander and the one, for which he should be rewarded, is the creation of a situation that does not require sacrifice, not even heroic sacrifice. There cannot be anything more important for an officer than that." (Ivanov, 1987, 15) He, therefore, does not trust to "luck" to complete the mission. Trunin trains his men hard even though he knows that they don't like it, because he knows that the harder they train and the more confident they are of themselves as soldiers, the more likely they are to go home at the end of their tour in Afghanistan. (Ivanov, 1987, 14-15) For him combat is not like an FTX, where, if you make a mistake, you can start all over again. "They are not firing blanks here, but live rounds that separate the quick from the dead." (Ivanov, 1987, 39) He weighs each decision carefully until he is sure that it is the only correct one for the given situation, preferring not to give any orders to his men until he is confident of his decision.

As a commander, there is nothing worse for Trunin than "when, on his orders, more danger falls on the shoulders of his subordinates than on his own." (Ivanov, 1987, 47) Trunin justifies putting his subordinates in harm's way, while keeping the commander safe, as something that is necessary to keep the whole unit alive. This justification is echoed by Lt. Negmatov in Valerij Povolyaev's "H" Hour. When Negmatov takes casualties, his first impulse is to rush to the aid of the wounded, but he suppresses it, reasoning that "the platoon cannot be left without a commander." (Povolyaev, 168) Trunin also has the same impulse when, despite his careful planning, he too takes casualties, but like Negmatov, he suppresses the impulse, because a commander's first duty is always to think of the living. (Ivanov, 1987, 66)

The positions of these two officers say a lot about the philosophy of command in the Soviet military in general. Despite the constant attention paid to interchangeability of unit members and the number of works of military fiction in which a subordinate successfully does take over for a "fallen" commander or leader, protecting the commander still remains an important goal in Soviet military operations, because he is the one with all the experience and knowledge of the situation.

Trunin comes off in the novella as a good commander, because over his two-year tour of duty as commander of the outpost at the pass, he suffers only one fatal casualty and one casualty resulting in a medevac to the USSR. He cares about his troops and it shows in the way that Ivanov has the troops react to him. Negmatov is more aloof than Trunin. Nevertheless, he too cares about his men. Povolyaev stresses his presence in combat and how he reacts in a firefight, placing more emphasis on the action than on Negmatov's character.

In his Hit Parade on the "Anaconda" which was written after the dissolution of the USSR and the loosening of the bonds of socialist-realism, Col. Nikolaj Kikeshev shows that not every commander was as concerned about his troops as were Trunin or Negmatov. Kikeshev takes the reader to a birthday party at a spetsnaz unit in Afghanistan that degenerates into a name-calling contest after a toast to fallen comrades. The tension at the party builds when Maj. Bogun comments: "that was a stupid way for Shchebnev to die" (Kikeshev, 1992, 52), referring to an enlisted man, who drowned when his BTR flooded during a forced river crossing. This leads to an exchange of accusations between Bogun and Maj. Bokov, who was Shchebnev's commander, over which of them has suffered the most casualties for stupid reasons.

Bogun accuses Bokov of treating his troops like expendable "paper soldiers" (Kikeshev, 1992, 53), instead of like people: if one of the old ones gets torn up, then just get some new ones. Bogun's conclusion is that it was Bokov's attitude about the inevitability of casualties in war that got Shchebnev drowned. This is the exact opposite of Trunin's philosophy. Khudakov joins Bogun in attacking Bokov, asking how Bokov could have done such a thing in view of the pitifully low level of experience among the troops. Bokov should not have pushed into the crossing straight from the march, but should have stopped to reconnoiter the river and check his vehicles before they started out. Bokov contends that he did not have time to do this, because of the tactical situation.

Kikeshev has Bokov explain this incongruously aggressive behavior between spetsnaz officers, in what should be a cohesive fighting unit, as an attempt by them to ease their bad consciences. "Don't try to make me feel guilty," retorts Bokov. "We're all really good, aren't we? Everyone of us has a sin on his conscience. That's why we are jumping down each other's throats. To assuage the pain." (Kikeshev, 1992, 53)

The low level of troop experience that Khudakov referred to is a recurring topic in Soviet military fiction that never seems to be entirely resolved, but is just a factor that needs to be reckoned with. It is a result of the draft cycle. The troops are only just becoming competent when they are released from the service. The recognition of this problem is, in part, at the root of Trunin's and Negmatov's reasoning as to why the commander should be kept out of harm's way to protect the unit.

In his novella *Storm over Gindukush Mountain*, Nikolaj Ivanov views the same issue from another angle, when he shows the reader how a colonel, who has already earned his spurs, reacts when it is time to leave Afghanistan and turn over his unit to a new commander. He feels a strong sense of responsibility to his subordinates and "is afraid" to turn his people over to someone new with "less experience." (Ivanov, 1986, 38) Col. Kulikov has been in command a long time, and wishes that he could leave all his experience, traditions and memories there for the new commander for the good of the people, who will be staying behind, when he goes home. (Ivanov, 1986, 38)

The issue of experience as viewed from the Afghan mountains looks no different than it did when it was raised by another generation of authors in their coverage of the changing of the guard during the seventies, the time frame in which the last of the World War II generation of officers were forced into retirement by their age and poor health. They too were concerned that the new officers replacing them, who had never been under fire, did not have enough experience to take over their jobs.

Viewed from the standpoint of an "experienced" commander turning over his unit to a new commander, there can only be one outcome; the orders have been cut and the old commander has to leave in the end, even if his departure is delayed. Viewed from the point of view of the men, who will follow the new commander into combat, there are a number of issues that can be raised—foremost of which is the question: will following this man's orders get me killed?

Confidence of the men in their leader is one of the pillars of the legitimacy of command and can be a very real problem for an army in combat. The leaders have to be respected by the troops, not because the Central Committee or the Congress said that they were officers and gentlemen, but because they are leaders and do care about the troops.

Aleksandr Prokhanov tackles this issue briefly, in his novella *The Mountains*. Through the eyes of his hero, Sgt. Vagapov, the reader sees a colonel, who has served his entire career in "ageless rear garrisons," never having been under hostile fire. As the colonel hesitates when it is time to move forward into the area of a firefight to survey the situation, Vagapov could see that the colonel needed to prove to himself that "he was not afraid of mines and bullets and therefore had the right to send others into battle" to face these same dangers. Vagapov, however, is riding on the skin of the BMP carrying the colonel into the battle area and resents being exposed to the danger of hostile fire just so this middle-aged officer can strengthen his character. (Prokhanov, 1989, 220) This is put a bit more succinctly by one of the bit players in Sergej Sokolov's *The Tiger's Claw* when, in a similar situation, he comments: "in general, all this heroism at somebody else's expense, stinks to high heaven." (Sokolov, 83) Even though Vagapov's colonel does eventually overcome his hesitation, the description of the incident highlights the concern of the front-line troops in Afghanistan, that a commander with no combat experience might just get them killed while he learns the ropes.

In *The Mountains*, Prokhanov further develops the theme of legitimacy of command, but at the platoon level. At this level, he describes the dislike of the troops for the new platoon leader, who had never led troops into battle before. The old platoon leader, who had served out his tour of duty and gone back to the USSR, is described as "smart, competent and brave," while Sgt. Vagapov sees the new platoon leader as "too loud." His orders are "abrupt and too much like he was on a parade field" (Prokhanov, 1989, 217), which in the vernacular of the American Army would have been expressed as he was "too mickey mouse."

In his novella *The Replacement*, Andrej Dyshev takes a look at a newly arrived senior lieutenant's revelations about the "mickey mouse" nature of garrison life in the USSR, when compared to the realities of combat in Afghanistan. Sr. Lt. Stepanov is only hours off the plane in Kabul and on his way to his unit, when the officer escorting him is killed in a firefight not far from his new unit. Stepanov realizes that his whole perception of military service, based on his garrison duty in the USSR, is out of line with the realities of combat in Afghanistan.

> What kind of stupid and senseless things I did there [in the USSR]! All that running around like a mouse that I wasted my nerves and time on is so very laughable. How naive I was, when I couldn't sleep all night before a pass in review and I thought that there was nothing worse in life than to slip on a wet cobblestone in full view of everybody. My tribulations when I was told to get a haircut were so simple. (A. Dyshev, 1989, 27)

This is the first necessary, but sometimes difficult, step to saving lives and getting the mission done, that not every officer can make.

In his novella *"Al'kor" Goes out of Action*, Nikolaj Ivanov accuses the "pretty boy officers" of the same kind of "mickey mouse" behavior. They come to Afghanistan with built up heels on their boots and cardboard stiffeners in their epaulets [Ivanov, 1990, 222), the American equivalent of spit-shine and starched fatigues in Vietnam. Ivanov then groups the "pretty boys" together with those afflicted with the pass-the-buck mentality so typical of collective decision making in the Soviet military: "put off the decision till tomorrow, prepare problems that have come to a head for discussion at the next meeting, delegate the matter to someone else." (Ivanov, 1990, 222) The realities of life in Afghanistan did not allow either kind of behavior.

Ivanov sees these two groups as *people* rather than *officers*, who just come to Afghanistan to get their tickets punched for their next promotion, and are astounded to find that they have to face hostile fire and go into the mountains with the troops to do that. Those of them, who cannot take the heat, are the ones who write Disposition Forms (DFs) and letters to get reassigned out of Afghanistan. Those who stay "change from people filling a position, into officers carrying out their duties." (Ivanov, 1990, 222)

While Ivanov wraps up the issue neatly with a socialist-realist happy ending in Afghanistan, he fails to address the source of the problem in the garrisons inside the USSR, where the "pretty boys" and pass-the-buckers exist with none of the pressures that combat in Afghanistan places on Ivanov's people to make them change. The Soviet presence in Afghanistan was limited and not every person filling an officer's job had a chance to be changed into an officer in the pressure cooker of combat. From Ivanov's comment about DFs and letters, it is most probable that a number of those sent to Afghanistan even managed to escape unrepentant. That leaves this an issue as yet to be resolved by the Soviet military.

Afghan military fiction is not without its descriptions of firefights and combat operations. The descriptions reveal more about the men participating in combat than about the weapons and tactics used, except for the area of combat vehicles. It is interesting to note the number of people in Afghan military fiction who ride on the skin of BMPs instead of inside. We see it in Prokhanov's *The Mountains*, in Andrej Dyshev's *The Replacement*, in Leonid Bogachuk's *Krez and Cleopatra* and Oleg Ermakov's *Baptism*. Sergej Sokolov provides the reasoning behind this seemingly illogical behavior in his short story *The Tiger's Claw*. Sr. Lt. Egorov explains why he likes to ride on the skin of his BMP or, at the very least, keep the hatches open if he is inside. He sees the trade off in safety as a good one.

> Inside the vehicle, of course, you are protected from sharpshooters and shrapnel, you won't get a cannon barrel in your back, if there's a tank behind you, you won't fall off and end up under the treads, but up top you can see better. There's more chance you can see the bad guys. As far as mines are concerned—that's clear: if one goes off under the vehicle, you get thrown off the skin and in the worst case you break something. Inside—you've had it. (Sokolov, 78)

In *Krez and Cleopatra*, Leonid Bogachuk's look at mines and BMPs is from the driver's point of view. The driver, after all, has to stay inside the vehicle. Pfc. Komissarov is detailed to drive a BMP into the mountains for an unnamed major. Before they start out, the major tells Komissarov to grab a couple of mattresses. The private's lips pale upon hearing this, because this meant that they were going into an area with mines. Placing mattresses under the seat was the accepted way to lessen the shock of a mine going off under the vehicle. The major dresses Komissarov down for his glum look. He tells him "even if there are mines, they are only antipersonnel mines and won't do anything to your iron box." (Bogachuk, 388)

As Sokolov shows later in *The Tiger's Claw*, mines are not the only problem for those inside a BMP. Rocket fire can be just as deadly as mines. Sr. Lt. Egorov sees the flash of the explosion. The next thing he knows, he is on the side of the road with shrapnel in his leg and his ears ringing. Inside the BMP, there are two wounded and one dead. The driver was hit in the arm and the lieutenant colonel from the Political Department, who was a passenger in the BMP, has a sprained wrist and some shrapnel in the face.

Both the lieutenant colonel and the driver were in open hatches when the rocket hit. The driver had his head out the driver's hatch so he could see better. The lieutenant colonel, though, had only stood up into a hatch, because he had not understood Egorov's shouted warning that they were about to take fire and wanted to ask what Egorov had said. If the lieutenant colonel had not stood up, he would have been dead. He was sitting directly opposite the place where the rocket penetrated the skin of the BMP. (Sokolov, 82) All in all, not a very good recommendation for the BMP as a combat vehicle.

Nikolaj Ivanov takes a shot at the Soviet-produced BTR as well in his novella *"Al'kor" Goes out of Action*. Ivanov has a crusty first sergeant giving a briefing to the newly arrived nurse and doctor. In his spiel to the ladies, delivered with a large dose of black humor, 1st Sgt. Starchuk discusses the comparative dangers of riding in or on a BTR. In a very matter-of-fact tone of voice he informs them that an explosion underneath the vehicle is a ticket straight to heaven, "but as far as he knows about religion, for some reason, nobody is in a hurry to get there." (Ivanov, 1990, 228) On the other hand, he continues, riding on the skin is not without its dangers. The bad guys have good sharpshooters too. His recommendation is, therefore, to sit in the hatch, half in and half out of the BTR.

> "If they start shooting, you can get inside quickly. If there's an explosion, you only lose your legs. ... And even better yet would be to only put one leg each in the hatch. Comrade Rita [the nurse], your left leg and you, Anna Nikolaevna [the doctor], your right. That way you can buy one pair of shoes between you and save on expenses." (Ivanov, 1990, 228)

In Valerij Povolyaev's *"H" Hour* we take a look at another field modification to a standard item in the Soviet military motor pool, the UAZ[3] general purpose vehicle. This modification was to take off the canvas top and saw off the metal supports that hold it up. All this made the UAZ look like a World War II jeep, but it also made it easier to bail out of the vehicle, when you came under fire. The vehicle offers no protection at all to hostile fire and the only thing to do, when you draw fire while in the vehicle, is to get out as fast as possible and dive in a ditch. It seems, however, that the doors on the UAZ are not designed with this in mind. "It is easy to get caught up in them." (Povolyaev, 166) When this happens and the door is blocked, people get killed or wounded. With the top off, you just jump out over the door and head for cover.

As the Soviets bailed out of Afghanistan and the USSR huddled on the verge of collapse, some works of military fiction began to show some very unsocialist-realist modifications to the standard style and content. Aleksandr Prokhanov's *The Mountains* released for publication in 1988, shows a very different view of Afghanistan than is found in earlier works of military fiction. Prokhanov presents a viewpoint that is more at home in Joseph Heller's *Catch-22* than in a socialist-realist work of fiction.

> Clevinger really thought he was right, but Yossarian had proof, because strangers he didn't know shot at him with cannons every time he flew up into the air to drop bombs on them and it wasn't funny at all. [4]

Prokhanov's hero, Sgt. Vagapov and his three men had just hit a group of seven bad guys, whom they suspected of planting the mines that had blown off their lieutenant's legs shortly before. They were getting even for their lieutenant. They had killed six of the seven in an ambush and were pursuing the seventh when they came under machine gun fire. Vagapov lost all three of his men and was cut off behind enemy lines.

Alone and out of ammo in a natural depression waiting for the mujahedeen to come get him, he comes to the conclusion that the war is an endless chain of killing—we kill them for killing us and they kill us for killing them and now Vagapov's turn has come to become a part of the chain. (Prokhanov, 1989, 242) This is a very sharp contrast to most military fiction, where the accent is on the sacrifice of the brave for the good of others, and the death of a bad guy is just another statistic and not of much consequence at that.

Valerij Povolyaev's main character in *"H" Hour*, Sgt. Knyazev, for example, always talks about the bad guys in the third person like "some sort of inanimate, but dangerous object." (Povolyaev, 147) That kind of mind-set precludes the concept of a chain of killing altogether. You cannot *kill* an inanimate object. You only have to count how many of them are lying on the ground when the action is over. Povolyaev supports this view of the bad guys as inanimate objects in a particularly vivid firefight scene in which Knyazev's platoon leader, Lt. Negmatov, is keeping score, much like you would in a soccer match: "One—nothing … two—nothing" (Povolyaev, 212-213), with no mention of the fact that he is counting kills or even that it is people that he is shooting at.

This is very much like the attitude expressed by Anatolij Polyanskij in his *The Right to Take Risks*, when Col. Korsunov's son confronts him with the question of whether or not he killed any "people" during the war. "No, son, I didn't kill people, but I had to [kill] the enemy. Learn to distinguish one from the other. They are different concepts." (Polyanskij, 1978, 176)

Povolyaev's characters have to have this kind of detachment from the enemy, because of the philosophical aside put in by Povolyaev's narrator in the description of the firefight. Only a pathological killer can pull the trigger on someone he knows. "When people recognize each other's faces, remember the color of their eyes, the shape of their nose, the warmth of their hand, the freshness of their thoughts, their goodness, their desire to see the sky blue and the earth green, then one person becomes, if you will, like another" (Povolyaev, 208), and killing becomes impossible. The narrator admits, however, that this is hardly possible in this day and age; there are too many weapons and might is too often right. (Povolyaev, 208)

By 1990, when his novella *The Muslim Wedding* was published, Aleksandr Prokhanov had become even more outspoken in his negative view of the war. *The Muslim Wedding* is a very personal, close-up view of the adversaries, told from the point of view of the translator for Lt. Col. Berezkin, the chief of intelligence, whose name evokes an image of Russianness through its meaning of "birch tree," a common symbol for the Russian Motherland. Berezkin came to Afghanistan from a tour in Germany, where he had "civilized" targets to work against. He feels that his assignment to Afghanistan faces him off against Asian, primitive targets, right out of the middle ages. (Prokhanov, 1990, 102 & 115)

Lt. Baturin is the translator for Berezkin. He is a Russian, who took area and language studies in college, and who, although the son of a career officer, provides a psychological counterpoint to Berezkin. He is trying to make sense out of what Berezkin considers primitive.

> His personal experience, built up bit by bit, his complex attraction to this country and its people, based on hunches and guesses, told him that there is an essence to the war and to the tragedy that he, that the newcomers, had not managed to guess at. Only love and patience and careful work could help him break through to the heart of the soul of the people and to guess what that essence was. Not destroying, but preserving. Not embittering, but winning over. Otherwise, the senseless killing will continue and the war will go on. (Prokhanov, 1990, 102)

For Baturin, the war was the collision of two worlds. One

> the endless line of death and birth of nameless Afghan peasants, living on these rocks and ridges, cut down and

massacred to the last man and boy and then coming back to earth like the grass, like water from a well, like the peak of a mountain chain. [The other was] a huge three-ocean country in torment and convulsion, in its power and naive ignorance, sending regiments into a throng of foreigners for a drawn-out, senseless war. (Prokhanov, 1990, 115)

He foresaw that, when the last Soviet crossed the border, things would go back to the way they had been and he would not have managed to guess the secret of the national soul and of a way of life, which was foreign and hostile to them. (Prokhanov, 1990, 106 & 115) The cost of not understanding this secret in Prokhanov's story is high. Berezkin had recruited Sejfuddin, a local warlord, to fight on the side of the Soviets against the mujahedeen, but at the end of the story, Sejfuddin has sworn eternal vengeance against the Soviets. If he ever takes a Soviet prisoner, he will personally slice a piece off of him every hour so that his dead son can hear the screams.

The cause of Sejfuddin's change of heart was a Soviet search and destroy mission initiated on uncorroborated information from a prisoner interrogation. Based on this information, they had shot up the wedding of Sejfuddin's son, killing not only the son, but many of Sejfuddin's relatives and followers as well. The prisoner had told them that this was the wedding of the son of Mullah Akram, a strong mujahedeen leader with a large fighting force. The prisoner knew that he would not leave Soviet captivity alive and he wanted to inflict as much damage on the enemy as he could before he went to meet Allah. He, therefore, appeared to sell out Akram, his leader, while, in fact, causing the Soviets to attack their own ally.

The prisoner's plan was hardly the kind of primitive case that Berezkin thought all his operations to be. It was as convoluted as many of the Cold War spy stories that played out against the background of Berlin. Berezkin only suspected that the prisoner might lead them into an ambush and, therefore, had him in the lead chopper so that they could kick him out the door, if the location that he gave them turned out to be a setup. It was setup alright, but too sophisticated for Berezkin to see. As the story ends and the Soviets confront him with the lie, the prisoner only yells out *Allah Akbar!* [Allah is Great!), which echoes repeatedly in the underground concrete interrogation chamber, the description of which bears a strong resemblance to Hell. This is the secret that the Soviets have been missing.

The ultimate in nonsocialist-realist criticism appears in a novella by Anatolij Polyanskij, a noted veteran of military fiction and laureate of the Fadeev prize, which was published in the organ of the Main Political Directorate of the Army and the Navy, *Kommunist vooruzhennykh sil* in 1990. In his *Afghan Syndrome*, Polyanskij says that the war in Afghanistan was a political mistake. (Polyanskij, 1990, No. 12, p. 81) Criticism is expected in a socialist-realist work, but it is expected to be directed to the proper (low) level of the hierarchy. Polyanskij's criticism is astounding in that it is directed at the highest levels of government and the military.

In Ivan Ivanyuk's short story *The Critical Approach*, the reader sees just how the process of socialist-realist criticism is supposed to work in military fiction. Ivanyuk follows the various revisions of a fictional short story as it is edited to adjust the level of command at which the criticism in the story is directed.

The fictional author, Capt. Pridykhajlo, wanted to write a story about a regimental commander who is "experienced and knowledgeable, but at the same time is not free of purely human weakness, and even occasionally makes mistakes." (Ivanyuk, 1990, 395) His first reviewer thinks that it is a good story, but the main character should be made a major instead of a colonel, because a major is younger and mistakes will seem more justified at his level and the criticism directed at the character will be more in place.

Pridykhajlo rewrites the story and sends it to another reviewer, who makes the character a senior lieutenant. The next reviewer reduces the character to the rank of private, "who has been justly subjected to criticism … [and] eventually may become a good squad leader." Before the story can be published, however, Pridykhajlo needs to resolve a problem with the text, the last reviewer says. It is the part where the character walks into his office and slams the door. That is not true to life. Who ever heard of a private with his own office?

Polyanskij skillfully qualifies the statement that the war was a "political mistake" with enough doubt to keep it from being a statement of fact. It is merely something that Ivan Pospekhin, an Afghan vet, has heard. Pospekhin does not agree with this judgment because of his personal stake in the war. If it is true, thinks Pospekhin, then all the Afghan vets are "wasted" people. Afghanistan has to mean something or all the sacrifice he and his buddies made there is in vain.

While Polyanskij denies the "political mistake" with the one hand, he confirms it with the other. As the story develops, it becomes clear that Pospekhin is wrong. "The leaders, who held sway over thousands of lives, have gone on to another world, leaving the lost, wandering souls—the victims of the leaders' failure to think the problem through—in a world of sin." (Polyanskij, 1990, No. 12, p. 81) The clear religious flavor of the wording of the accusation only serves to subtly throw salt in the wound that it creates. Polyanskij shows that this is indeed the case in his description of the lives of his three Afghan vets back in the USSR after their tour in Afghanistan.

At every turn Pospekhin and his crippled comrade in arms, Sergej, run into another bureaucrat, who does not want to help them. Sergej lost a leg in Afghanistan, but he's still number 37 on the waiting list for an apartment, and has to share a room with Ivan. Ivan cannot keep a job because of his sense of initiative and intolerance for bureaucratic stupidity that was well-developed in Afghanistan. This change in his psychology has made Ivan a mental cripple, who no longer fits in with Soviet society. They are both attacked by a crowd in line for shoes as "bogus war-heroes" (Polyanskij, 1990, No. 13, p. 84), when they try to use their privilege as war vets to go to the head of the line. Eventually Ivan falls in with a criminal element and is killed by his former commander during a raid on an arms depot at the base near by.

Polyanskij does not stop with Pospekhin and Sergej, who have completed their tours of service and are now civilians. He shows the same kind of reactions to Afghan vet Capt. Pavel Kretov, who is eventually forced to resign his commission and leave the service, because he too has outgrown the peacetime, garrison mentality of the Soviet military and refuses to revert to it when his tour in Afghanistan is over. Polyanskij's view, as presented in *Afghan Syndrome*, is that the system has rejected the experience of Afghanistan that it paid for in blood, in favor of the old, tried-and-true, SOPs that it feels comfortable with, rather than undergo the upheaval of change.

NOTES

1. "2 Soviet Deserters, Back Home Depicted as Heroes," *New York Times*, 2 December 1984, Section 1, part 1, p. 13; "Soviets Admit Defection of Soldier in Afghanistan," *Los Angeles Times*, 17 January 1985, part 1, p. 1; "5 Soviet Defectors in Afghanistan Write to Reagan for Asylum," *New York Times*, 17 October 1986, Section A, p. 20.

2. The monetary unit in Afghanistan.

3. UAZ is the designator for the Soviet-produced version of a military general purpose passenger vehicle.

4. Joseph Heller, Ulovka-22 [Catch-22]. Moscow: Military Publishing House, 1967, p. 24.

Appendix

The newspaper articles calling for the formation of LOKAF were signed by:

- L. Degtyarev (*Red Star*), Osepyan, Kivertsev, and Berlin (of the Political Directorate of the Workers' and Peasants' Red Army [PURKKA]), Ehjdeman (of the Military Academy), Mutnykh (of the Central Officers' Club of the Soviet Army), Panirovskij (of the Red Army Theater), Podsotskij (*Red Warrior*), Krasnopol'skij and Shchipaev (from *Krasnoarmeets* and *Krasnoflotets*);
- I. Shcherbakov, P. Fedotov, David Lin, Mikh. Polyak, Nik. Svirin and V. Lapinskij (from the "Red Star" literary group of the Leningrad Military District);
- Vs. Vishnevskij, Adam Dmitriev, I. Zal'tser and Abriozi (of the literary group of the Baltic Fleet);
- Simen, Demyan Bednyj, Kanatchikov, Feliks Kon, Mikhail Kol'tsov, Yanka Kupala, B. Ol'khovyj, A. Khalatov and Ef. Zazulya;
- Yurij Libedinskij, Isbakh, Makar Pasynok, Al. Bezymenskij, V. Sayanov, Mikh. Chumandrin, G. Gorbachev, Iv. Molchanov, A. Surkov, V. Stavskij, Mikh. Luzgin, S. Mikhajlov and G. Korenev [the organizational Secretary] (of The Russian Association of Proletarian Writers [RAPP]);
- I. Batrak, P. Zamojskij, I. Dorogojchenko, Leonid Il'inskij and M. Karpov (of The All-Union Organization of Peasant Writers [VOKP]);
- V. Kirillov, S. Mstislavskij, Gekht, Yu. Olesha, N. Aseev, S. Tret'yakov, E. Sergeev, Bol'shakov and N. Ognev of the Federation of Associations of Soviet Writers (of the Federation of Soviet Writers [FOSP]);
- Sannikov (of the literary group "Kuznitsa");
- Al. Malyshkin, Iv. Kataev, E. Vikhrev, S. Pakentrejger and Boris Guber (of the literary group "Pereval");
- Yan Kalnyn' (of the literary group "Rezets").

Annotated Bibliography and Anthologies

Afinogenov, Vladimir Dmitrievich. Накат штормовой волны [The Storm Wave Breaks]. Moscow: DOSAAF Publishing House, 1985. A collection of documentary sketches and novellas about the Navy.

──────── Грозно шумело море [The Sea Was Ominously Noisy], in В мирные дни [In Peacetime],* 1971, pp. 257-259.

──────── Победители «белой смерти» [The Victors over the "White Death"], in Живёт солдат ... [A Soldier Lives ...],* 1982, pp. 360-367.

──────── Залив семи бурь [The Gulf of Seven Storms], in Труба зовёт [The Trumpet Calls],* 1973, pp. 57-90.

Andreev, Vladimir Mikhailovich. Мой лейтенант [My Lieutenant]. Moscow: Moskovskij rabochij Publishing House, 1987. This edition contains an afterword written by Anatolij Mednikov. Guards Capt. (ret.) Andreev was awarded a special certificate by the Ministry of Defense for his novel *My Lieutenant*.

──────── Острый сигнал [Urgent Signal], in Родины солдаты [Soldiers of the Motherland],* 1983, pp. 7-42.

Andrianov, Sergej Vasil'evich. Полёт продолжается [The Flight Continues]. Moscow: Military Publishing House, 1984. A collection of short stories and novellas.

─────────────────

* See section on "Anthologies" for full publishing details of the anthologies cited in the Bibliography.

————— Четвёртый поединок [The Fourth Duel]. Moscow: Military Publishing House, 1975. A collection of short stories.

————— Взлёт [Take Off], in Живёт солдат ... [A Soldier Lives ...],* 1982, pp. 228–243. Andrianov flew in World War II as a navigator and afterward worked as a flight instructor.

Asanov, Nikolaj Aleksandrovich. Катастрофа отменяется [The Disaster is Cancelled]. Moscow: Military Publishing House, 1968. Republished in 1984. One of the novellas in this collection tells of how troops come to the aid of the civilian populace following a major landslide. Was awarded the second place MOD prize for literature in 1970.

Reviewed in: Col. Ya. Ershov, Подвиг мирного времени [Feat of Arms in Peacetime], *Red Star*, 9 June 1970.

Avdeenko, Yurij Nikolaevich. Год любви [A Year of Love]. Moscow: Molodaya gvardiya Publishing House, 1981.

Azov, Dmitrij. Какого цвета земля [What Color Is Earth?]. Moscow: DOSAAF Publishing House, 1980. The story of an EOD man after the war. Azov holds the rank of colonel.

Reviewed in: Semen Borzunov, Чуткая тишина [The Sensitive Silence], Литературная россия [Literary Russia], No. 25, 1981; and in: Semen Borzunov, Взрывы мирные [Peaceful Explosions], Коммунист вооружённых сил [Armed Forces Communist], No. 20, 1981, pp. 90-91.

Babaev, Stanislav. Между нами офицерами [Just Between Us Officers], Литературная учёба [Literary Studies], No. 1, 1982 pp. 56-60.

————— Конфликт [Conflict], in Поиск-86 [Search-86], pp. 160-195. A reworking of *Just Between Us Officers*.

————— Серёзные игры [Serious Games]. Moscow: Sovremennik Publishing House, 1989.

Babich, Valentin Vladimirovich. В студеных просторах [In the Icy Reaches]. Moscow: DOSAAF Publishing House, 1984. A collection of documentary short stories and novellas about the silent service.

Bakhtin, Boris Borisovich. Сержант и фрау [The Sergeant and the Frau], in Так сложилась жизнь моя ... [That's the Way My Life Turned out ...]. Leningrad: Sovetskij pisatel' Publishing House, 1990, pp. 316-324.

Baranov, Yurij Aleksandrovich. Минная гавань [The Mined Harbor]. Moscow: Military Publishing House, 1985. A collection of novellas and short stories about the Navy.

Baranov was himself a serving naval officer.

Baruzdin, Sergej Alekseevich. А память всё зовёт ... [And My Memory Continues to Call ...]. Moscow: Military Publishing House, 1981.

Belikov, Sergej. Чужое небо [A Foreign Sky], Подвиг [Feat of Arms], No. 34, 1989, pp. 65-74.

Belyaev, Aleksandr Pavlovich. Взлётная полоса [The Runway]. Moscow: Military Publishing House, 1979. The story of the creation of a night vision device for the Armed Forces.

Reviewed in: Yu. Idashkin, Роман о новаторах, творцах [A Novel about Innovators and Creative People], Коммунист вооружённых сил [Armed Forces Communist], 1980, No. 9, p. 91; and in: V. Verstakov, Люди, которых я люблю [People I Love], *Pravda*, 14 January 1980; and in: Col. V. Khobotov, Устремлённость в завтра [Reaching for Tomorrow], Советский воин [Soviet Warrior], No. 14, 1976, p. 23.

——— Танкодром [The Tank Range], in Мы - военные [We Are Military Men], 1974, pp. 216-238. A reworked version of *The Tank Range* makes up the first half of *The Runway*.

Belyaev was on active duty in the rank of colonel in 1974. He is a graduate of the Airborne Academy. Later in his career he worked as a military journalist.

Berestov, Evgenij. Караван специального назначения [Special Purpose Caravan]. Moscow: Molodaya gvardiya Publishing House, 1986. A story from Afghanistan.

Berezko, Georgij Sergeevich. Сильнее атома [Stronger than the Atom]. Moscow: Sovetskij pisatel' Publishing House, 1970. First published in Знамя [The Banner], Nos. 9, 10 and 11, 1959, pp. 3-64, 56-139 and 3-50.

Besschetnikov, Evgenij Ivanovich. Тают снега [The Snows Are Melting]. Moscow: DOSAAF Publishing House, 1986. The story of engineering troops of the Turkestan Military District, who helped the populace during a flood.

Biryukov, Valerij Grigor'evich. Всего три дня [Only Three Days]. Moscow: Military Publishing House, 1975. The story of the reequipping of an artillery unit in the Turkestan Military District.

——— Дублер [The Backup], in Труба зовёт [The Trumpet

Calls], 1973, pp. 153–160.

　　　　　Biryukov is a graduate of the Gorkij Literary Institute. In 1972, he held the rank of captain.

Bogachuk, Leonid. Крез и Клеопатра [Krez and Cleopatra], in Эхо афганских гор [Echo of the Mountains of Afghanistan], 1987, pp. 381–399.

Bogatov, Viktor Vasil'evich. К высоте подняться своей [Rise to Your Own Level]. Moscow: Military Publishing House, 1988. The story of how a young officer finds himself.

Boltromeyuk, Valerij Vladimirovich. Юность командиров [Youth of the Commanders]. Moscow: DOSAAF Publishing House, 1983. A collection of sketches.

Borich, Leonid. Третье измерение [The Third Dimension], Звезда [Star], Nos. 1 & 2, 1975, pp. 73-148 & 5-82. The story of the impact of the Scientific and Technological Revolution on the submarine Navy.

　　　　　Reviewed in: Iv. Andreev, Подводники в художественном изображении [An Artistic View of Submarines], Коммунист вооружённых сил [Armed Forces Communist], No. 15, 1976, pp. 90-92.

Boriskin, Nikolaj. Туркестанские повести [The Turkestan Novellas]. Moscow: Military Publishing House, 1971. Contains: Знойная параллель [The Hot Parallel], about a young enlisted man in the rocket troops, and Чрезвычайное происшествие [The Incident], a spy novel about the Air Force.

　　　　　Reviewed in: Il. Okunev, Короткие рецензии [Short Reviews], Октябрь [October], No. 2, 1973, p. 219.

————　 Друзья Ивана Вишнякова [The Friends of Ivan Vyshnyakov], in Мы - военные [We Are Military Men], 1974, pp. 239-249.

　　　　　Boriskin held the rank of lieutenant colonel (res.) in 1974.

Borodin, Vladimir. Восьмой комбат [The Eighth Battalion Commander], Советский воин [Soviet Warrior], No. 8, 1981, pp. 20-23.

————　 Самый застенчивый лейтенант [The Shyest Lieutenant], Советский воин [Soviet Warrior], No. 24, 1980, pp. 18-21.

Borovik, Artem Genrikhovich. Спрятанная война [The Hidden War]. Moscow: PIK Publishers, 1992. Postsocialist-realist stories about the war in Afghanistan.

Burbyga, Nikolaj. Агитотряд [The Pacification Detachment], in Поиск–90 [Search-90], pp. 262-289. A story from the war in Afghanistan.

Bychkov, Capt. A. Суровая романтика [Harsh Romance], in Дни мирные – подвиги боевые [Danger in Peacetime], 1965, pp. 32-38. An explosive ordinance disposal (EOD) story.

Cherginets, Nikolaj. Тайна черных гор [The Secret of the Black Mountains]. Minsk, Mastatskaya literatura Publishing House, 1987. A story from the war in Afghanistan.

Davydov, Il'ya Yul'evich. Назначение [The Assignment]. Moscow: Military Publishing House, 1983. The story of the initial years of the antiaircraft Rocket Forces of the PVO.

Demidov, V. Мы уходим последними ... записки пиротехника [We Leave Last ... The Diary of an EOD man]. Moscow: Molodaya gvardiya Publishing House, 1967. This story, which takes place in the early sixties, describes the life of an EOD man in the postwar period.

    Demidov served as an officer in the Leningrad EOD group, which removed over 30,000 explosive devices after the end of the war.

Dicharov, Zakhar L'vovich. Глубины сердца [The Depths of a Heart], Советский воин [Soviet Warrior], No. 13, 1962, pp. 3-6. The winner of the second prize of the *Soviet Warrior* literary contest for 1962.

Dyshev, Andrej. Замена [The Replacement], Подвиг [Feat of Arms], No. 34, 1989, pp. 17-64. A young officer's first encounter with the realities of war in Afghanistan.

    This novella was probably also written by Sergej Dyshev. Even though the table of contents and the title page list him as Andrej/A. Dyshev, the photo credits are for S. Dyshev.

Dyshev, Sergej Mikhailovich. Пуля на ладони [A Bullet Resting on the Hand], Подвиг [Feat of Arms], No. 32, 1988, pp. 37–100. A story from Afghanistan.

——— Да воздастся ... [Grant Unto Them ...], in Юность [Youth], No. 8, 1989, pp. 2-21. The story of an Afghan veteran.

——— Марш стальных чудовищ [The March of the Steel Monsters], in Литературная Россия [Literary Russia], No. 52, 1995, pp. 8-10.

    Dyshev is a graduate of the L'vov Advanced Military-

Political Academy (1977) and the Military-Political CGSC (1987). He served several tours in Afghanistan.

Egorov, Anatolij. Шагнуть на линию огня [Step onto the Line of Fire], in Я – солдат, мама ... [I am a Soldier, Mama ...], 1988, pp. 57-61.

——— Ждите нас в мае [You Can Expect Us in May], Подвиг [Feat of Arms], No. 26, 1984, pp. 78–93.

Egorov, Nikolaj. Всадник на вороннем коне [Rider on a Black Horse], Дон [Don], Nos. 11 & 12, 1973, pp. 8-49 & 14-67. The story of an enlisted man.

Ehkonomov, L. Готовность номер один [Readiness Condition Number One]. Moscow: Military Publishing House, 1968. Presents an enlisted man's view of the introduction of the new, all-weather interceptor aircraft into the Soviet Air Force.

Ekimov, Boris. Наш солдат [Our Soldier], Литературная Россия [Literary Russia], No. 21, 1995, pp. 8-9. A story from Chechnya.

Elkin, Anatolij Sergeevich. Атомные уходят по тревоге [The Nuclear (Subs) Depart on Alert]. Moscow: Military Publishing House, 1984. The story of the formation of the Soviet Nuclear Submarine Fleet.

Ermakov, Oleg. Афганские рассказы [Afghan Tales], in Крещение [Baptism], 1991, pp. 320-461.

——— *Afghan Tales*, New York: William Morrow, 1993.

——— Последний рассказ о войне [The Last Story about the War], Знамя [The Banner], No. 8, 1995, pp. 10-25. The war in this case is Afghanistan.

Fejgin, Ehmmanuil Abramovich. Солдат, сын солдата [Soldier, Son of a Soldier]. Moscow: Military Publishing House, 1975. The story of military service in the Transcaucus Military District.

Filatov, Viktor Ivanovich. На вертикалях [Power Climb], Молодая гвардия [The Young Guard], No. 5, 1975, pp. 148-236.

——— На вертикалях [Power Climb]. Moscow: Military Publishing House, 1978. Contains two novellas. The title novella is the story of Air Force cadets. The second novella, entitled Новобранцы [Recruits], tells the story of enlisted men in a motor rifle company. *Recruits* also deals with the problem of religion in the military.

Reviewed in: Yurij Belichenko, Школа мужества

[The School of Heroism], Знамя [The Banner], No. 5, 1980, pp. 230-237.

———   Курсантское небо [A Cadet's Sky], Подвиг [Feat of Arms], No. 30, 1986, pp. 53-87.

When he published *Power Climb* in 1975, Filatov held the rank of lieutenant colonel and was working as a correspondent for *Red Star*.

Ganibesov, Vasilij Petrovich. Эскадрон комиссаров [A Squadron of Commissars]. Moscow: Sovetskij pisatel' Publishing House, 1959. A story of the Red Army.

Ganibesov was a member of LOKAF. He died in a German prison camp in 1943.

Gastello, Viktor. Служить – не тужить [In the Service—Don't Be Nervous]. Moscow: Military Publishing House, 1985. A humorous look at life in the service.

Godenko, Mikhail. Вечный огонь [Eternal Fire]. Moscow: Molodaya gvardiya Publishing House, 1987. The story of a reactor accident on a nuclear submarine.

Gorbachev, Nikolaj Andreevich. Ракеты и подснежники [Rockets and Snowdrops]. Moscow: Military Publishing House, 1963.

Reviewed in: Maj. A. Khorev, Влюбленный в службу [In Love with the Service], Советский воин [Soviet Warrior], No. 24, 1963, p. 12.

———   Звездное тяготение [The Pull of the Stars]. Moscow: Military Publishing House, 1965. *The Pull of the Stars* tells the story of the self-sacrifice of Gosha Kol'tsov, who risks his life to save the lives of his comrades when a Soviet test rocket malfunctions.

Reviewed in: G. Zabelok, Две повести о ракетчиках [Two Novellas about the Rocket Troops], Вестник противовоздушной обороны [Bulletin of the PVO], No. 11, 1965, pp. 78-80.

———   Дайте точку опоры [Give Me a Fulcrum], Москва [Moscow], Nos. 2 & 3, 1969, pp. 3-73, 3-77.

Reviewed in: Дайте точку опоры [Give Me a Fulcrum], Советский воин [Soviet Warrior], No. 9, 1970, p. 36.

———   Дайте точку опоры • Ударная сила [Give Me a Fulcrum • Striking Force]. Moscow: Military Publishing House, 1973. Together with *The Battle*, *Give Me a Fulcrum*

Reviewed in: Aleksej P'yannov, Точка опоры [The Fulcrum], *Pravda*, 4 March 1983.

——— Битва [The Battle]. Moscow: Military Publishing House, 1977.

Reviewed in: Iv. Andreev, Люди с пламенными сердцами [People Whose Hearts Are on Fire], Коммунист вооружённых сил [Armed Forces Communist], No. 15, 1977, pp. 86-91; and in: Col. (ret.) V. Arkhipov, Во имя будущего [In the Name of the Future], Советский воин [Soviet Warrior], No. 18, 1977, pp. 32-33.

——— Любовь моя—армия [My Love is the Army]. Moscow: DOSAAF Publishing House, 1978. Sketches, documentary short stories and journalistic articles. Also contains a biographic sketch of the author by B. Leonov.

——— Иду в шинели [I Wear an Army Greatcoat]. Moscow: DOSAAF Publishing House, 1983.

——— Возвращение [Going Back], in Родины солдаты [Soldiers of the Motherland], 1983, pp. 80-87. The story of life in a remote, northern garrison.

——— Классическое правило [The Classic Rule], in Родины солдаты [Soldiers of the Motherland], 1983, pp. 89-97.

——— На всём пространстве [Over the Entire Surface], in В солдатской шинели [In a Soldier's Greatcoat], 1985, pp. 488-495.

——— При свете северного сияния [By the Light of the Aurora Borealis], in Мы - военные [We Are Military Men], 1974, pp. 36-46.

——— Испытатели ракет [Rocket Testers], in Дни мирные – подвиги боевые [Danger in Peacetime], 1965, pp. 53-61.

Lt. Col. (ret.) Gorbachev served as an engineering specialist officer in the rocket troops. He was a participant in the development of the first rocket systems and his trilogy is based on that experience. He is a laureate of the Ministry of Defense prize for literature.

Interview in: Valentina Zhegis, Подснежники и ракеты [Snowdrops and Rockets], *Sovetskaya Kul'tura*, 10 March 1981, p. 6.

Gorlov, Aleksandr Georgievich. Служу во внутренних войсках [I Serve in the Internal Troops]. Moscow: Military Publishing

House, 1983. Includes the short story: Мера мужества [The Measure of Bravery].

Gribanov, Stanislav Vikent'evich. Тайна одной инверсии [The Secret of an Inversion]. Moscow: Military Publishing House, 1985. A collection of stories and novellas about the Air Force.

Gryaznov, Evgenij Nikolaevich. Там, где рождаются молнии [Where Lightning Is Born]. Moscow: DOSAAF Publishing House, 1981.
        In 1979, Gryaznov held the rank of lieutenant colonel.

Gubanov, Gennadij. Рябина зреет на морозе [Ashberries Ripen in the Frost], Советский воин [Soviet Warrior], No. 23, 1981, pp. 39-41.

——— Рябина зреет на морозе [Ashberries Ripen in the Frost]. Moscow: Military Publishing House, 1986.
        Gubanov held the rank of colonel in 1981.

Igumnov, ALeksandr. Выстрелы в долине [Shots in the Valley], Подвиг [Feat of Arms], No. 37, 1990, pp. 148-155.

Il'inskij, Yurij Borisovich. Взрыв на рассвете [Blast at Dawn]. Moscow: Sovremennik Publishing House, 1982. The story of EOD teams cleaning up after World War II.

——— В прославленной Таманской [In the Glorious Taman Division], in Мы – военные [We Are Military Men], 1974, pp. 144-150.
        Il'inskij held the rank of captain (res.) in 1974.

Ionin, Sergej. В тихом кишлаке [In a Peaceful Village], Подвиг [Feat of Arms], No. 37, 1990, pp. 130–147.

Ivankov, Evgenij. Старшина Кошкарев [First Sergeant Koshkarev], Советский воин [Soviet Warrior], No. 14, 1962, p. 24.

Ivanov, Nikolaj Fedorovich. Гроза над Гиндукушем [Storm over Gindukush Mountain], in Солдаты мира [Soldiers of Peace], 1985, pp. 380-414. This novella first appeared in Октябрь [October], No. 12, 1984, pp. 3-25.

——— Гроза над Гиндукушем [Storm over Gindukush Mountain], in Поиск-86 [Search-86], pp. 8-49.

——— Перевал [The Mountain Pass], in Эхо афганских гор [Echo of the Mountains of Afghanistan], 1987, pp. 3-70.

——— «Алькор» выходит из боя ["Al'kor" Goes out of Action], in Поиск-90 [Search-90], pp. 208-261.

——— Рассветы Саура [Saur's Sunrises], in По горячей земле [Over the Hot Earth], 1986, pp. 97-140.

All four of the works above are about the war in Afghanistan.

———   Только тебе одной [Only for You Alone], Литературная Россия [Literary Russia], No. 38, 1995, pp. 8-9. A story from Chechnya.

     Ivanov is a graduate of the Suvorov Military Academy and of the L'vov Advanced Military-Political Academy. He served a tour in Afghanistan. He was an editor of Советский воин [Soviet Warrior]. As of 1995, he was serving in the Tax Police with the rank of colonel.

Ivanyuk, Ivan. Критический подход [The Critical Approach], in Поиск-90 [Search-90], pp. 395-396.

———   Сонет [The Sonnet], in Поиск-86 [Search-86], pp. 325–326.

Izyumskij, Boris Vasil'evich. Алые погоны [Scarlet Shoulder Boards]. Moscow: Molodaya gvardiya Publishing House, 1975. The story of the lives of graduates of the Suvorov Military Academy.

Kaledin, Sergej. Стройбат [Construction Battalion], in Крещение [Baptism], 1991, pp. 268-319.

Kalmykov, Maj. Nikolaj. Запах сирени [The Smell of Lilac], Советский воин [Soviet Warrior], No. 14, 1974, pp. 14-16.

Kambulov, Nikolaj. Разводящий ещё не пришёл [The Corporal of the Guard Has Not Come Yet]. Moscow: Military Publishing House, 1966.

———   Ракетный гром [The Rocket's Thunder]. Moscow: Military Publishing House, 1969. These two novels form a single unit describing the reorganization of an artillery regiment into a rocket unit and the effect the Scientific and Technological Revolution has on the lives of the members of the unit.

     The Corporal of the Guard Has Not Come Yet is reviewed in: S. Savel'ev, Всегда в строю [Always in the Ranks], Коммунист вооружённых сил [Armed Forces Communist], No. 1, 1965, pp. 89-92.

———   Верность [Faithfulness]. Moscow: Military Publishing House, 1970. Republication of *The Corporal of the Guard Has Not Come Yet* and *The Rocket's Thunder* (two volumes).

     Reviewed in: A. Kochetov, Ракетный гром [The Rocket's Thunder], Коммунист вооружённых сил [Armed Forces Communist], No. 3, 1970, p. 92.

———— Ротмистр Пижма [Captain Pizhma], in Труба зовёт [The Trumpet Calls], 1973, pp. 254-266.

———— Огонёк [The Campfire], in В мирные дни [In Peacetime], 1971, pp. 108–129.

———— Мужской разговор [Man to Man Talk], in Родины солдаты [Soldiers of the Motherland], 1983, pp. 98-120.

Colonel of Aviation (ret.) Nikolaj Kambulov is laureate of the Ministry of Defense prize for literature.

Karpov, Vladimir Vasil'evich. Эстафета подвига [The Baton of Glory]. Moscow: DOSAAF Publishing House, 1980.

Reviewed in: В бою и труде [In Combat and at Work], Октябрь [October], No. 9, 1981, pp. 221-222.

———— Мужают не только в бою [Not Only Combat Makes You a Man]. Moscow: Sovetskaya Rossiya, 1981. A collection of sketches and short stories, including the novella Не мечом единым [Not by the Sword Alone] and the short story Новенький [New Guy].

Reviewed in: Col. G. Solov'ev Воспитать гражданина и воина [Indoctrinate a Citizen and Soldier], Коммунист вооружённых сил [Armed Forces Communist], No. 15, 1981, pp. 89-91.

———— Стать солдатом нелегко [It Is not Easy to Become a Soldier], in Родины солдаты [Soldiers of the Motherland], 1983, pp. 121-147.

———— Исскуство быть командиром [The Art of Being a Commander], in В солдатской шинели [In a Soldier's Greatcoat], 1985, pp. 381-386.

———— Командовал ротой... [He Commanded a Company ...], in В солдатской шинели [In a Soldier's Greatcoat], 1985, pp. 461-465.

Guards Col. (ret.) Karpov, a twenty-five-year veteran of the service, is a graduate of the Gorkij Literary Institute and laureate of the Ministry of Defense Fadeev prize for literature. He was the editor in chief of Новый мир [New World]. Biographic sketch in Советский воин [Soviet Warrior], No. 4, 1963.

Khalturin, Fedor Nikolaevich А поезда всё идут [And the Trains Are Still Running], in Родины солдаты [Soldiers of the Motherland], 1983, pp. 189-202.

———— Соловьиные зори [A Nightingale's View]. Moscow: Moskovskij rabochij Publishing House, 1977. Contains *And the Trains are Still Running*.

———— Песня [The Song], Советский воин [Soviet Warrior],
No. 16, 1980, pp. 7-8. A rewrite of Человек и гаубица
[The Man and the Howitzer], which was first published in
Соловьиные зори [A Nightingale's View].

———— Три сердца [Three Hearts]. Moscow: DOSAAF
Publishing House, 1984.
In 1980, Khalturin held the rank of colonel.

Khandus', Oleg. Он был мой самый лучший друг [He Was My
Very Best Friend], in Крещение [Baptism], 1991, pp.
242-250.

———— Полковник всегда найдётся [You Can Always Find a
Colonel]. Moscow: PIK Publishing House, 1992. Both are
stories about the war in Afghanistan.

Kikeshev, Col. Nikolaj. Хит-парад на «Анаконде» [Hit Parade on
the "Anaconda"], Армия [Army] (formerly Коммунист
вооружённых сил [Armed Forces Communist]), No. 15,
1992, pp. 52-55. A story of the spetsnaz in Afghanistan.

———— Встань и иди [Stand Up and Walk]. Moscow:
Международная ассоциация писателей
баталистов и маринистов [International Association
of Military Fiction Writers], 1995. A novel about the
spetsnaz in Afghanistan.
Reviewed in: Col. Igor Lebid'ko, После «Афгана»
[After "Afghan"], Литературная россия [Literary
Russia], 12 May 1995, p. 5.
Kikeshev began his service as an artillery officer,
serving as a political officer and later as a military
journalist.

Kireev, Aleksej Filippovich. Сосны гудят тревожно [The Pines Roar
Ominously]. Moscow: Military Publishing House, 1983.
Includes the novella Течёт река Эльба [Flows the River
Elbe], which tells the story of life in GSFG at the beginning
of the fifties. Kireev was awarded a special certificate by
the Ministry of Defense for *Flows the River Elbe*.

Klimovich, Liliya Mikhailovna. Успеть до боя [To Make it to the
Battle]. Moscow: Molodaya gvardiya Publishing House,
1984. Also printed by Children's Literature Publishing
House in 1980. The story of an enlisted man in the Air
Force.

Klyuev, Maj. Viktor. В зимний день [On a Winter's Day], Советский
воин [Soviet Warrior], No. 19, 1970, pp. 25-28.

——————   В зимний день [On a Winter's Day], in Труба зовёт
           [The Trumpet Calls], 1973, pp. 161-171.
——————   Комбат [The Battalion Commander], Советский воин
           [Soviet Warrior], No. 10, 1971, pp. 24-27.
——————   Комбат [The Battalion Commander], in Труба зовёт
           [The Trumpet Calls], 1973, pp. 91-102. Stories about
           armored troops.
Kolosov, M. Записки лейтенанта [A Lieutenant's Diary], in В
           мирные дни [In Peacetime], 1971, pp. 140-169.
Komissarov, Vladimir Sergeevich. Гвардий лейтенант [Guards
           Lieutenant]. Moscow: Military Publishing House, 1956.
Kondrashov, Vasilij Pavlovich. Небо выбирает нас [The Sky Chooses
           Us]. Moscow: Molodaya gvardiya Publishing House, 1983.
           Tells the story of the formation of the character of young
           flying officers. Kondrashov served as a pilot himself.
Konetskij, Viktor Viktorovich. Третий лишний [Three's a Crowd].
           Leningrad: Sovetskij pisatel' Publishing House, 1983. Story
           of a naval deployment to the Antarctic.
Konovalov, Leonid. Серебряный журавль [The Silver Crane],
           Советский воин [Soviet Warrior], No. 3, 1981a, pp. 20-
           22.
——————   Длинная ночь [The Long Night], Советский воин
           [Soviet Warrior], No. 7, 1981b, pp. 13-15.
——————   Брод через Серебрянку [Ford Across the Serebryanka
           River], Советский воин [Soviet Warrior], No. 21, 1981c,
           pp. 27-29.
——————   Левый фланг [The Left Flank], in Труба зовёт [The
           Trumpet Calls], 1973, pp. 172-183.
——————   Хмурное небо [The Overcast Sky], in Труба зовёт
           [The Trumpet Calls], 1973, pp. 340-351.
——————   Солдатский поклон [A Soldier's Bow], in Родины
           солдаты [Soldiers of the Motherland], 1983, pp. 259-271.
Kovalenko, Rimma Mikhailovna. Рядовой Яковлев [Pvt. Yakovlev],
           in Конвейер [Conveyer]. Moscow: Sovetskij pisatel'
           Publishing House, 1981, pp. 3-40. Story of a young boy
           growing up during his tour in the Army.
Kozlov, Valdimir. Ночной звонок [The Night Call], in Поиск-80
           [Search-80], p. 310.
Krajnij, Andrej. Курсант Касьянов [Cadet Kas'yanov], Юность,
           [Youth], 1982, No. 1, pp. 62-67.The short story of a young
           cadet's loves and tribulations.

Kulakov, Col. A. Командир ракетной [Commander of a Rocket
          Unit], in Мы - военные [We Are Military Men], 1974,
          pp. 105-120.
Kuleshov, Aleksandr Petrovich. Голубые молнии [Blue Lightning],
          Знамя [The Banner], Nos. 1, 2 & 3, 1972, pp. 7-47, 3-78
          and 6-48.
               Reviewed in: F. Rezinkov, Эстафета воинской
          доблести [Continuing the Tradition of Military Valour],
          Литературная россия [Literary Russia],
          23 June 1972, p. 16; and in: S. Savel'ev, Становление
          офицера-современника [The Formation of a Modern
          Officer's Character], Коммунист вооружённых сил
          [Armed Forces Communist], No. 6, 1978, pp. 86-87.
———   Белый ветер [The White Wind]. Moscow: Military
          Publishing House, 1977a; and in Знамя [The Banner],
          Nos. 4 & 5, 1977b, pp. 62-140 & 91-136.
———   Ночное солнце [The Nighttime Sun]. Moscow: Military
          Publishing House, 1981. All three of the above works tell
          the story of the airborne.
               Reviewed in: Gennadij Alifanov, Солдаты мира
          [Soldiers of Peace], *Literaturnaya Gazeta*, 1 December 1982.
               Interview in: Nikolaj Dobronravov, Верный курс
          [A True Course], Советский спорт [Soviet Sport], 9
          June 1981.
Kuplevakhskij, Valerij Evgen'evich. Разведчики [Recon], Знамя [The
          Banner], No. 2, 1983, pp. 66-117; and Moscow: Sovetskij
          pisatel' Publishing House, 1985. The story of the
          development of a young man's character in the airborne.
          Reprinted in Солдаты мира [Soldiers of Peace], 1985,
          pp. 302-379.
               Reviewed in: Irina Bogatko Становясь солдатом
          [Becoming a Soldier], *Literaturnaya Gazeta*, 16 March 1983.
———   Суетность пристрастия [The Vanity of Partiality].
          Moscow: Molodaya gvardiya Publishing House, 1990.
          Contains the novella Без вести вернувшийся [Missing
          in Peacetime] about the war in Afghanistan and the short
          story Маленький клоун Мань [Man', the Little Clown]
          about the war in Vietnam.
               Lt. Col. Kuplevakhskij is a graduate of the Suvorov
          Military Academy, the Advance Engineers Radiotechnical
          Academy and the Military Engineering Radiotechnical

Academy.

Kuz'michev, Anatolij Petrovich. Ночная проверка [Nighttime
      Check]. Minsk: Mastatskaya literatura Publishing House,
      1982. Tells the story of a young officer in the Rocket
      Forces. Reprinted in Отвага [Daring]. Moscow: Molodaya
      gvardiya Publishing House, 1987, pp. 277-392.
————   Год службы [A Year's Service]. Moscow: Military
      Publishing House, 1979.
             Reviewed in: Col. A Solov'ev, Окрыленность
      [Inspiration], Советский воин [Soviet Warrior], No. 4,
      1981, p. 32.

Lutskij, Sergej Artemovich. У себя в части [At Home in the Unit],
      Советский воин [Soviet Warrior], No. 22, 1973, pp. 4-6.
————   Двое суток из десяти [Two Days out of Ten],
      Октябрь [October], No. 12, 1975, pp. 40-75.
————   Десять суток, не считая дороги [Ten Days, not
      Counting Travel Time]. Moscow: Sovremennik Publishing
      House, 1980. Contains У себя дома [At Home], a reprint
      of *At Home in the Unit*.

Makhnev, Nikolaj. Поправка на Камильянова [Match up to
      Kamil'yanov], in Горячие высоты [The Hot High
      Ground], 1983, pp. 332-344.

Mamontov, Lt. Col. Viktor. Цветы на краю окопа [Flowers on the
      Edge of a Foxhole], Советский воин [Soviet Warrior],
      No. 21, 1979, pp. 28-30.
————   Не послужишь, не узнаёшь [If You Don't Serve,
      You'll Never Know], Советский воин [Soviet Warrior],
      No. 15, 1980, pp. 16-19. Also in Живёт солдат ... [A
      Soldier Lives ...], 1982, pp. 299-309.
————   Замполит [The Political Officer], in Поиск-83 [Search-
      83], pp. 197-212.

Marchenko, Vyacheslav Ivanovich. Год без весны [A Year Without a
      Spring]. Moscow: Sovetskij pisatel' Publishing House,
      1978.
————   Север [The North]. Moscow: Military Publishing House,
      1981.
             Reviewed in: Capt. II V. Likashevich По долгу
      мужества и чести [A Debt of Bravery and Honor], *Red
      Star*, 13 June 1981.
————   По местам стоять [Fall In]. Moscow: Military
      Publishing House, 1985. Tells the story of the modern-day

Navy. Marchenko served in the Navy himself.

Matreshin, Maj. V. Маленько [Just a Bit], Советский воин [Soviet Warrior], No. 15, 1961, pp. 5-8.

Mikson, I'lya L'vovich. И на всю жизнь [For All Your Life]. Moscow: Military Publishing House, 1976. Contains the novella Офицеры [Officers], which relates the story of life in the modern-day Soviet Army in a remote garrison.

Mitroshenkov, Viktor Anatol'evich. Приказано испытать [Ordered to Test]. Moscow: Sovremennik Publishing House, 1983. A collection of novellas that tell the story of test pilots in the Air Force. The title novella was first published in 1975. In 1974, the author held the rank of colonel.

Nekrasov, Gennadij Mikhajlovich. Пограничный причал [Dock on the Border]. Moscow: Military Publishing House, 1985. The story of the Coast Guard.

Nikolaev, Lev Nikolaevich. Кабульские рассветы [Kabul's Dawns], in Эхо афганских гор [Echo of the Mountains of Afghanistan], 1987, pp. 231–335.

——— Кабульские рассветы [Kabul's Dawns]. Moscow: Sovetskaya Rossiya Publishing House, 1985.

Nikol'skij, Boris. Повесть о солдатской службе [A Novella About a Soldier's Service], Юность [Youth], No. 7, 1967, pp. 2-22. Reviewed in: E. Bogdanov, О солдатской службе [About a Soldier's Service], Советский воин [Soviet Warrior], No. 6, 1968, p. 20.

——— Повесть о солдатской службе [A Novella about a Soldier's Service], in Горячие высоты [The Hot High Ground], 1983, pp. 82-132.

Pakhomov, Yurij К оружию, эскулапы! [To Arms, Medics!], Звезда [Star], No. 7, 1978, pp. 5-77, also published by Molodaya gvardiya Publishing House, 1984. The story of cadets in a military medical academy. Reviewed in: Yurij Belichenko, Школа мужества [The School of Heroism], Знамя [The Banner], No. 5, 1980, pp. 230-237.

——— Драконова кровь [Dragon's Blood]. Moscow: Sovremennik Publishing House, 1986. Also contains К оружию, эскулапы! [To Arms, Medics!].

Parmuzin, Boris Sergeevich. Сабля в отблесках огня [Sabre Reflected in the Fire]. Moscow: Military Publishing House, 1978. Excerpts from the novel were printed in Советский воин [Soviet Warrior], No. 23, 1977, pp. 36-39.

———— Кист винограда [A Bunch of Grapes], Одна царапина [One Scratch], Неожиданные слёзы [Unexpected Tears], Старый мост [The Old Bridge], Обелиск независимости [The Obelisk of Independence], Рождение картины [The Birth of a Picture], all in Труба зовёт [The Trumpet Calls], 1973, pp. 382-390.

Perventsev, A. Остров надежды [The Island of Hope]. Moscow: Military Publishing House, 1969. The story of coping with the introduction of nuclear powered submarines into the Soviet Navy.

Reviewed in: V. Grishanov, Неразведанным курсом [Uncharted Course], *Pravda*, 22 March 1968; and in: I. Strelkova, Хождение за четыре океана [The Passage of Four Oceans], *Literaturnaya Gazeta*, 10 April 1968, p.4.

Interview in: Mikhail Vershin, Вровень с веком [In Step with His Time], Советский воин [Soviet Warrior], No. 2, 1980, pp. 34-35.

Petl'ovannyj, Vitalij. Сурми грають зорю [The Trumpets Play Retreat], in Collected works, Vol. 1. Kiev: Dnipro Publishing House, 1984. Relates the story of the life of the military in the immediate postwar period.

Petrov, Vladimir Nikolaevich. Философия боя [The Philosophy of Battle], Советский воин [Soviet Warrior], No. 14, 1971, pp. 14-16.

———— Философия боя [The Philosophy of Battle], in Труба зовёт [The Trumpet Calls], 1973, pp.143-152.

———— Горечь таежных ягод [The Bitterness of the Tajga's Berries], in Труба зовёт [The Trumpet Calls], 1973, pp. 7-56.

———— Тревожно мерцают экраны [The Screens Shimmer Ominously]. Moscow: Military Publishing House, 1975. The story of the PVO. Also contains Философия боя [The Philosophy of Battle].

———— Гарнизоны первых сирен [Garrisons of the First Sirens]. Moscow: Military Publishing House, 1977.

———— Дочь Кассиопеи [Cassiopeia's Daughter], in Родины солдаты [Soldiers of the Motherland], 1983, pp. 214-241.

Vladimir Petrov holds the rank of guards lieutenant

colonel (res.).

Petukhov, Yurij Dmitrievich. ... Через две весны [... Two Springs
        from Now]. Moscow: DOSAAF Publishing House, 1983.
        The story of motor-rifle troops.

Pinchuk, Arkadij Fedorovich. Однажды и навсегда [Once and for
        All]. Moscow: Military Publishing House, 1985. The story
        of the PVO.

———   Билет на «Лебединое озеро» [A Ticket to "Swan
        Lake"], Советский воин [Soviet Warrior], No. 11, 1971,
        pp. 20-23.

———   Приглашение на «Лебединое озеро» [An
        Invitation to "Swan Lake"], in Труба зовёт [The
        Trumpet Calls], 1973, pp. 309-316. Reprinted in Горячие
        высоты [The Hot High Ground], 1983, pp. 158-176.

———   Всё только начинается [It's Only Just Begun], in
        Горячие высоты [The Hot High Ground], 1983,
        pp. 177-191.

———   Я живу хорошо [I Live Well], in Поверка [Roll Call],
        1988, pp. 148-244
                In 1971, Pinchuk held the rank of lieutenant colonel.

Pishchulin, Vladimir Pavlovich. Воскресный день [A Sunday],
        Советский воин [Soviet Warrior], No. 7, 1976, pp. 13–15.

———   Ракетный наш дивизион [Our Rocket Battalion].
        Moscow: DOSAAF Publishing House, 1978.
                Reviewed in: Lt. Col. Evgenij Gryaznov, Будни
        ракетчиков [Everyday Life in the Rocket Troops],
        Коммунист вооружённых сил [Armed Forces
        Communist], No. 9, 1979.

———   Знойное лето [The Hot Summer]. Moscow: DOSAAF
        Publishing House, 1982.

———   После боя [After the Battle], in Живёт солдат ... [A
        Soldier Lives ...], 1982, pp. 290-298.

———   Расставание [Parting], in Мы - военные [We Are
        Military Men], 1974, pp. 176-181.
                In 1976, Pishchulin held the rank of lieutenant
        colonel.

Plotnikov, Aleksandr Nikolaevich. Звёзды над рубкой [Stars over
        the Conning Tower]. Moscow: Military Publishing House,
        1983. The story of the silent service.

———   Бушлат на вырост [A Pea-coat to Grow into], in
        Родины солдаты [Soldiers of the Motherland], 1983, pp.

322-327.

Aleksandr Plotnikov holds the rank of captain first class (Navy) in the reserves. He is a laureate of the Ministry of Defense Fadeev prize for literature as well as the Ministry of Defense prize for literature.

Polityko, Georgij Pavlovich. Твои сыновья [Your Sons]. Moscow: Sovremennik Publishing House, 1977. Contains the novella Товарищы офицеры [Comrade Officers], which tells the story of the reequiping of the Army after World War II.

Polyakov, Yurij Mikhajlovich. Сто дней до приказа [One Hundred Days till the Order]. Moscow: Molodaya gvardiya Publishing House, 1988. Also in Крещение [Baptism], 1991, pp. 86-175. The story of Grandpa-autocracy.

Polyanskij, Anatolij Filippovich. Право на риск [The Right to Take Risks]. Moscow: Military Publishing House, 1978. The story of the airborne.

Reviewed in: V. Evpatov, Преемственность [Continuity], Советский воин [Soviet Warrior], No. 10, 1979, p. 34; and in: Capt. II V. Likashevich, По долгу мужества и чести [A Debt of Bravery and Honor], *Red Star*, 13 June 1981.

——— Тайфун [Typhoon], Советский воин [Soviet Warrior], No. 1, 1982, pp. 27-29.

——— Право на риск [The Right to Take Risks]. Moscow: Military Publishing House, 1988. Reprint of the title novel plus the author's new novella, Плацдарм [The Bridgehead].

——— Армия — любовь моя [The Army is My Love]. Moscow: Sovetskaya Rossiya, 1983.

——— Просто служба [Just My Duty]. Moscow: DOSAAF Publishing House, 1984. A collection of short stories about the airborne.

——— Афганский синдром [Afghan Syndrome], Коммунист вооружённых сил [Armed Forces Communist], Nos. 11, 12 & 13, 1990, pp. 81-86, 78-84 & 80-87.

Polyanskij joined the Army in 1944. A graduate of the Artillery Academy, he served as a platoon leader and battery commander. Later he became a military journalist, working for regional military newspapers. He served tours in the Far East, Turkestan and the Caucasus. He is a laureate of the Fadeev prize for military literature.

Povolyaev, Valerij. Время «Ч» ["H" Hour], in Эхо афганских гор
[Echo of the Mountains of Afghanistan], 1987, pp. 146–230.

Prokhanov, Aleksandr Andreevich. Дерево в центре Кабула [A
Tree in the Center of Kabul], Октябрь [October], Nos. 1 &
2, 1982, pp. 3-73 & 74-137. The first novel about
Afghanistan.

——— Светлее лазури [Brighter than Azure], Октябрь
[October], No. 9, 1986, pp. 3-55.

——— Записки на броне [Diary on Armor Plate]. Moscow:
Pravda Publishers, 1988. Contains the novella Светлее
лазури [Brighter than Azure], which relates the story of
Soviet soldiers in Afghanistan.

——— Там, в Афганистане ... [There, in Afghanistan ...].
Moscow: Military Publishing House, 1988. Contains the
novels: *A Tree in the Center of Kabul*, and Рисунки
баталиста [Drawings of Combat]. One of the portraits
from *Drawings of Combat* is *The Grey-headed Soldier* (pp. 267-
311), which was later published seperately as a novella.

——— Южный знак [Southern Marker], in В солдатской
шинели [In a Soldier's Greatcoat], 1985, pp. 446-451.

——— На севере теплом... [Warmth of the North ...], in В
солдатской шинели [In a Soldier's Greatcoat], 1985,
pp. 466-470.

——— Горы [The Mountains], Подвиг [Feat of Arms], No. 34,
1989, pp. 214-244.

——— Мусульманская свадьба [The Muslim Wedding],
Подвиг [Feat of Arms], No. 37, 1990, pp. 97–129.

——— Седой солдат [The Grey-headed Soldier], in Эхо
афганских гор [Echo of the Mountains of Afghanistan],
1987, pp. 336-380.

——— Седой солдат [The Grey-headed Soldier], in По
горячей земле [Over the Hot Earth], 1986, pp. 141–190.

Pronyakin, Yurij. Курсанты [Cadets]. Moscow: Military Publishing
House, 1954. One of the earliest postwar works of this
genre.

——— Ставка на совесть [Counting on Conscience]. Moscow:
Military Publishing House, 1967. The story of the
development of a battalion commander.

Reviewed in: A. Kochetov, Ставка на совесть
[Counting on Conscience], Коммунист вооружённых

сил [Armed Forces Communist], No. 24, 1967, p. 88.

——— Суд чести [Court of Honor]. Moscow: Military Publishing House, 1974. Includes the short stories: Магнетическое отклонение [Magnetic Deviation], Срочное задание [Urgent Mission], Строгий командир [The Strict Commander] and Облако [The Cloud].

——— В Средиземном и дальше [In the Mediterranian and Further], in В мирные дни [In Peacetime], 1971, pp. 219-234.

——— За синей далью [Beyond the Blue Horizon]. Moscow: Military Publishing House, 1983.

Pustynin, Ehduard. Афганец: Роман в тридцати пяти главах [The Afghan Vet: a Novel in Thirty-Five Chapters], Знамя [The Banner], No. 12, 1991, pp.103-114.

Rezik, Vitalij. Небо над твоим домом [The Sky over Your Home], in Горячие высоты [The Hot High Ground], 1983, pp. 381-387.

Rodichev, Nikolaj Ivanovich. За сиреневыми звёздами [Beyond the Lilac-colored Stars]. Moscow: Moskovskij rabochij Publishing House, 1970. Contains short stories about the airborne.

Romanov, Boris. Музей [The Museum], Литературная россия [Literary Russia], No. 49, 1995, pp. 8-9. A story of the Strategic Rocket Forces.

Roshchin, Boris Alekseevich. Тревога [Alert]. Leningrad: Sovetskij pisatel' Publishing House, 1977. The story of a young officer in the engineers.

——— Голова на плечах [A Head on His Shoulders], in Горячие высоты [The Hot High Ground], 1983, pp. 3-81. The story of an engineering academy cadet and how his character develops.

——— Блины на лопате [Pancakes on an Entrenching Tool], in Поверка [Roll Call], 1988, pp. 5-40.

Roshchin served a ten-year stint in the Armed Forces before being discharged to the reserves in the rank of captain. During his period of active duty, he served as a platoon leader in an EOD unit and as a text and photo journalist. He completed the Gorkij Literary Institute by correspondence.

Ryadchenko, Sergej. Полоса препятствий [Obstacle Course], Литературная учёба [Literary Studies], No. 2, 1979, pp. 10-74. Reprinted by Sovetskij pisatel' Publishing House, 1987.

Reviewed in: Belichenko, Yurij, Школа мужества [The School of Heroism], Знамя [The Banner], No. 5, 1980, pp. 230-237.

———   Время мира [A Time of Peace]. Moscow: Molodaya gvardiya Publishing House, 1986.

Rybakov, Vladimir. Афганцы [The Afghanies]. London: Overseas Publications Interchange, 1988. The disillusionment of a career officer when he gets to Afghanistan.

Rybin, Anatolij Gavrilovich. Рубеж [The Boundary Line]. Moscow: Military Publishing House, 1984. The story of the modernization of the Armed Forces.

———   Люди в погонах [People with Epaulets]. Moscow: Military Publishing House, 1968.

Selikhov, Kim. Эхо афганских гор [Echo of the Mountains of Afghanistan], in Эхо афганских гор [Echo of the Mountains of Afghanistan], 1987, pp. 71-145.

Semenikhin, Gennadij Aleksandrovich. Взлёт [Take Off], Октябрь [October], Nos. 10 & 11, 1973.

Reviewed in: Col. Viktor Mitroshenkov, Молодая гвардия [The Young Guard], No. 8, 1974, pp. 316-317.

———   Collected Works (in 3 volumes). Moscow: Military Publishing House, 1981. Novels and stories about the Air Force.

———   Финиширует смелость [Courage Wins], in В мирные дни [In Peacetime], 1971, pp. 197-201.

———   Финиш смелости [The Win Goes to Courage], in Мы - военные [We Are Military Men], 1974, pp. 65-70.

Semenikhin was in reserve status in the rank of colonel in 1974.

Silakov, Aleksandr Semenovich. Внимание: Воздушный мост [Attention: an Air Lift]. Moscow: Military Publishing House, 1983. The story of the airborne and the pilots that fly the planes that carry them.

Simanchuk, Il'ya Semenovich. Шаг вперёд! [One Step Forward!] Moscow: Moskovskij rabochij Publishing House, 1987. The story of an enlisted Comsomol activist in an artillery unit in the mid-sixties.

Skul'skij, Grigorij and L. Zajtsev. В далёкой гавани [In a Distant Harbor]. Moscow: Naval Publishing House, 1952. Reprinted by Molodaya gvardiya Publishing House, 1954.

Snegirev, Lev Anatol'evich. Две весны [Two Springs]. Kiev, Radianskii
        Pis'mennik Publishing House, 1978. A collection of short
        stories.

Sobko, Vadim. Залог мира [The Guarantee of Peace]. Moscow: State
        Fiction Publishing House, 1951. Winner of the Stalin prize
        for literature, third class, 1950. Originally published in
        Ukrainian. Action in the story begins on 10 May 1945, the
        day after the German capitulation.

Sokolov, Sergej. Тигровый коготь [The Tiger's Claw], Подвиг [Feat
        of Arms], No. 34, 1989, pp. 75-98.

Sorokin, Evgenij Aleksandrovich. Наследники [The Inheritors].
        Moscow: Sovetskaya Rossiya, 1982.

Sosnovskij, Vladislav. Холодно-жарко [Cold and Hot], Октябрь
        [October], No. 12, 1976, pp. 29-53.

Stadnyuk, Ivan. Максим Перепелица [Maksim Perepelitsa] in
        Collected Works, Vol. 2, pp. 373-498. Moscow: Molodaya
        gvardiya Publishing House, 1983.
        Reviewed in: Boris Leonov, Главный объект [The
        Main Subject]. Moscow: Moskovskij rabochij Publishing
        House, 1978.
        Stadnyuk retired from the Army in 1958 in the rank
        of colonel. He served on the editiorial staff of *Soviet
        Warrior* from 1952 to 1958.

Stepanenko, Vladimir Ivanovich. Девять дней без тревог [Nine
        Days without an Alert]. Moscow: Sovetskaya Rossiya,
        1977. The story of the PVO.
        Stepanenko is a veteran of the second Air Army.

Stepanov, Viktor Aleksandrovich. У Бранденбургских ворот [At
        the Brandenburg Gate], Знамя [The Banner], No. 5, 1973,
        pp. 81-144. The author examines the Soviet dilemma of the
        "good Germans" and the "bad Germans" when a war
        veteran visits his son serving in GSFG.
        Reviewed in: I. Kozlov, Неотстывающая память
        [Living Memory], *Pravda*, 3 February 1974, p. 3; and in: Lt.
        Col. V. Khalipov, В едином ритме [In a Single
        Rhythm], Советский воин [Soviet Warrior], No. 9, 1978,
        p. 35.
———— Рота почётного караула [Honor Guard Company],
        Юность [Youth], Nos. 5 & 6, 1976, pp. 25-40 & 19-40.
        Reviewed in: N. Kizimenko Рота почётного
        караула [Honor Guard Company], Октябрь [October],
        No. 4, 1977, pp. 221-222.

——— Обратный адрес –– ОКЕАН [Return Address is the OCEAN]. Moscow: Military Publishing House, 1977. Also contains the novella Рота почётного караула [Honor Guard Company].

Reviewed in: S. Zonin, Глубины человеческих душ [The Depth of Human Hearts], Советский воин [Soviet Warrior], No. 10, 1979, p. 34; and in: V. Verstakov, Люди, которых я люблю [People I Love], *Pravda*, 14 January 1980.

——— Венок на волне [Wreath on a Wave], in Солдаты мира [Soldiers of Peace], 1985, pp. 9-95.

——— Звездные мгновения [Stellar Moments], Октябрь [October], No. 5, 1979, pp. 152-169. The story of conquering Space.

Stepanov served as an officer in the Soviet Navy and is a graduate of the Gorkij Literary Institute. He is a laureate of the Ministry of Defense Fadeev prize for literature.

Strekhnin, Yurij Fedorovich. Завещаю тебе • Вечный пропуск [I Bequeath You • Permanent Pass]. Moscow: Military Publishing House, 1977. The novel *I Bequeath You* was awarded a special certificate by the Ministry of Defense in 1974.

——— Находка [Nakhodka], in В мирные дни [In Peacetime], 1971, pp. 239-246.

——— Служу за границей [I Serve Overseas], in Родины солдаты [Soldiers of the Motherland], 1983, pp. 148-180.

Lt. Col. (ret.) Yurij Strekhnin is a winner of one of the literary contests of the Ministry of Defense of the USSR.

Studenikin, Petr. Дорога в Кабул [The Road to Kabul], in По горячей земле [Over the Hot Earth], 1986, pp. 191–240.

Sul'yanov, Anatolij Konstantinovich. Расколотое небо [The Sundered Sky]. Moscow: Military Publishing House, 1984. The story of the Air Force.

——— Замполит [The Zampolit], in Живёт солдат ... [A Soldier Lives ...], 1982, pp. 91-156.

——— Симфония мужества [A Symphony of Bravery], in Мы - военные [We Are Military Men], 1974, pp. 21-35.

Sul'yanov was on active duty in the rank of colonel in 1974.

Sul'zhenko, Galina. Письмо тебе [A Letter for You], in Горячие высоты [The Hot High Ground], 1983, pp. 329-331.

Svetikov, Viktor. Жаркий месяц Саратан [The Hot Month of
        Saratan]. Moscow: DOSAAF Publishing House, 1988. The
        story of Afghanistan.

Sviridov, Georgij Ivanovich. Победа даётся нелегко [Victory Does
        Not Come Easy]. Moscow: Military Publishing House,
        1969. Republished by Sovetskaya Rossiya Publishing
        House, 1982. Consists of the novellas Рядовой
        Коржавин [Private Korzhavin] and Солдат всегда
        солдат [A Soldier Is Always a Soldier]. They tell the
        story of how a young enlisted man adapts to service in the
        Soviet Army on the background of how the Army aided
        the populace of Tashkent after an earthquake. Was
        awarded the third place Ministry of Defense prize for
        literature in 1970.
                Reviewed in: V. Starikov, Выший долг [Highest
        Duty], Литературная россия [Literary Russia],
        4 May,1969, p. 16; and in: Col. I. Davydov, Солдатский
        характер [A Soldier's Character], *Red Star*, 9 June 1970.

Sviridov, Col. Mikhail. На рассвете [At Dawn], Советский воин
        [Soviet Warrior], No. 5, 1974, pp. 13-15.

———   Русакову верьте! [Believe Rusakov!], Советский
        воин [Soviet Warrior], No. 22, 1980, pp. 18-21.

———   За синими туманами [Beyond the Blue Horizon],
        Советский воин [Soviet Warrior], No. 1, 1982, pp. 18–21.

———   Тихонова лазурь [Tikhon's Azure], in Живёт солдат
        ... [A Soldier Lives ...], 1982, pp. 244-251.

———   Магистраль [The Railroad], in Живёт солдат ... [A
        Soldier Lives ...], 1982, pp. 252-258.

Teplov, Yurij. Среди афганских гор [In the Mountains of
        Afghanistan], in По горячей земле [Over the Hot
        Earth], 1986, pp. 241-283.

Timrot, Vladimir. Убиенного воина Сергея [(Soul) of the Fallen
        Warrior Sergej], Альманах Истоки [Sources Annual].
        Moscow: Molodaya gvardiya Publishing House, 1990,
        pp. 77-92. A post-Afghanistan story.

Tkachenko, A. Сигнал оповещения [Alarm Signal], Юность
        [Youth], No. 7, 1974, pp. 30-59.

Tyurin, Vladimir Mikhajlovich. Слушать в отсеках [To Listen in the
        Compartments]. Moscow: Military Publishing House,
        1982. The story of a young sailor in the silent service.

Umnov, Mikhail. Поле [The Field], in Крещение [Baptism], 1991, pp.

225-242.

Usol'tsev, Al'bert Kharlampievich. Громкая тишина [The Loud
    Silence]. Moscow: Sovremennik Publishing House, 1974.
    The story of the PVO.

───── Солдатская земля [A Land of Soldiers]. Moscow:
    Military Publishing House, 1981. Stories and novellas
    about the PVO.

Uspenskij, Vladimir D. Ухожу на задание ... [Going out on a
    Mission ...]. Moscow: Military Publishing House, 1987.
    Stories about Afghanistan.

───── Птенцы и ракеты [Fledglings and Rockets], in В
    мирные дни [In Peacetime], 1971, pp. 67-75.

───── Птенцы и ракеты [Fledglings and Rockets], in
    Родины солдаты [Soldiers of the Motherland], 1983, pp.
    7-42.

───── Трудный перевал [The Hard Mountain Pass], Подвиг
    [Feat of Arms], No. 28, 1985, pp. 11-28. A classic doing-
    our-international-duty piece about the war in Afghanistan.

Ust'yantsev, Viktor Aleksandrovich. Автономное плавание
    [Independent Cruise]. Moscow: Sovremennik Publishing
    House, 1973. The story of the silent service.

───── Только один рейс [Only One Cruise], in Родины
    солдаты [Soldiers of the Motherland], 1983, pp. 328-360.

───── Старпом [First Mate], in Мы - военные [We Are
    Military Men], 1974, pp. 195-215.
        Capt. first class (Navy) Ust'yantsev was the editor of
    the fiction department of the Military Publishing House.

Vanshenkin, Konstantin Yakovlevich. Десантники [Airborne].
    Moscow: DOSAAF Publishing House, 1970.

───── Десантники [Airborne], in В мирные дни [In
    Peacetime], 1971, pp. 44-48.

───── Через всю жизнь [Throughout Your Life], in В
    солдатской шинели [In a Soldier's Greatcoat], 1985,
    pp. 568-572.
        Vanshenkin served in airborne units during World
    War II and is a graduate of the Gorkij Literary Institute.

Verstakov, Viktor. Без отметки на календаре [Not Marked on the
    Calendar], in По горячей земле [Over the Hot Earth],
    1986, pp. 3-96.

───── Возвращение афганца [The Return of the Afghan
    Vet], Альманах Истоки [Sources Annual]. Moscow:
    Molodaya gvardiya Publishing House, 1990, pp. 4-76. A

post-Afghanistan story.

Volkov, Maj. V. Жду тебя, солдат [I'm Waiting for You, Soldier], Советский воин [Soviet Warrior], No. 23, 1980, p. 13.

Vozovikov, Vladimir. Сын отца своего [His Father's Son], Октябрь [October], No. 5, 1977, pp. 16-93. Republished in Солдаты мира [Soldiers of Peace], 1985, pp. 199-301.

> Reviewed in: Capt. II V. Likashevich, По долгу мужества и чести [A Debt of Bravery and Honor], *Red Star*, 13 June 1981; and in: S. Savel'ev, Становление офицера - современника [The Formation of the Character of a Modern Officer], Коммунист вооружённых сил [Armed Forces Communist], No. 6, 1978, pp. 87-89; and in: I. Okunev, Спасибо, сын [Thank You, Son], Советский воин [Soviet Warrior], No. 18, 1977, p. 41.

——— Время алых снегов [The Time of the Scarlet Snows], Советский воин [Soviet Warrior], No. 18, 1972, pp. 21-25.

——— Голос земли [The Voice of the Earth], in Труба зовёт [The Trumpet Calls], 1973, pp. 123-131.

——— В снегах [In the Snows], in Труба зовёт [The Trumpet Calls], 1973, pp. 194-204.

——— Перед экраном [In Front of the Screen], in В мирные дни [In Peacetime], 1971, pp. 97-108.

——— Река не может молчать [The River Cannot Be Silent], in Родины солдаты [Soldiers of the Motherland], 1983, pp. 43-79.

——— Первый горизонт [The First Horizon], in Живёт солдат ... [A Soldier Lives ...], 1982, pp. 205-227.

——— Товарищ экипаж [Comrade Crew], in Мы - военные [We Are Military Men], 1974, pp. 151-170.

> Lt. Col. (res.) Vozovikov is a graduate of the Tashkent, Order of Lenin Tank Academy and of the Gorkij Literary Institute. He is a winner of the Ministry of Defense literary contest.

Vsevolodov, Vyacheslav. Девять граммов свинца [Nine Grams of Lead], in Поверка [Roll Call], 1988, pp. 334-348.

Yakovlev, Yurij Ya. Семеро солдатиков [Seven Little Soldiers]. Moscow: Children's Literature Publishing House, 1983.

Zen'kovich, Nikolaj Aleksandrovich. Друзья мои, ракетчики [My

Friends, the Rocket Troops]. Alma Ata: Zhalyn Publishing
House, 1988. © 1983 Yunatstva Publishing House.

Zhdanov, Igor' Nikolaevich. Ночь караула [Night of the Guard].
Moscow: Sovremennik Publishing House, 1978. This
edition includes a foreword by Yurij Bondarev.

ANTHOLOGIES

В добрый путь: сборник рассказов, удостоенных премий
на конкурсе журнала «Советский воин» [On the Good
Path: A Collection of Stories That Won the *Soviet Warrior*
Literary Contest], Библиотека солдата и матроса
[Soldiers' and Sailors' Library]. Moscow: Military Publishing
House, 1959.

В мирные дни [In Peacetime], Yurij Fedorovich Strekhnin, ed.
Moscow: Sovetskaya Rossiya Publishing House, 1971.

В солдатской шинели [In a Soldier's Greatcoat], T.A. Gajdar,
compiler. Moscow: Political Publishing House, 1985.

Горячие высоты [The Hot High Ground], Petr Iosifovich Kapitsa
and Riza Khalitovich Khalitov, compilers. Leningrad:
Lenizdat, 1983.

Дни мирные – подвиги боевые [Danger in Peacetime], Col. (ret.)
Ivan Ivanovich Gaglov, compiler. Moscow: Military
Publishing House, 1965.

Живёт солдат ... [A Soldier Lives ...], Aleksandr Dmitrievich
Aristov, compiler. Moscow: Military Publishing House, 1982.

Крещение: повести и рассказы молодых писателей о
современной армии [Baptism: Novellas and Short Stories
by Young Authors about the Modern Military],
L.A. Teplova, compiler. Moscow: Pravda Publishing House,
1991. All the authors have served in the military as enlisted
men. Most of the stories are about Afghanistan.

Мы – военные [We Are Military Men], I. V. Chernyaeva, ed.
Moscow: Sovetskaya Rossiya Publishing House, 1974.

На страже границ [Guarding the Borders], V. A. Mel'nichuk and P.
M. Sobolev, compilers. Moscow: Military Publishing House,
1978.

Океан [The Ocean], V. M. Tyurin, compiler. Moscow: Children's
Literature Publishing House, 1981. Stories of the Navy.

Поверка [Roll Call], Arkadij Fedorovich Pinchuk and Riza
Khalitovich Khalitov, compilers. Leningrad: Lenizdat, 1988.
Commemorative anthology of stories and poems for the

seventieth anniversary of the Soviet Armed Forces.

По горячей земле [Over the Hot Earth], V. G. Verstakov, compiler. Moscow: Molodaya gvardiya Publishing House, 1986. Stories about Afghanistan.

Поиск-80 [Search-80], Moscow: Sovetskij pisatel' Publishing House, 1980. A collection of novellas and short stories from participants of the Dubulty seminars.

    Reviewed in: Boris Leonov, Главний поиск – впереди [The Main Search is Still Ahead], *Red Star*, 3 June 1981.

Поиск-83 [Search-83], S. P. Benke, compiler. Moscow: Military Publishing House, 1982. A collection of novellas and short stories from participants of the Dubulty seminars.

Поиск-86 [Search-86], Yu. I. Chernov, compiler. Moscow: Military Publishing House, 1986. A collection of novellas and short stories from participants of the Dubulty seminars.

Поиск-90 [Search-90], Yu. I. Chernov, compiler. Moscow: Military Publishing House, 1990. A collection of novellas and short stories from participants of the Dubulty seminars.

Правофланговые [The Best], I. Skarinkin, compiler. Minsk: Belarus', 1970.

Родины солдаты [Soldiers of the Motherland], Valentin Erashov, compiler. Moscow: Molodaya gvardiya Publishing House, 1983. Contains a biographical sketch of the authors and an introduction.

    Valentin Erashov is retired in the rank of Guards major.

Солдаты мира [Soldiers of Peace], N. I. Netesina, compiler. Moscow: Sovetskaya Rossiya, 1985. Includes a foreword by Boris A. Leonov and a short biographical sketch of the authors.

Труба зовёт [The Trumpet Calls], Aleksandr Dmitrievich Aristov, compiler. Moscow, Military Publishing House, 1973. A collection of stories and novellas from the pages of Советский воин [Soviet Warrior].

Эхо афганских гор [Echo of the Mountains of Afghanistan], N. P. Kuz'min, compiler. Moscow: Military Publishing House, 1987.

Я - солдат, мама ... [I Am a Soldier, Mama ...], A. A. Volkov, compiler. Leningrad: Lenizdat, 1988.

Ялта-91: сборник стихов и прозы армейских и флотских литераторов [Yalta-91: A Collection of Poetry and Prose by Army and Navy Writers], Библиотека журнала «Советский воин», Нр, 11/894 [The *Soviet Warrior Library*, No. 11/894]. Moscow: Sovetskij voin Publishing House, 1991.

Index

About the Author

MARK T. HOOKER served as a linguist and Soviet/East-European area specialist with the U.S. Armed Forces and as a Department of Defense civilian. He is a Visiting Scholar at the Russian and East-European Institute at Indiana University.

ISBN 0-275-95563-X

EAN

9 780275 955632

90000>

HARDCOVER BAR CODE